ON RESISTANCE

ALSO AVAILABLE FROM BLOOMSBURY

A New Philosophy of Society, Manuel DeLanda
Dissensus, Jacques Rancière
The Universal Exception, Slavoj Žižek

Yoko Ono
Play It By Trust
1966/*date of your show*
Mixed media, no. 2/3
Collection Serge Ziegler Galerie

ON RESISTANCE

A Philosophy of Defiance

Howard Caygill

B L O O M S B U R Y
LONDON • NEW DELHI • NEW YORK • SYDNEY

Bloomsbury Academic

An imprint of Bloomsbury Publishing Plc

50 Bedford Square
London
WC1B 3DP
UK

1385 Broadway
New York
NY 10018
USA

www.bloomsbury.com

Bloomsbury is a registered trade mark of Bloomsbury Publishing Plc

First published 2013
Reprinted 2013, 2014

British Library Cataloguing-in-Publication Data
A catalogue record for this book is available from the British Library.

ISBN: HB: 978–1–4725–2258–0
ePDF: 978–1–4725–2656–4
ePUB: 978–1–4725–2966–4

Library of Congress Cataloging-in-Publication Data
A catalog record for this book is available from the Library of Congress.
Caygill, Howard.
On resistance: a philosophy of defiance/Howard Caygill.
pages cm
Includes bibliographical references and index.
ISBN 978-1-4725-2258-0 (hardover: alk. paper) – ISBN 978-1-4725-2656-4 (ebook (pdf): alk. paper) – ISBN 978-1-4725-2966-4 (ebook (epub): alk. paper) – ISBN 978-1-4725-2309-9 (pbk.: alk. paper) 1. Resistance (Philosophy) I. Title.
B105.R47C39 2013
172'.1–dc23

2013023968

Typeset by Fakenham Prepress Solutions, Fakenham, Norfolk NR21 8NN
Printed and bound in Great Britain

For Piero

CONTENTS

As a protest of men attacked in their honour and the right idea
that they hold of truth, this resistance has a meaning that exceeds
the circumstances in which it was asserted and that it is now
important to recapture, no matter how things turn out.

DECLARATION OF THE RIGHT TO INSUBORDINATION IN THE
ALGERIAN WAR (MANIFESTO OF THE 121)

'Now is the time to resist'

CALL TO RESIST ILLEGITIMATE AUTHORITY, 1967 CHOMSKY,
MARCUSE, SONTAG ET. AL.

But what if my decision to make my years with the resistance
public were a sign that it was soon to disappear? Some
inexplicable feeling warned me that the rebellion was fading,
flagging, was about to turn into the path and disappear. It would
be made into epics. I looked at the resistance as if it were going to
vanish at any moment.

JEAN GENET, *PRISONER OF LOVE*

"It is a difficult case. What do you think I ought to do – resist?
Eh? I want no more than justice"…He wanted no more than
justice – no more than justice.

JOSEPH CONRAD, *HEART OF DARKNESS*

OCTOBER 27TH 1960

The riots in Paris on October 27th 1960 inaugurated a sequence of events that culminated in the outright defiance of 1968. Proclaimed as a Day for Peace in Algeria by the Left and Trade Unions, the eruption of police violence against demonstrators was continuous with the intensification of the anti-colonial struggle in Algeria and the migration of its violence to the colonial metropolis (Tartakowski 1997, 671–7). It followed closely the publication of the *Declaration of the Right to Insubordination in the Algerian War* or 'Manifesto of the 121' on September 5th, which cited the French Resistance in a call for civil disobedience and was contemporary with the trial of the resistant Jeansen Network and Jean-Paul Sartre's uncompromising Preface to Frantz Fanon's *The Cursed of the Earth* (subsequently banned in France). The calculated use of state violence against the Algerian community in Paris planned and executed by the Parisian *préfect de police* Maurice Papon – whose qualifications for office included the persecution of the Jews of Bordeaux under Vichy and ruthless colonial repression in Morocco and Algeria (see House and Macmaster) – culminated in the hunt and murder of over 200 demonstrators by the police in Paris a year later on 17 October 1961 and the murder of demonstrators at the Charonne Metro Station on 8 February 1962. The official repression was complemented by un- or semi-official acts of terror including bomb attacks on Jean-Paul Sartre's home (9 July 1961 and 7 January 1962) and the offices of *Les Temps Modernes on* 13 May 1961.

These violent episodes from the last days of the Algerian War were haunted by the memory of the French resistance to Nazi occupation and collaboration during the Second World War. The 'Manifesto of the 121' asked how a state whose legitimacy rested on the morality of the resistance to Nazism could resort to Nazi methods in its dirty war against the Algerian resistance (Blanchot 2010, 15–17). The same question was asked by those French citizens of the Jeansen and other resistant networks who took the decision to support the Algerians in their struggle against the French state and who saw their actions as continuous with the resistance to Nazism (see

Evans 1997). Yet they could share this perspective with the *Organisation de l'armée secrète* or OAS, the paramilitary terrorist group of the right that was also 'immersed in resistance imagery' (Evans 1997, 187); they too considered their counter-insurgent *guerre révolutionnaire* or guerrilla war from above as continuous with the wartime resistance. Who then, were the true resistants? What was the connection between the collaborationist past of the Parisian *préfet de police* and the extreme but calculated exercise of state violence against anti-colonial demonstrators? And how was it possible that the man who issued the legendary call for resistance on June 18th 1940 should now be cast as the 'grand sorcerer' (Sartre) or manifestation of the 'essential perversion' (Blanchot)? And what of the hero of the resistance who received the *Croix de guerre* in 1945 for his heroic service and who now, in *The Cursed of the Earth*, called for absolute resistance to the colonial French Republic? Informing such questions is a perplexity about the nature of resistance: is it reactive and part of an escalating reciprocal movement of repression provoking resistance that in turn intensifies counter-resistance … or is it the perennial defiance of oppression and injustice?

Sartre's 1961 essay 'An Unprivileged Painter' written for the catalogue of an exhibition by Robert Lapoujade – 'Paintings on the Theme of the Riots, Tryptich on Torture, Hiroshima' – held at Galérie Pierre Domec between 10 March and 15 April 1961 and then collected in *Situations IV*, views the painting of a riot 'October 27th' in the context of a perplexed resistance.

> And then, suddenly, there is a streak of asphalt: the void. This overflows and runs off to the bottom of the canvas. But is there a top or a bottom? The space is itself a *meaning*; it is composed by the crowd and is determined as a function of the crowd's acts. This streak is, simultaneously, a thick downward plunge and a flight to the horizon; it matters little which. It is the sudden opening-up of the void: the police are charging. Are we going to run or resist? Whatever we do, the space exists with all its dimensions in one: it is distance – which shrinks on one side and on the other, seems interminable. (Sartre, 569)

It is a familiar scenario, one replayed recently in the Arab insurgencies, the resistance of the *indignados* and *aganaktismenoi*, the global eruption of the Occupy movement, the 'Taksim Republic' and their violent repression. Sartre reads Lapoujade's mark as a moment of decision: the viscosity and void of the 'streak' of paint condenses the intensified experience of space and time characteristic of the moment of resistance and the formation of a capacity to resist. Sartre sketches a phenomenology of this defiant moment in which street and square are suddenly no longer unobtrusively 'present at hand' but are instead invested with ambivalent and threatening properties. With the rapidly diminishing distance between the police charge and the stand or *stasis* of the immobile demonstrators, the urban space becomes void, at once contracting and expanding to the horizon. Sartre identifies this experience as a 'function of the crowd's acts', and the stretching and contraction of urban space manifests the crowd's indecision. At the moment of a Kierkegaardian either/or – 'Are we going to run or resist?' – the street assumes dramatic spatial and affective properties routinely inconspicuous but now captured in the artist's mark. The 'meaning' of the space has changed from routine to exception and the question of flight or defiance envelops the entire scene, making it seem the ritual space for staging either an authentic resistance or an inauthentic flight.

Yet perhaps the properties of this scene are not as clear as they seemed to Sartre and the question of meaning not the most important. Sartre's scenario of meaning presupposes a prior opposition of forces themselves the outcome of a prior act of resistance. That Sartre does not see this clearly is betrayed by his over-insistent claim that the 'meaning' of the space is first *composed* by the crowd and then *determined* as a *function* of its *acts*. This equation may hold for meaning but does not reach the dynamics of political force. The latter remain unobtrusive since in this scenario one of the opposed forces does not manifest itself as a discrete force but as the given state of things. By focusing on one element in a dynamic scenario and looking for its meaning, Sartre makes the error that Newton already warned against with his example of a horse drawing a stone in the statement of the 3rd law of motion in the *Principia*: 'If a horse draws a stone tied to a rope, the horse will (so to speak) also be drawn back equally towards the stone...' (Newton, 417). Newton is illustrating the principle that 'to any action there is always an opposite and equal reaction', or that the stone, indeed, draws the horse. In the case of 27 October 1960 the meaning of the space is already informed and undercut by a complex field of applied and resistant forces, with the properties of the space determined as much by the force of the police charge as by the crowd's resistance to it. In terms of political dynamics, the crowd's stand is the reciprocal of the police charge: to defy or take a stand assumes a capacity to resist, which is the outcome of previous stands within previous scenarios of opposed forces.

Hegel's description of how the collision of forces is obscured by the question of meaning or 'law' in the section *Kraft und Verstand* of *The Phenomenology of Spirit* criticises in anticipation Sartre's gesture in 'An Unprivileged Painter'. An important step in Hegel's account of the occlusion of force describes how one of the opposed forces in a dynamic scenario manifests itself less as a discrete force than as a neutral 'medium':

> The soliciting force, e.g., is posited as a universal medium, and the one solicited, on the other hand, as Force driven back into itself; but the former is a universal medium only through the other being Force that is driven back into itself; or, it is really the latter that is the soliciting Force for the other and is what makes it a medium. (Hegel 1977, 84)

On 27 October 1960 the crowd adopts the posture of the force 'driven back into itself' when forced to decide whether to resist or run, a decision 'solicited' by the 'universal medium' or the force of the police whose charge seems continuous with its routine and legitimate exercise of force. The force that appears as a neutral 'universal medium' in the state's routine maintenance of order appears at this moment in Paris, but is also at work in seemingly distant Algeria. Yet the scenario was far more complicated than that remembered by Sartre before the painting of Lapoujade. The demonstration of 27 October 1960 had been banned by the authorities and the ban respected by the trade unions, socialist and communist organisations. While *outdoor* demonstrations were banned, meetings *indoors* were permitted. Accordingly the French National Student Organisation held a mass meeting in the Salle de la Mutualité which was attacked by militants of the right with tear gas grenades, calculatedly *forcing* the students onto the streets and into a 3 hour conflict with the police waiting for them outside (the fighting taking place on the left bank, not the Place de la République as recalled by Sartre) with 60 casulties among the demonstrators, 25 among the police and 527 arrests.

Sartre's moment of decision is only possible, as Hegel shows, in an already established context of opposed forces. Indeed, a Clausewitzean reading of Sartre would find his neglect of the reciprocal character of force a fatal strategic error: by placing the decision of whether to resist or run at the level of meaning and authentic decision, Sartre overlooks the quality of the opposed forces. From the dynamic point of view, *resistance* understood in terms of the preservation or enhancement of the capacity to resist cannot be reduced to a binary opposition of 'run or resist', but must be situated instead within a complex and dynamic spatio-temporal field that manifests itself in postures of domination and defiance. The military doctrine of resistance pioneered by Clausewitz with its central conflict between imperial and guerrilla war disdains romantic, chivalric, deeply *meaningful* but doomed gestures such as taking a stand and never retreating. Sartre's description of 27 October 1960 implicitly respects the logic of what Hegel called the *'verkehrte Welt'* or upside-down world: while implicitly acknowledging the initiative of the police – 'the police are charging' – he nevertheless proceeds as if initiative rests entirely with the crowd and that it is their decision that counts. Yet at the same time the crowd is placed in a posture of reacting to applied force, their response in Hegel's terms has been 'solicited'. This predicament is betrayed in the very form of the question *'are we* going to run or resist?', in which initiative is at once possessed and renounced. The students are running from the (well equipped and planned) attack of the extreme right, and their flight drives them into a posture of defiance against the medium of resistance that is the police. Yet Sartre cannot see that the initiative lay in the attack of the extreme right – or elements within the police itself given the use of tear gas grenades – which choreographed the confrontation of students and police captured in Lapoujade's painting and his own reflection on its meaning. From this perspective, that of the reactionary *guerre révolutionaire* of the OAS, 27 October 1960 was a spectacularly successful exercise in the resistance to decolonisation, *forcing* the anticolonial demonstrators into a violent and unwinnable confrontation with the state.

The upside-down world of solicited and soliciting force disclosed in Sartre's response to the collision of repression and defiance on 27 October 1960 is difficult to analyse or bring to full visibility. There is never a moment of pure resistance, but always a reciprocal play of resistances that form clusters or sequences of resistance and counter-resistance responding to each other in surrendering or seizing initiative. The blows of the police and the resistance of the demonstrators take their place within a spatial scenario that extends from the Left Bank in Paris to Algiers and in a temporal sequence that includes among its terms the Paris of the Liberation, Dien Bien Phu, and the Battle of Algiers. The police are called to *resist* the anti-colonial demonstrations as much as the demonstrators are resisting the police. The equilibrium of forces is deliberately disturbed by the extreme right who took the intiative in attacking the meeting and forcing the demonstrators into a spectacular confrontation that they could only lose.

My thanks to students and colleagues at the Centre for Research in Modern European Philosophy Kingston University, the Department of Philosophy at the University of Paris 8, the Departments of English and Political Science at the University of Delhi, the Centre for Linguistics, Jawaharlal Nehru University, the organisers and participants of the Attakkalari India Biennial 2011, Bangalore and the members of the seminar in Contemporary Thought at Goldsmiths College for their encouragement and critical discussion of many of the themes of this book.

Introduction

Resistance was one of the most important and enduring expressions of twentieth-century political imagination and action and one ever more important in the struggles of the present century. And yet, despite the proliferation of texts dedicated to provoking, sustaining or repressing it, resistance remains strangely unanalysed and indeed *resistant* to philosophical analysis. Resistance, it seems, is rooted in practice and articulated in tactical statements and justifications addressing specific historical contexts, from the Swiss Army manual of the 1950s *Total Resistance* to the Greenham Common Women's Peace Camp's *Resist the Military* and, most recently, Gene Sharp and Bruce Jenkins' influential *Anti-Coup*. Such specificity is not necessarily a disadvantage, since defining a concept of resistance risks making it predictable, open to control and thus lowering its resistance. A key moment for reflecting upon this risk is the event of the French Resistance and the attempt in 1943 by Jean Moulin to organize existing spontaneous resistances into a Resistance structured according to the functions of military resistance, propaganda and intelligence-gathering and co-ordinated centrally in the form of a legitimate proto-state. Crucial to this step was the invention of a unified concept of resistance and the foundation of an institution that would give it historical expression, the *Conseil national de la Résistance* (CNR). De Gaulle's summary of Moulin's achievement is revealing: 'Without the CNR, there would not have been *a* resistance, but *several* resistances.'[1] The unification of practices of resistance into a concept and institution of *the* Resistance, while tactically necessary in certain contexts, risks emptying resistance of its very capacity to resist. The tormented history of the French Resistance and its posterity exemplifies the dangers of disarming resistances in the name of a Resistance, and the perhaps unavoidable subordination of its centripetal activities and initiatives to a centralised military and/or political logic. Nevertheless, without the constant reinvention of the resistances a sustained Resistance would not have been possible.

A philosophy of resistance has itself to resist the pressure of concept-formation, of reducing the practices of resistance to a single concept amenable to legitimation and appropriation by the very state-form that it began by defying. Yet, while remaining attentive to such risks, it cannot renounce the responsibility for seeking a certain consistency in the practices of resistance: while resistance has continually to be reinvented, its history of inventions demands philosophical reflection. Kant's formula from the first *critique* 'Thoughts without content are empty, intuitions without concepts are blind' (Kant 2003, A51/B75) is a good point of departure for such reflection, but not in the sense that he intended it: the mutual restitution of plenitude and sight. Recognizing the dangers of the extremes of conceptual unification and historical dispersal, Kant's formula may contribute to organizing the historical archive of resistances and so making the experience of resistance theoretically available to future calls and occasions for it. Making available such experience and avoiding the conceptual unification of '*a* Resistance' and the empirical dispersion of several historically discrete resistances requires an understanding of conceptuality that permits consistency without imposing unity. The 'concept' of resistance then exemplifies a conceptuality that includes within it a counter-movement to both unification and dispersal. Perhaps it should be thought of as a variant of Kantian reflective judgement, but one in which the individual case does not only demand a change in the concept or rule of judgement, but actively *resists* its subsumption under such a concept or rule.

The resistance of resistance to analysis is the point of departure for the two most significant recent philosophical attempts to understand the peculiar properties of this concept: Jacques Derrida's *Resistances of Psychoanalysis* (1996) and Foucault's work with resistance from the mid–1970s. Derrida speaks of resistance as

> This word, which resonated in my desire and my imagination as the most beautiful word in the politics and history of this country, this word loaded with all the pathos of my nostalgia, as if, at any cost, I would like not to have missed blowing up trains, tanks, and headquarters between 1940 and 1945 – why and how did it come to attract, like a magnet, so many other meanings, virtues, semantic or disseminal chances. (Derrida 1998, 2)

The Derridean dream of resistance is also the dream *of* resistance or the resistant, unanalysable dream in which resistance comes to stand as the limit at which analysis falters and breaks off. Every point where resistance is encountered reveals itself as already a counter-resistance, thus definitionally eluding any thought of a unitary and pure Resistance.

Some years earlier Foucault, too, attempted to find a place for resistance, this time by the side of power. In one of his last interviews in 1984, on the gay movement and the practices and pleasures of S/M, Foucault responds to the citation of a by now notorious passage from the *History of Sexuality*, 'There where there is power, there is resistance', with the comment:

Look, if there was no resistance there would be no relations of power. Because everything would be simply a question of obedience. From the moment an individual is in the situation of not doing what they want, they must use relations of power. Resistance thus comes first, it remains above all the forces of the process, under its effect it obliges relations of power to change. I thus consider the term 'resistance' to be the most important word, the key word of this dynamic. (Foucault 2001, 1559–60)

The term is identified as 'an element of the strategic relation that is power' and is recognized as 'always relying on the situation that it combats' (Foucault 2001, 1560). Yet as a peculiar condition of possibility of both power and defiance, resistance remains intangible: without it there is no power, but exactly what, when, where and how it is remains resistant to analysis. Foucault, like Derrida, recognizes the resistance to resistance as a limit point to analysis, but only if the latter is understood according to the juridical model of analysis.[2]

Foucault left some very suggestive clues about another model for analysing power and resistance. One appears in an interview with B-H. Levy in *Le Nouvel Observateur* from March 1977 that picks up from an earlier (1975) interview in *L'imprévu* entitled 'Politics is the Continuation of War by Other Means'. After some discussion of the strategy and tactics of power, once again a propos of the maxim 'there where there is power, there is resistance,' Levy succumbs to irritation and complains: 'power and resistance ... tactics and strategy ... why these background military metaphors? Are you thinking that power from now on should be thought under the form of war?' (Foucault 2001, 267). Foucault appears to back off from the reproach of having an undue fascination with things military, but pleading ignorance he continues disingenuously:

I know practically nothing about it at the moment. But one thing appears certain, that to analyse relations of power we only have at our disposal two models at the moment: that given us by law (power as law, prohibition, institution) and the military or strategic model in terms of relations of forces. The first has convincingly shown, I believe, its inadequacy: we know that law does not describe power. (Foucault 2001, 268)

Foucault was, in fact, already very well advanced in the project of knowing power through the strategic model of analysis. His Collège de France lectures of 1973–4, *Psychiatric Power*, had abandoned the juridical understanding of power and described power relations in an asylum in terms of military strategy – 'So what is organised in the asylum is actually a battlefield' (Foucault 2006, 7). But it is in the introduction to the 1975–6 lectures of the year preceding the interview with Levy, *Society must be Defended*, that Foucault advances the explicit hypothesis that 'Power is war, the continuation of war by other means' (Foucault 2003, 15) thus inverting Clausewitz's classic definition, cited by Mao and prominent in the *Little Red Book*, that 'war is the mere continuation of politics by other means'. The implications of this turn to a 'strategic model' of analysis for revolutionary politics are underlined by the statement 'It is necessary to invent another [politics] or something else that will substitute itself for it' (Foucault 2001, 267). Foucault is silent as to what this substitute may be, but a politics of resistance is clearly an important candidate. The stakes involved in understanding resistance are thus raised very high, promising no less than a new or other politics, and yet its character remains obscure and intangible.

The arrival at a politics of resistance provokes even further perplexity with respect to this term. Its frequently cited etymology in Latin *stare* – to *come* to a stand or to *cause* to stand – relates it to the ancient Greek term *stasis* which Nicole Loraux (1986) has shown names the occasion for the invention of democracy and what was subsequently called 'politics'. The ambivalent experience of a blocking or *aporia* that is also an uprising or insurrection – an experience that might be called the *state* of resistance – locates it on the crossroads between violence and speech. At issue here is the desire of resistance, its orientation towards a future that can as easily be ruinous as constructive, a desire that will be played out in war and politics but also, as testified by the role of tragedy in the Athenian democracy, in what was subsequently called 'art'. Jacqueline Rose's recent analyses of the contemporary *stasis* that is the state of Israel and the Palestinian resistance in *The Last Resistance* charts the playing out *and* working through of ambivalent resistant desire in political fantasy and in literature. By locating literature at a tangent to the intersection of violence and speech – war and politics – she is able to show how it is at once cathartic and formative, able to dissolve and confirm resistance. Her insight into the uncanny location of literature with respect to the crossing over of violence and speech that is resistance informs the marginal readings of Genet, Pasolini and Kafka in what follows.

My analysis of resistance will pursue three broad strategies: the first traces the refractions of the concept of resistance through the various discourses according to which it has been framed. By showing the persistence of certain frames and their limits it will become possible to attempt a *critique* of resistance – for these frames have provided and continue to provide the conditions of possibility for the thinking of resistance while, nevertheless, not exhausting its capacity. They include the framing of resistance in terms of force, consciousness, violence and subjectivity. The second strategy describes some of the features of historical resistances, their character and habitual gestures, showing how these point to a typological consistency informing its practice, while the third strategy explores the *valencies* of the concept of resistance, its ties and affinities, sympathetic and antipathic, to other concepts such as repression, reform and revolution.[3] These strategies will be pursued through a reading of resistant texts from the long twentieth century punctuated by reflections on their place beside historical acts of resistance.

The most pervasive framing discourse of resistance is *force,* one which ranges beyond the political to the spheres of electromagnetic, immuno-logical and military resistance. The equivocal character of force and thus resistance contributes to the intractability of the concept, but also to its resourcefulness. When Derrida evokes the resistance within resistance he does so by appealing to the sophisticated discourse of immunology and likens counter-resistance to 'an auto-immune process' (1998, viii), but this discourse itself is closely yet intangibly complicit with the military doctrine of resistance and its focus on enmity. Indeed resistance has its place within a project of *political physics* or *immunology* that manifests itself above all in a clash of forces understood in terms of relations of enmity theorized most candidly by the military doctrine of resistance. In this respect, an approach to the work of Clausewitz is unavoidable in any attempt to philosophize upon the theme of resistance. As the first theorist of the war of resistance, although for long mistaken as the theorist of the wars of nation states, Clausewitz's insight that modern politics and war pivot upon the 'capacity to resist' is crucial to a philosophy of resistance and complicates its relation to the discourse of force. Already on the first page of his posthumous 1832 *On War* we meet a definition of war framed in terms of a pure relation of enmity – a duel or a pair of wrestlers – in which the object of the mutual application of force is to render the other 'incapable of further resistance'. Clausewitz is very clear about the implications of this definition, and devotes much of *On War* to showing that the war of resistance is bivalent: it is dedicated not only to compromising or annihilating the enemy's capacity to resist, but also to preserving and enhancing one's own capacity in the face of the enemy's application of force.

While the thought of resistance remains indebted to its origin in the discourse of force and the opposition of forces characteristic of Newtonian mechanics and later electromagnetics – a provenance which remained largely unquestioned in late twentieth-century philosophy's fascination with the idea of force – it was also carried over into and grafted onto other powerful discourses. The grafting of the experience of resistance onto the philosophy of consciousness proved a powerful and resourceful alliance, especially in classic Marxist theory, but one with its own internal limits and difficulties. The introduction of resistance into the contexts of national and, later, class consciousness energized but at the same time diverted the potential or capacity to resist by fixing it on objects such as nation and class. The enlisting of resistance into revolutionary national and class struggles and processes of identity formation through the philosophy of consciousness produced a number of theoretical and strategic problems exposed in Georg Lukács' attempt to reconcile the positions of Lenin and Luxemburg on the relation between resistance and revolution in *History and Class Consciousness* (1923), as well as in Freud's charting of the workings of unconscious resistance.

The alignment of resistance and consciousness was complicated by the dependence of the concept of resistance on the discourse of force and opposed forces. As Clausewitz clearly showed, the opposition of forces directly entails the exercise of violence. The relationship between resistance and violence was and remains one of the fundamental questions of the politics of resistance. One option is to follow Clausewitz in identifying resistance and violence, an identification that leads directly to the proposition repeated in various forms throughout *On War* that war is politics by other means. This position was embraced by Lenin, Mao and Che Guevara, who saw resistance as a preliminary step towards a revolutionary class war whose objective, a classless society, legitimates the violence necessary to achieve it. Another option challenged the identification of resistance with violence while maintaining a strong conception of enmity; this position was elaborated by Gandhi in the South African and Indian anti-colonial struggles and non-violent resistance remains in the hands of Gene Sharp, Bruce Jenkins and others an effective strategic option. It is not altogether removed from Clausewitzian considerations, since it possesses a clear concept of enmity along with a developed strategic sense of the importance of preserving and enhancing the capacity to resist. Engaging on the terrain of what Clausewitz described as moral rather than physical force, non-violent resistance is a powerful strategic option in the struggle to preserve its own and to compromise its enemy's capacity to resist.

One way in which the preservation and enhancement of the capacity to resist has been thought and practiced is through the invention of resistant subjectivity. In *On War*, Clausewitz returns repeatedly to this problem, even developing an anthropology of violent or resistant subjectivity. The practice of resistance contributes to the formation of resistant identities, exemplary resistants, who inhabit and foster a broader culture of defiance. The reflection upon violent resistant subjectivity was developed in the work of Mao, Giap and Fanon, but may be contrasted with the non-violent resistant subjectivity pioneered once again by Gandhi and taken further by the American Civil Rights Movement under the leadership of Martin Luther King Jr and the Greenham Common Women's Peace Camp's resistance to military violence. A surprising feature of resistant subjectivity is its mobilization of the theory of the traditional cardinal virtues of justice, courage/fortitude and prudence in the understanding of resistance. Resistance is motivated above all by a desire for justice, its acts are performed by subjectivities possessed of extreme courage and fortitude and its practice guided by prudence, all three contributing to the deliberate preservation and enhancement of the capacity to resist.

The discourses of consciousness, violence and subjectivity inform the theory of resistance as well as intersecting in the historical reflections on its practice. They may be translated into the typology of resistance drawn from historical movements of resistance, especially in the extreme case of resistance to National Socialism exemplified by the Polish and French Resistances. The organization of the activities of the French Resistance according to violent paramilitary action, propaganda and intelligence-gathering activities and training suggested at the outset by Henri Frenay and adopted by Jean Moulin may be understood in terms of the conceptual structure of violence, consciousness and subjectivity. The first group of paramilitary actions include assassinations, sabotage, banditry, mass demonstrations, urban and rural guerilla actions and terror, but also a broad range of everyday non-violent practices whose extent has been emphasized in recent work on the French Resistance (see Marcot 2006).[4] Many of these actions served a propaganda function, supplemented by theatrical gestures such as the V sign and its variants in the Second World War, and what may be described as the carnival of resistance.[5] Linked to this is the theme of prudence or cunning, very subtly analysed by the resistant Jean-Pierre Vernant and, as is clear from his memoir, practiced with devastating effect in the context of the French war of resistance.[6] Intelligence activities range from classical models of espionage, disinformation, secrecy, counter-propaganda such as clandestinely listening to the BBC during World War II and, more recently, hacking and the work of Wikileaks. The paradigm here in both its historic and contemporary expressions is the raising of consciousness through resistance to state secrecy, the making public of the state's secret actions in the context of its manipulation of communications and media.

The concept of resistance is also constituted by its valencies, molecular binding and antipathy with other concepts. Prominent among these are the affinities of resistance and repression, resistance and constitution, resistance and revolution and its place in the oppositions of action and reaction, sovereignty and the partisan, legitimate and illegitimate violence, *ressentiment* and affirmation, slave and noble morality. In these compounds, the concept of resistance is shaped by that which it opposes or complements. The role of valencies is significant for a critique of resistance since it raises the possibility of the concept itself being determined to some degree by its resistance. This is especially the case with the discourse of force, in which resistance as a force is essentially determined by the forces that oppose it.

The discourses, historical typology and conceptual valencies of resistance form the matrix of the readings of largely twentieth-century texts and practices that constitute the archive of resistance visited in this book. It opens with Clausewitz's search for a way to theorize resistance to the Napoleonic Empire and then follows a sequence that begins with the evocation of a global civil war of Empire and Commune in the work of Marx and Nietzsche and terminates in the experience of Nazism and the possibility of the extinction of the capacity to resist expressed in the defiant despair of Pasolini during the making of his last film, *Salò*. The pioneering invention of new strategies of resistance in the anti-colonial struggles will be emphasized in this account and a case made for their significant impact on modes of philosophizing apparently far removed from the immediate context of anti-colonial struggle. The final chapter will reflect on recent and contemporary resistances, asking how far they are continuous with historical experience and how far they present a new understanding of resistance.

1 CONSCIOUS RESISTANCE

The *Disasters of War*

Carl von Clausewitz (1780–1831) and Francisco di Goya Lucientes (1746–1828) from opposite ends of Europe were forced to bear witness to the emergence of something new and terrible in their lifetimes. The military observer in Prussia and the artist in Spain testified in their different mediums to the advent of a new warfare of unprecedented violence and mass, ruthless killing. They witnessed not only the devastatingly successful military adventure of Revolutionary and Napoleonic France that swept away entire armies and states of the *Ancien Régime* but also the challenge of the 'little war' or *guerrilla* of resistance that opposed it with most deadly effect in the Peninsular War (1808–14). Clausewitz and Goya strove to understand and to represent the novel complicity of the revolutionary/imperial and resistant/guerrilla wars, both evoking in different ways the 'people armed', recognizing in the new warfare the emergence of an unprecedented and deadly logic of terror and violent escalation.[1] Although the title of the engravings making up Goya's *Disasters of War* was attributed posthumously,[2] the term *disaster* well describes the new predicament of violence in which European and, later, global populations now found themselves, one in which offensive war and resistance seemed inextricable.[3]

Clausewitz's sustained reflection on the new warfare is presented in his posthumously published *On War*. In this classic of strategy Clausewitz not only analyses Napoleonic warfare, in the hope better to know his enemy, but also – and more significantly – explores the options for resisting it. Indeed *On War* might more properly be entitled *On Resistance*, since its prime theoretical motivation is to invent a means of resisting Napoleonic strategy. This ambition is evident in the infamous but ill-understood opening definition of the aim (*Zweck*) of war as rendering the enemy 'incapable of further resistance' ('*zu jedem ferneren Widerstand unfähig zu machen*') (2010, 24).[4] At issue in war is the *capacity to resist*, understood by Clausewitz as the sum of material means along with the moral will to resist the enemy. War, whether offensive or defensive, is oriented towards compromising or resisting any attempt to compromise the capacity to resist. We shall see that the peculiar logical properties of an act dedicated to attacking another's or defending its own future capacity to resist account for many of the conceptual peculiarities of resistance and its strategies.[5]

The conceptual privilege granted to resistance is inseparable from the specific historical circumstances that provoked Clausewitz's reflections on organized violence. *On War* distils Clausewitz's thoughts regarding his own experience of the defeat of Prussia by Napoleonic France in the Battle of Jena in 1806 and his subsequent work alongside his mentor Scharnhorst in the military and civil reforms of Prussia in response to this defeat. Clausewitz complemented his work on the Prussian military reforms with an extended reflection on the reasons for defeat and the character of the new warfare that had emerged with the French Revolution. This was by no means a retrospective 'grey on grey' meditation on the passing of the *Ancien Régime*, but an urgent exploration of the possibilities of resisting the seemingly invincible Napoleonic armies. Like Hegel, but more sceptically, he recognized the world-historic significance of Napoleon and the French Revolution but was preoccupied not only with understanding what it meant but also with how to resist its violent, imperial expression.[6] Clausewitz dedicated himself not only to understanding how Napoleon, building on the total mobilization of the people ostensibly in the defence of the revolution during the early 1790s, had invented a new mode of warfare, but also with how to develop the capacity to resist it. He hypothesized that the fusion of politics and war in the French Revolutionary nation created its opposite in the invention of political and military resistance though guerrilla warfare, first in the Vendée then in Spain, Russia and Germany. Stimulated by the Tyrolean and Spanish resistances to Napoleon (Clausewitz is first to describe them as 'resistance'), *On War* arrived at the theory of the People's War of Resistance. Yet in order to understand historic and potential future resistances and to theorize how to resist and preserve the capacity to resist in the face of the Imperial nation state and its arms, Clausewitz was required to revise the concepts through which war had hitherto been understood.

The new warfare demanded a new conceptual structure in order to comprehend and defeat it, one which Clausewitz found in the philosophy of Immanuel Kant. A further alternative title to *On War* could have been *The Critique of Military Reason,* for it is not only an original understanding of the conditions of possibility of modern warfare and its limits but also a significant contribution to the history of post-Kantian philosophy. Clausewitz's understanding and use of Kantian concepts is quite distinct from the more canonical Fichtean and Hegelian developments of the critical philosophy. Like his fellow military post-Kantian Heinrich von Kleist, Clausewitz approaches the critical philosophy from the standpoint of a reason confronted with danger, insecurity and the violence of chance. Departing from a predicament of danger and insecurity, Clausewitz puts in question Kant's insistence on justifying the legitimate possession of concepts, noting that such justification would not be necessary were possession not already endangered, in a state of war. His description of a logic of escalation and the dangers of absolute war is Kantian in its appreciation of the risks to thought and happiness involved in moving from the realm of the spatio-temporally limited (armed observation) to the unlimited absolute of total war. His refusal to pursue or concede dialectical mediation and resolution anticipates later critics of Hegelianism,[7] as does his distinctly unspeculative view of resistance as a concept dedicated to preserving its own capacity or conditions of possibility.

Clausewitz's renown as a strategist and theorist of war has obscured this debt to the critical philosophy. A post-Kantian philosopher trained at the Berlin military academy by the first generation Kantian Kiesewetter, and contemporary with Hegel (1780–1831), he is very rarely – if ever – situated in the tradition which includes Fichte, Schelling and Hegel. This is not too surprising, since his work in many ways faithful to the critical philosophy nevertheless diverged radically from the paths followed by other contemporary readers of Kant. His central and most influential concept of escalation rephrases the orthodox Kantian concern with the dangers of moving from spatio- and temporally limited appearances to the absolutes of reason – in this case, from 'armed observation' to 'absolute war'. His focus on actuality, energy and *Aktus* testifies to his fascination with Kant's modal category of actuality, which distinguishes him and his teacher Kiesewetter from the contemporary fascination with Kant's modal category of possibility (the third modal category – necessity – was left to the 'Spinozans'). The modal categories describe the relation of a subject to the totality of appearances; a focus on possibility leads directly to the centrality of the idea of freedom – that a subject is free with respect to appearances. In different ways this fascination with freedom was shared by Fichte, Schelling and Hegel but not by Clausewitz, who rarely uses the term. In place of freedom, Clausewitz is interested in the Akt or actuality of war: in Book One Chapter 2, he describes how the 'whole Akt of war is permeated by spiritual forces and actualities'; or in Book One, Chapter 1 war is described less as the actualization of violence than the actualization of politics. The relationship of the Clausewitzian subject to the sum of appearances was characterized by the insecurity provoked by the power of chance and the effects of enmity. Clausewitz's model of historical action was less the realization of freedom through the exercise of free will than the management of violence released by the workings of chance and enmity. These were not effects that could be carried through to some dialectical resolution and brought to yield a positive result; indeed, chance and enmity stand as a sign for the ruin of any dialectical endeavour.

The distance of Clausewitz's view of Kant from those of Fichte and Hegel is also evident in his confrontation of reason with history: history is understood as the realm of chance and accident that resists easy subordination to rational sequences or progressions. In Hegel's philosophy of history the accident is a stage or moment in a rational historical sequence, while for Clauswitz it is the interruption or the thwarting of any aspiration to such a rational sequence. The rule of chance and enmity consequently governs the entire argumentative progression of *On War*, structuring its eight books covering the nature and theory of war, strategy, tactics, attack and defence as well as the relationships between absolute and real war and between war and politics.[8] *On War* is in no respect an apology for the workings of reason in history, but is rather an intensification of Kant's reflective judgement in which the case *resists* the application of a rule, puncturing its legitimacy and providing an occasion for a meditation on the impact of chance and enmity on reason.

The importance of resistance for Clausewitz's specific understanding of the new warfare – both Napoleonic offensive and guerrilla resistant war – is underlined by the importance Book Six holds in the architecture of *On War*. It is the largest single book, twice the length of the others, and is dedicated to proving the proposition that '*defence is a stronger form of war than attack* ' (Clausewitz 2010, 335). Clausewitz claims that the defensive war of resistance mounted by a people 'as in Spain' (Clausewitz 2010, 342) shows that a new power (*Potenz)* has arisen which is the 'people armed' or *Volksbewaffnung* (in the Prussian context the *Landsturm)* that now confronts the 'armed people' of the French Republic/Empire. The form of warfare most appropriate to this emergent new power is *Widerstand* or resistance. In Chapter 8 dedicated to analysing the 'Forms of Resistance' (*Widerstandsarten)* Clausewitz reiterates that the people's war of resistance has become the most powerful form of contemporary warfare. The Spanish resistance was the intimation of a new power and a new epoch in the history of war, one of imperial violence and the resistance to it. It is one closely linked with the primacy of the political, discussed most extensively by Clausewitz in Books One and Eight of *On War*.

In Chapter 6B of Book Eight of *On War*, 'War is an Instrument of Politics', Clausewitz proposes a Kantian 'regulative idea' that will unite the otherwise heterogeneous concepts of war and peace: '*war is a part of political action, and by no means a self-sufficient one*', or more precisely, war is 'the continuation of political action through its mixture with other means (Clausewitz 2010, 591). In this proposition politics and war do not have the same status – war is an approximation to the 'logic' or the thought of politics, its analogue, but expressed in 'a different writing, a different speech' – 'It has admittedly its own grammar, but not its own logic' (Clausewitz 2010, 591). The laws of politics and peace may be articulated through logic, but war is the grammatical actualization of this logic, its actuality as an event. Clausewitz continues by claiming politics to be the whole of which war is but a part. The outcome of this metonymy is a strange anamorphosis in which politics turns 'the overwhelming element of war into a mere instrument' transforming the violent event into a logical calculation: the murderous sword of war 'raised with both hands with all physical force' becomes the dagger or a fencing blade of logic and politics. War actualises political logic, while obeying its own grammar; it is a supplement of politics, the substitution of the sword for the pen, of one kind of violent expression for another.

War as a means for continuing or actualizing political logic threatens to take the place of the politics that it should serve: 'As much as politics is magnificent and more powerful, so too war, and this can rise to the heights where war can assume its absolute form' (Clausewitz 2010, 593). The notion of absolute war, often understood as an approximation of war to its Platonic idea, has in fact a very different, unplatonic sense. It is the actualisation of a politics which in its absolute form is no longer politics but a fusion of politics and war, described apocalyptically by Virilio and Girard and figured by Goya as a terrifying Colossus (Lecaldano, 88). Specifically Clausewitz is thinking of the impact of the energies released by revolutionary politics on the intensity of warfare. In his view, war is a grammatical expression, it does not have an ideal essence, and while its expression has degrees of intensity – from minimum to maximum – these are not understood in terms of levels of participation in an idea but as degrees of actualization. Absolute war is the most intense expression of a revolutionary political logic, its fullest actualization and Clausewitz will use the term 'energy' in its classical Aristotelian, pre-thermodynamic sense to describe this actualization. War is the actualisation or the bringing to event of a political logic with varying degrees of intensity which *On War* describes in terms of energy or the capacity to create or to resist the creation of events.

It is only after a series of variations on the theme of war and politics that Clausewitz reveals the historical event that prompted his invention of a new conceptual framework for understanding this relationship, the French Revolution. In a passage of extraordinary clarity Clausewitz observes that 'The monstrous effects (*ungeheueren Wirkungen*) of the French Revolution abroad are clearly less due to the new means and perspectives of its military leadership than to the completely changed state and art of administration, to the character of the regime and the condition of the people' (Clausewitz 2010, 597). The opposing armies of the *Ancien Régime* did not understand this novelty and responded in conventional ways to a new enemy, necessarily for Clausewitz, since even if the enemy had been understood 'philosophically' the existing political constitution did not possess the capacity to resist the new energies released by the nation in arms and its new grammar of war.

The new art of war that 'brought (war) close to its absolute shape' or maximum intensity was only possible following the 'new political (*Politik*) that emerged in France and Europe' (Clausewitz 2010, 597). This 'new political', Clausewitz continues, summoned 'new means and new forces and has made possible an energy of warfare which without it would not have been thinkable' (Clausewitz 2010, 597).[9] The change in the political conditions of possibility (*Politik* or 'the Political') allowed a previously unthinkable actualization of war to take place, one which swept aside the spatio-temporally limited wars that actualized pre-revolutionary polities. This intensification of war, one that approaches the limit of absolute war, is characterized by its capacity to escalate the intensity of violence beyond the limits of political logic. Clausewitz, especially in the opening chapter of *On War*, probably written latest, contemplated the possibility of a political logic (revolution) capable of actualizing a military energy of sufficient intensity to consume and destroy the political itself, a movement exemplified for him in the transformation of revolutionary into imperial France.

Many readings of Clausewitz stop at this point, seeing his theoretical object as limited to the political form of the nation-state and the extreme intensity of its warfare. This is the Clausewitz of a military *energeia* capable of drawing political logic into a self-destructive escalation of violence directed against its enemy and itself. The prospect of escalation would fascinate post-war nuclear strategists and game theorists of the USA and USSR, provoking at once the alarmed efforts of Raymond Aron to theorize the political basis of arms control in the renewed subordination of the grammar of escalation to political logic as well as the apocalyptic gaze of René Girard. Yet in *On War* Clausewitz had already moved beyond Napoleonic warfare to reflect on the new wars of resistance to it, above all the little war or *guerrilla* waged by the Spanish against the French. This was a form of warfare that avoided the seduction of escalation, or the temptation of trying to oppose the Napoleonic enemy by using Napoleonic means. *On War* can be read as a treatise on the philosophical implications of this strategy of resistance, proposing at once a new political logic and a new military grammar and then new ways of thinking the relationship between them.

With this step Clausewitz remained true to his method: societies resisting the Revolution invented new grammars of resistant warfare. But the difficulty arose of how the new grammar of guerrilla warfare and its implications for political logic could be represented theoretically.[10] The philosophical apparatus inherited from Kant, Fichte and above all Hegel was adapted to the political logic of revolution and its view of freedom as autonomy that privileged granting oneself laws. Since Rousseau, laws were legitimated by being our laws given to ourselves and which it would be literally folly to oppose. Kant adopted this logic in the Introduction to the *Critique of Pure Reason* when he famously distinguished the 'critical age' from despotic and nomadic constitutions and their philosophical regimes primarily through its institution of a 'critical tribunal' that gave itself laws while assessing claims brought before it. For Clausewitz this political logic was incapable of comprehending the violence it had itself actualized, let alone a violence which rejected it along with all the privileges it gave to autonomy and reason. Clausewitz was aware that his philosophical debts to Kant and Fichte placed him, like Hegel, in a strong position to understand the political logic actualized in Napoleonic offensive warfare, but not the grammar of the violence that resisted it; in the light of the commitment to a political logic of freedom and autonomy, any resistance to the violence that actualized it could only appear as accidental and irrational folly in the face of the necessity of actualizing reason and freedom in history.

Clausewitz's *On War* finds itself in the same predicament as Goya's *Disasters of War*, namely that of having to make visible a new form of violence and warfare. It was not only a question of describing or analysing the monster or colossus of Napoleonic warfare whose self-consuming escalation of violence was allegorically represented by Goya in terms of Saturn devouring his own children, or a monster prowling the land,[11] but also resistance and the horrors of the *guerrilla*. Goya's etchings invent a new language to express with appropriate intensity this new, terrible warfare. The erosion of the distinction between civil and military expressed in the armed nation met a resistance which affirmed it by not recognizing any distinction between the military and civilian enemy.

Goya's Massacres or *Disasters of War* are exercises in moral disaster, exhibiting the conduct of the new warfare between partisans and Napoleonic troops. Uniformed figures execute civilians as in the second engraving of the series with the the the motto *con razón o sin ella* (with or without reason), while resistant partisans kill uniformed soldiers with axe and dagger in the complementary third engraving with the motto *lo mismo* (the same).[12] The breakdown of the distinction between civilian and soldier is emphasized in the fifth engraving which shows a mother with child engaging in the unmaternal act of spearing an enemy soldier, who, what is more, is wounded in the same place as Christ when speared by the centurion during the crucifixion. The mother kills, the enemy becomes a Christ-like martyr or forsaken son of another mother, and all this revaluation of values takes place above the title *y son fieras* (they are proud). Images such as engraving 36 of a soldier contemplating a hanged civilian (reworked to great effect by the Chapman Brothers)[13] shows the importance of an aesthetics of terror and the display of horror in the actualization of the new warfare, one which employed 'terror' or moral in addition to physical force.

Goya's mottoes and the preservation of legibility in the orientation of the images from left to right emphasize his attempt to make visual sense of the horrific sights provoked by the war of resistance. The first image of the series prepares for this venture with its 'Sad Presentiments of What is to Come', referring not only to the images from this war, but also to those of the new and even more terrible wars on the horizon. Occasionally the consistency of the orientation and legibility of the image utterly breaks down, as in the totally disoriented engraving 30 – described by Todorov as the 'most astonishing' of the *Disasters of War* and which seems to capture the moment of the explosion of a shell in a domestic environment.[14] The disorientation of all familiar settings and the total insecurity this brings exemplifies Goya's attempt to describe the 'Ravages of War'. In this attempt Goya tries to make visible the collision of two emergent grammars of the people's war: the revolutionary/imperial nation-in-arms and the nation of armed resistance. While his testimony was based on direct experience of the invasion and guerrilla resistance – he added to two of his engravings 'I saw that' – Todorov is right to insist that the images of the *Disasters of War* are less an anticipation of war reportage than the attempt to think visually about the 'fatal consequences' of the war and to express the intimation he shared with Clausewitz that with this war something new and monstrous had been born.[15]

The Critique of Pure Resistance

At the same time as Goya was sketching the emergent shape and consequences of the war unfolding before his eyes, Clausewitz was watching and thinking carefully about the lessons to be drawn from events in Spain. In February 1812 when close to the Prussian reformers he chose the form of *Bekenntnisdenkschrift* or Profession of Faith to articulate what he had learnt from the Spanish resistance about strategies for resisting Napoleonic violence.[16] The first profession states that submission to Napoleonic dominance in the form of a 'superficial hope for salvation through the hand of chance' or hoping 'for the future' or trying to avoid provoking 'the rage of the tyrant' will 'undo and undermine the force of the generations to come' (Clausewitz 1966, 689) thus compromising the survival of the capacity to resist while the second calls for Prince and People to mount 'an ultimate and courageous resistance' (Clausewitz 1966, 703–4). It is striking that this resistance is declared against the odds, as a gesture not necessarily expected to succeed in the short term, even if 'this resistance (*Widerstand*) should be viewed as the last and only means for salvation.' (Clausewitz 1966, 704). Resistance itself remains inchoate, and is initially given almost apocalyptic qualities; yet in the third profession Clausewitz turns to the concrete strategic considerations of mounting a People's War while maintaining the monarchic regime. The third profession provides an inventory of the Prussian material capacity to resist while citing the moral and strategic precedents of the *Landsturm* in the Tyrol, the Vendée and Spain.[17] Clausewitz cites these precedents with considerable admiration and does not flinch from their lesson in the terroristic logic of escalation: 'Let us pay back terror with terror, violence with violence. It will be easy for us to outbid the enemy and to lead him back into the limits of moderation and humanity.' (Clausewitz, 1966, 734) Clausewitz defends this 'gloomy intimation' of the logic of escalating violence later analysed in *On War* on the grounds that in the case of ultimate or *absolute* resistance, with nothing to lose, defenders should always trump the aggressors in their preparedness to escalate violence and terror. Yet even here, this eventuality is tempered by his conviction that the terror of People's War can be controlled by the Government or monarch and ultimately brought under political or diplomatic control.

This view of warfare as involving the escalation of terror or moral violence is far removed from the professional warfare of the *Ancien Règime* and responds to the violence unleashed by the revolutionary and Napoleonic armies. The warfare of the *Ancien Règime*, which resembled a carefully choreographed and complicit movement of solid masses, was destroyed by what Clausewitz described in *On War* as the liquid, wave-like offensives of the revolutionary armies.[18] In some of his etchings of the consequences of the war Goya shows the flotsam left by the flood of the passing revolutionary army: destroyed buildings, crops and heaps of mutilated bodies. How could such an irresistible force, this flood of violence, be resisted? When reflecting on this question in Chapter 16 'On the Armed People' of Book Six 'On Defence', Clausewitz counters the metaphor of liquid violence with one of vaporization and condensation. From the defeat of the massed solids of the armies of the *Ancien Régime* by the liquid mass of the revolutionary army emerges the People's War (*Volkskrieg*) of episodic and pointillist attacks, momentary condensations of an intangible political vapour or cloud that is the actualization of a new capacity to resist.

Clausewitz opens his chapter on the 'Armed People' by specifying that in Europe this politico-military phenomenon is 'a manifestation of the nineteenth century', carefully locating it as a response to Napoleonic violence. This proximity to the revolution is underlined in his response to unnamed critics who object that arming the people is a 'revolutionary means' associated with 'anarchy' and consequently as great an internal risk to the social order as any external enemy against whom it might be directed. To this political objection is added the strategic objection, in one of the earliest critiques of the concept of resistance, that the outcomes of People's War are not proportionate to the forces it expends.

Clausewitz responds to both political and strategic objections by arguing that People's War is the actualization of the same political conditions of possibility that brought forth Napoleonic warfare, observing that 'People's War is in general to be seen as a consequence of the warlike element's breaking down its old artificial confines, an extension and intensification of the process of fermentation that we call war' (Clausewitz 2010, 460). People's War intensifies and accelerates the decomposition of the distinction between military and civil society inaugurated by the revolution, reaching a point of intensity sufficient to vaporize the liquid element of war – 'an intensification of the element of war in humanity' (Clausewitz 2010, 461). Clausewitz leaves the question of whether this process is desirable 'to the philosophers', accepting the revolutionizing of society as a political fact with literally incalculable consequences for the grammar of war. His unsentimental reply to the objections against

People's War, as much in the *Bekenntnisdenkschrift* as in *On War*, is that the revolution has already happened, that People's War is its consequence and not its cause, and finally that it is a phenomenon – the actualization of a new intensity of violence – that cannot be submitted to conventional military calculus nor understood in terms of its obsolete grammar.

It is when turning his attention to this new form of warfare that Clausewitz identifies it with resistance. As part of Book Six on 'Defence', the doctrine of resistance emerges in the context of Clausewitz's position that defence is to be preferred over attack, a position that puzzled many of his nineteenth-century readers who did not fully appreciate that Clausewitz was not simply theorizing Napoleonic offensive warfare but also its intensification into the People's War of resistance. He raises new questions appropriate to a new grammar of warfare: 'We no longer ask: what is the cost to itself of the resistance (*Widerstand*) mounted by an entire people with weapon in hand? Rather we ask, what influence can this resistance have, what are its conditions and how is it to be applied?' (Clausewitz 2010, 461). It is these new questions that will speak to the radical movements and thinkers of the nineteenth and twentieth centuries, who also saw the revolution as an intensifying fact, an irreversible event actualizing itself with unpredictable intensities – most notably Lenin, Mao Zedong and Che Guevara.

In venturing to answer these new questions Clausewitz found himself having to think not only beyond the physics of opposed solid bodies axiomatic for traditional military doctrine but also beyond the liquid military body of the revolution. He begins with the problem of describing the actuality of resistance: 'That a resistance so distributed is not suited to achieving the effect (*Wirkung*) of major blows concentrated in space and time is evident' (Clausewitz 2010, 461); instead of physical presence in solid or liquid form, the actualization of People's War must be compared to 'the physical process of vaporisation' (Clausewitz 2010, 461). Clausewitz's use of the doctrine of the four elements has not often been remarked, but there is a consistent alignment of war with fire, with the intensity of its expression graded according to the low degree of solid matter (earth), the intermediate degree of liquid matter (water) and the highest degree of vaporization (air). Absolute warfare, its highest degree of intensity, is on this scale the vaporized violence of People's War.[19] In this high-intensity warfare, actualizations of violence are pointillist and erosive, taking effect in the repetition of small but accumulative attacks extended in space and protracted over time, condensing and vaporizing. Such war

destroys like a swelling Glut the foundations of enemy armies. Since success requires time, a state of tension emerges while both elements work on each other, one that can either be gradually resolved, if the People's War is extinguished at one point and gradually ignited at another, or lead to a crisis when the flames of the general conflagration fall on the enemy army… (Clausewitz 2010, 462).

The fate of Napoleon's army in Spain and Russia was clearly foremost in Clausewitz's mind, but the latter example leads him, in the case of European warfare, to a rare alleviation of his thought in subordinating the new grammar of violence to an existing political logic, one in which it was conceivable for People's War to supplement the regular army.

An ambivalence pervades Clausewitz's discussion, one expressed in the attempt to align People's War with conventional warfare at the same time as appreciating it on its own terms as a novel intensification of violence. In terms of the latter he is remarkably prescient in his analysis of the peculiar difficulties facing People's War:

> According to our representation of People's War, it must be like a foggy or cloudlike being that will never allow itself to be concentrated into a resistant body, otherwise the enemy will apply an appropriate force to this kernel, destroy it and take a number of prisoners: thus morale will sink, all will consider that the main question has been decided, further effort useless and the weapons fall out of the hands of the people. (Clausewitz 2010, 464)

Strategists of People's War must maintain its nebulous state and resist the temptation to assume solid form and enter into conventional conflict; yet for success it cannot remain constantly suspended in the air: 'On the other hand it is however necessary that this fog condenses at certain points and forms threatening clouds from which powerful bolts of lightning can emerge' (Clausewitz 2010, 464).[20] Not only must these points of condensation be without constant presence and manifest themselves at unpredictable intervals, they must also appear where they are least expected, and then disappear without ever engaging in a frontal confrontation with the enemy. Resistance is effected by means of threat, surprise, unpredictable manifestation and disappearance, namely by the refusal to accept the military grammar of the enemy.[21] Violence is thus directed against the margins of the enemy; the war of resistance does not seek to gain territory but to make the enemy's hold of it costly in terms of material and life, with attacks on the system of communication, bridges, passes, fords recommended, but only in order to disrupt the enemy's lines and to be abandoned when counter-attacked, moving the point of condensation to another unpredictable location. Clausewitz predicts the error of all future guerrilla wars (including the Polish at the beginning and the French in the middle of the Second World War) when he warns the forces of resistance against 'confining themselves in a narrow, last refuge, condensing into a defensive posture and being trapped' (Clausewitz 2010, 465).

Clausewitz gives his most extended reflection on the strategy on resistance in Chapter 2 of the first book of *On War* 'On Ends and Means in War' in his discussion of 'pure resistance'. This chapter is a meditation on the inverse of the axiom that the objective of war is to render the enemy incapable of 'further resistance'. What then are the strategic advantages of viewing this objective from the other side, that is, pursuing the objective of 'preserving' the capacity to resist in the face of enemy attack? Is the strategy of defence, of preservation, in fact an effective form of indirect attack on the enemy's own 'capacity to resist'? Clausewitz opens a series of subtle meditations on the war of resistance by situating it in terms of a protracted 'attack' upon the enemy's material and moral resources, pointing out that in this form of war, time is crucial; it is in the interest of resistance to extend the conflict for as long as possible. The 'end' or purpose (*Zweck*) of the pure war of resistance is solely the preservation of the capacity to resist over time and through this eroding the material resources and political will of the enemy.

Against the positive and articulated campaign plans of the logistically superior enemy Clausewitz poses the '*kleinste Zweck*' or minimal end of '*pure resistance,* that is, the struggle without a positive purpose' (Clausewitz 2001, 46). Adopting one of Kant's aesthetic formulations for disinterested beauty, '*Zweckmässigkeit ohne Zweck*', Clausewitz embarks on an analysis of the character of pure resistance, asking first 'how far can this negation extend?' Negation, thought here as the absence of a positive end or purpose, does not reach the point of 'absolute passivity', since pure passion would no longer be a struggle' (Clausewitz 2010, 46). This characteristic reflection on the limit case, only seemingly analogous to Hegel's focus on negation, allows him to claim that the negation of pure resistance is nevertheless 'an activity, through which as much of the enemy's forces are destroyed as to make them surrender their purposes' (Clausewitz 2010, 46). It is a negative activity aimed at undermining the material and moral resources of the enemy – in short, its capacity to mount an effective counter-resistance. Clausewitz then affirms that this grammar of war is characterized by its surrender of 'effectivity through a single act' (*Wirksamkeit im einzelnen Akt*) in favour of an extended time or 'duration of the struggle'. Anticipating what Mao would later call the 'protracted war of resistance', Clausewitz links the war of resistance – now called 'mere' or 'bare' resistance (*bloßen Widerstand*) – to a fight in and for time which pursues the minimal aim of 'exhausting' the enemy through sheer persistance, through the political calculation that its intended military objective would in the long term become too costly to sustain in terms of material and morale. In this way the enemy's capacity to counter-resist is fatally compromised.[22]

By the end of the chapter Clausewitz seems to have settled on a distinction between positive war – aimed at destroying the enemy's capacity to resist – and negative war aimed at eroding or exhausting this capacity. With this Clausewitz arrives at an insight which will reappear in Nietzsche's aligning of resistance and ressentiment in the *Genealogy of Morals*:

> For mere resistance lacks positive purpose, and thus cannot direct our forces to other objects, but is only determined (*nur bestimmt sein*) to the destruction of the purposes of the enemy. (Clausewitz 2010, 52)

For Clausewitz the play of the positive and the negative are reciprocal but not dialectical. If dialectic and dialectical resolution characterize the 'positive' struggle of opposed armies dedicated to achieving a result through sublation in battle, the 'negative' posture of pure resistance and its objective of preserving the capacity to resist undermines rather than sublates:

> The effort to destroy enemy forces has a positive end and tends to positive results, ultimately the overthrow of the enemy. The preservation of one's own forces has a negative end and leads to the destruction of the enemy's objectives, that is, it is pure resistance for which the ultimate aim can only be to prolong the duration of the action and so exhaust the enemy. (Clausewitz 2010, 52)

The aim of exhausting an enemy rather than attaining victory through a Napoleonic-Hegelian struggle for recognition challenges not only the force of the enemy but also the foundations of their political logic and strategic grammar. The liquid flow of the Napoleonic armies required a steady supply of material that could only be appropriated from a static enemy; this would not be possible when facing the vaporous adversary of the guerrilla who would ensure the maximum disruption of supply without carrying any resources whose capture could in any way aid the enemy.

The war of pure resistance is not a detail in Clausewitz's wider philosophy of war, but an essential conceptual link between war and politics. The war of resistance is directed to disengaging the grammar of war – the kind of war that needs to be waged against a guerrilla army – from the political logic of the enemy understood materially and morally. The inability to fight like the guerrillas introduces political logic and political considerations into the field, overriding purely strategic and tactical evaluations. In the case of a deliberately protracted war, the initiative of the enemy is sapped, its military momentum undermined, and the conduct of war transferred from the battlefield to the realm of politics. The war of resistance brings into relief the triad of forces and capacities that Clausewitz at the end of his life saw constituting the anatomy of modern political-war: the people, the commander and the politician. The passion of the people at the moment of war may complement the soul or genius of the commander in overcoming the calculations of the politician, but if the war is extended then the role of political calculation – what Clausewitz repeatedly calls the 'balance' of cost and benefit – reasserts itself. The war of resistance is thus explicitly conducted at both military and political levels, a theoretical insight on Clausewitz's part that would be repeatedly confirmed in practice during the revolutionary wars of the twentieth century. The protracted war of resistance – armed or unarmed – directed at compromising the material and moral resources of the enemy, as we shall see, characterizes both Mao and Gandhi's violent and non-violent strategies of resistance.

In his later work from the 1960s Carl Schmitt recognized the significance of Clausewitz's analysis of the People's War and developed it further in his reflections on Marxist-Leninist and Maoist doctrines of the revolutionary war and the Swiss defensive doctrine of 'total resistance'. *The Theory of the Partisan* and his later essay on Clausewitz develop the thesis that People's War is war approaching its absolute degree of intensity, intimating an actualization of violence that intensifies as it is raised to the level of global class war. At a global level, People's War can no longer sustain its vaporized, unpredictable expressions against the movements of a regular army – its tactics of condensation and surprise become predictable and fall back on secured territory, as in Maoist doctrine. We shall return to Schmitt's analysis of the global partisan and his view of Mao Zedong as the *catechon* or restrainer of global civil war as well as the legislator of a new 'law of the earth' in Chapter 3. Schmitt was writing after the experience of a century and a half of wars of revolution and resistance, while for Clausewitz, the grammar of revolutionary and imperial warfare and the art of resistance to it was a new phenomenon which he helped begin to examine and understand. Yet in doing so, in reflecting historically and philosophically on the Napoleonic wave of violence and resistance to it, he fundamentally transformed the scenario of modern war and politics.

Resistance to Empire

Marx, in an article 'Truth Testified' written for the *New York Daily Tribune* in 1859, cites Clausewitz as an exemplary critic of ideology, one who saw through the illusions of the logic of politics to the truth of the actuality of violence: 'victories and defeats, if contemplated with the eye of science, look rather the reverse of the picture of them reflected on the brains of the political gossip' (Marx and Engels 1980, 435; see also 444). This view of the strategist bereft of political illusions to the point of cynicism was shared by both Marx and Engels. In a letter to Marx of January 7th 1858 written while re-reading *On War*, Engels referred to Clausewitz's 'odd way of philosophising, but *per se* very good', appreciating his analogy that 'Combat is to war what cash payment is to commerce; however seldom it need happen in reality, everything is directed towards it and ultimately it is bound to occur and proves decisive' (Marx and Engels 1983, 242). Marx agreed, replying 'The fellow possesses a common sense bordering on the ingenious' (Marx and Engels 1983, 247). Yet in spite of this appreciation of Clausewitz's almost macabre candour and his cold distance from any dialectic, his disillusioned insight into the actuality of violence might seem at first hand remote from the enthusiasm of revolutionary politics.

Yet the insight into the ubiquity of war was fully compatible with a view of the ubiquity of class war.[23] Marx and Engels brought the emblems of the French Revolution and imperial expansion so despised by Clausewitz – liberty, equality and fraternity – under the aegis of resistance and proletarian revolution. Both Marx and Engels saw class war taking place behind the slogans of the 'idealism of the state' and sought to bring Clausewitz's testimony to the implacable truths of war to the history, actuality and future of class war. It is perhaps more Clausewitz's non-dialectical analysis of enmity and its consequences than the Hegelian dialectic of master and slave that informs their understanding of the conduct and consequences of class struggle. At the beginning of the *Communist Manifesto* the history of class struggle is understood to end 'either in a revolutionary constitution of society at large, or in the common ruin of the contending classes' (Marx 1973, 68), that is to say, with either an Hegelian or a Clausewitzian ending. The outcome of class war – reconstitution of society or escalating mutual destruction – largely depends, in Clausewitzian terms, on the plan of war adopted by the resistance. The *Communist Manifesto* is an attempt to provide such a plan, to rephrase the quotidian resistance of the workers to bourgeois rule according to the grammar of the actuality of class war and the political logic of revolutionary Communist consciousness. The first part of the manifesto describes the formation of the warring parties, the second the alliance of resistant workers with the Communists, the third the rejection of competing Communist plans of war, and the fourth, the articulation of class war as the people's war of resistance with the project or plan of war for the revolutionary reconstitution of society.

In Section IV of the *Communist Manifesto* Marx and Engels propose an alignment of the workers' resistance with Communist revolutionary logic, an alliance that would dominate the Communist movement for over a century. This involved translating resistance into the logic of a conscious political project oriented to the future:

> The Communists fight for the attainment of the immediate aims, for the enforcement of the momentary interests of the working class; but in the movement of the present, they also represent and take care of the future of that movement. (Marx and Engels 1973, 97)

The supplement, or 'also', marks the linkage between present resistance and the care for the future; the tactics of resistance are thus oriented according to a revolutionary future already present to Communist consciousness. While the Communists support the immediate resistance of workers to the rule of the bourgeois class, they do not neglect the duty of care for the future of the movement. This duty is legitimated by and pursued in the name of the Communists' conscious grasp of the meaning and sense of the workers' pre-conscious resistance.

The alignment of immediate tactical resistance with broader conscious strategic objectives would perplex the Communist movement for well over a century. One approach to it involved the construction of an historical constellation between the struggles of the workers' movement and the experience of the early Christian resistance to the Roman Empire – what might be described as the evangelical view of Communism's historical mission.[24] The resistance of early Christians to the Roman Empire was cited as an anticipation of the workers' socialist resistance to the empire of capital. In the last third of the nineteenth century this parallel metamorphosed into the opposition between the political figures of the Commune and Empire. In *Capital* Marx describes and endorses the workers' tactical resistance to capital – factory acts, struggles over the length of the working day, prohibition of child labour – while his Addresses on the Paris Commune and critiques of nascent social democracy formed part of his care for the Communist future of the workers' movement. Yet it is in the Addresses on the Commune that Marx looked beyond the distinction between resistance in the present and the conscious revolutionary aspirations for a Communist future towards the future-oriented but not necessarily *conscious* resistance embodied in the Commune.[25]

Marx responded immediately to the event of the Paris Commune with a text (and two drafts) of an Address on the Commune to the International Working Men's Association. The history of the Paris Commune and Marx's texts on would assume a mythic near-sacred character in the socialist and communist movements of the early twentieth century. Lenin saw in them a series of indispensable lessons in the strategy and tactics of revolution, an 'historical analysis' characterized by 'genius'.[26] Their repute remains untouched by the remarkable reassessment of the work of Marx undertaken after the collapse of the 'real existing socialist' regimes in 1989. The recognition of a plurality of voices in the Marxian text proposed in Blanchot's attending to the 'Three Voices of Marx' was taken further by Jacques Derrida in *Spectres of Marx* (1993) and in Daniel Bensaïd's *Marx for Our Times* (1995). Yet *The Civil War in France* has remained innocent of this reassessment, underestimating some of the extraordinary departures that Marx made in his reflections on the actuality of the Commune. These may be approached by confronting the logics and voices at work in Marx's commune with Nietzsche's genealogy of 'the Commune' in *ressentiment* and the desire for vengeance.

Marx was a close student of French politics: his analyses of the 1848 Revolution and the 1851 *coup-d'etat* of Louis Napoleon remain classics of history and political theory. He followed closely the institution of the Second Empire in 1851 and described its internal tensions provoked by speculative finance capital, an inflated bureaucracy and sustained police repression. On July 19th 1870 the Empire declared war on Bismarck's Prussia and was rapidly defeated, surrendering on 2 September. Already in July Marx gave his first Address to the International Working Men's Association in London on events in France. He prophesied accurately that the war was the 'death knell of the 2nd Empire' and announced that 'in contrast to the old society, with its economic miseries and its political delirium, a new society is springing up, whose international rule will be *Peace*, because its national ruler is everywhere the same – *Labour*! The pioneer of that new society is the International Working Men's Association' (Marx 1974, 176). He saw an international society emerging from the ruins of Empire in the same way as the Church emerged from the ruins of the Roman Empire, except this time the parallel is complicated by the very material analogy of the International Working Men's Association with the 'pioneers' who were laying the track for the global railway network.

The French surrender was succeeded by the proclamation of a Republic on 4 September, closely followed by Marx's Second Address of 9 September calling on the workers critically to support the Republic in its resistance against the German invasion of France while building up the presence of workers' institutions within it: 'They have not to recapitulate the past, but to build up the future. Let them calmly and resolutely improve the opportunities of republican liberty, for the work of their own class organisation' (Marx 1974, 185). Paris came under German siege on September 19th and was largely abandoned by the Republican government's capitulation on 28 January 1871. Parisians began to organize their own resistance with committees of vigilance and the strengthening of the National Guard: with these initiatives, according to Marx, Paris 'heroically resolved to run all the hazards of a resistance against the French conspirators' (Marx 1974, 200). The Parisians repulsed an attempt by the army to invade the capital on March 18th 1871 and held elections to the Commune on March 26th. The Commune passed a number of measures, including Courbet's demolition of the Vendôme Column celebrating the Imperial military victories that had earlier so alarmed Clausewitz, but even more significantly it actualized the principle of a democratically accountable non-bureaucratic administration sustained by a people's army or militia. The Commune lasted 72 days before the invasion of Paris brought it to a bloody end in barricade fighting (600 barricades), setting on fire of parts of Paris and the taking and execution of hostages. It was succeeded by a brutal repression in which it is estimated that at least 100,000 people were executed, condemned to prison or deported. The final barricade of the Commune fell on 28 May and it was on 30 May that Marx gave his third – and now valedictory – address, in English, which was then rapidly published in June.

How did Marx understand this act of resistance and how does he further it by means of his address? What logic does he bring to bear in organizing the historical materials that he gathered through newspapers and correspondents and to what end? Putting Marx's *The Civil War in France* to the test of Nietzsche's *The Genealogy of Morals* and the latter's own view of the Commune and socialism in the fragments collected in *The Will to Power* allows some initial critical orientation. Marx and Nietzsche are rarely read together, but in this case the experiment of confronting the two authors and texts is warranted by a number of points of historical proximity. Both Marx and Nietzsche address the conflict of Empire and Commune and both set the resistance of the Paris Commune to Empire in an historical constellation that extends to the Christian resistance to the Roman Empire.[27] But Nietzsche reads both the ancient and modern resistances in terms of a logic of vengeance and *ressentiment* which Marx on some occasions confirms but on others decisively exceeds.

The confrontation of *The Civil War in France* with *The Genealogy of Morals* puts Marx's address to the test of *ressentiment* at the same time as putting Nietzsche's genealogy to the test of Marx's assessment of the significance of the Commune. Nietzsche's analysis of *ressentiment* seems to apply to only one strand of Marx's account of the Commune's resistance to Empire. In the first essay of *The Genealogy of Morals* Nietzsche distinguishes between the creation of values in 'noble' morality and that of the 'slave revolt of morals'. The latter begins

> [...] when *ressentiment* itself becomes creative and gives birth to values: the *ressentiment* of natures that are denied the true reaction, that of deeds, and compensate themselves with an imaginary revenge. While every noble morality develops from a triumphant affirmation of itself, slave morality from the outset says No to what is "outside", what is "different," what is not itself, and *this* No is its creative deed. (Nietzsche 1969, I, 10)

While noble morality begins with an affirmation of difference, slave morality departs from its negation. The two modalities – one proceeding from affirmation to negation, the other from negation to affirmation – determine two moralities, one organized around good and bad, the other around good and evil.

Nietzsche describes with great clarity the two moral orientations and their genealogies. He begins with *ressentiment*, saying that 'in order to exist, slave morality always first needs a hostile external world; it needs, physiologically speaking, external stimuli in order to act at all – its action is fundamentally reaction' (Nietzsche 1969, I, 10). Slave morality, in other words, is resistant; by contrast

> The reverse is the case with the noble mode of valuation: it acts and grows spontaneously, it seeks its opposite only so as to affirm itself more gratefully and triumphantly – its negative concept "low," "common," "bad" is only a subsequently-invented pale, contrasting image in relation to its positive basic concept – filled with life and passion through and through... (Nietzsche 1969, I, 10)

The affirmation of the noble

> [...] conceives the basic concept "good" in advance and spontaneously out of himself and only then creates for himself an idea of the "bad"! This "bad" of noble origin and that "evil" out of the cauldron of unsatisfied hatred – the former an after production, a side issue, a contrasting shade, the latter on the contrary the original thing, the beginning, the

distinctive *deed* in the conception of a slave morality – how different these words "bad" and "evil" are, although they are both apparently the opposite of the same concept "good". But it is *not* the same concept of "good". (Nietzsche 1969 I, 11)

The affirmative evaluation of good and bad and the negative and reactive evaluation of good and evil diverge fundamentally on the issue of the desire for revenge. This desire is essential to *ressentiment*, which for Nietzsche is the morality of resistance, but it has no role in the origins of noble morality which defines itself affirmatively in creating a new world with little thought for resisting the old. Nietzsche here intensifies Clausewitz's thought that resistance is defined by negation, by the desire to preserve itself in the face of attack, and that sentimentality is dangerous in this context of enmity and revenge.[28]

Nietzsche moves from the formal part of his genealogy of morals to an historical analysis of Christianity in its conflict with the Roman Empire, seeing the desire for vengeance concealed in Christian calls for justice and the hope that 'their kingdom too shall come' (Nietzsche 1969, I, 15). He cites those vengeful Christians Tertullian and Aquinas who claim that 'The blessed in heaven will see the punishments of the damned, in order that their bliss shall be more delightful for them' (Nietzsche 1969, I, 15). Nietzsche gives a different perspective on the socialist vision of a parallel between the christian resistance to the Roman Empire and the workers' resistance to the empire of capital, judging its significance quite differently. The appeal by socialists to the precedent of christian resistance to Empire brought it under Nietzsche's broader critique of *ressentiment*. In response to the question 'Nihilism stands at the door: whence comes this uncanniest of all guests?' (Nietzsche 1968, § 1), Nietzsche answers 'The end of Christianity' and its survival in socialism: 'Residues of Christian value judgements are found everywhere in socialist and positivist systems' (Nietzsche 1968, § 1). Socialism is the 'this-worldly solution, but in the same sense – that of the eventual triumph of truth, love and justice...' (Nietzsche 1968, § 30). It pursues christian values under a different guise, but for Nietzsche it remains motivated by the same *ressentiment*, the same slave morality or desire for revenge. Just as contemporary socialism draws inspiration from early Christianity, so too may the historic christian resistance to Empire be identified retrospectively as socialist:

The gospel: the news that a gateway to happiness stands open for the poor and lowly – that all one has to do is free oneself from the institutions, traditions, guardianship of the upper classes: to this extent the rise of Christianity is nothing more than the *typical socialist doctrine*. (Nietzsche 1968, § 209)

Nietzsche sees in the resistance to injustice and to the traditions and institutions of class rule a disowned violence and desire for revenge: 'In the background is insurrection, the explosion of a stored-up antipathy towards the "masters"...' (Nietzsche 1968, § 209), a *ressentiment* that for him marks the elective affinity of Christianity and socialism, one he identifies as 'passive nihilism'. This condition is characterized by a desire to punish, an insurrection driven by the desire for vengeance:

> The socialist, the anarchist, the nihilist – in as much as they find in their existence something of which someone must be *guilty*, they are still the closest relations of the Christian, who also believes he can better endure his sense of sickness and ill-constitutedness by finding someone whom he can make responsible for it. The instinct of revenge and *ressentiment* appears here in both cases as a means of enduring, as the instinct of self-preservation. (Nietzsche 1968, § 373)

Nietzsche locates the Paris Commune in this context of socialist *ressentiment*, seeing it as a vengeful insurrection. His disclosure of the hatred and desire for revenge masked in the professions of peace, love and justice of Christian and socialist *ressentiment* is applied in his critique of the Commune. The latter is but the harbinger of a major, modern slave revolt in morals: 'the Paris Commune, which has its apologists and advocates in Germany too, was perhaps no more than a minor indigestion compared to what is coming' (Nietzsche 1968, § 125). In this dictated fragment from 1885 Nietzsche sees the Commune as announcing what he elsewhere called the *grosse Politik* of the coming twentieth century, in which the socialist experiment would violently refute itself, a *demonstrandum ad absurdum*, nevertheless still worthwhile 'even if it were gained with a tremendous expenditure of human lives' (Nietzsche 1968, § 125). The future is resentful, the pursuit of revenge in the name of justice and fraternity would eventually destroy itself in an accelerated version of the self-destruction of Christianity. Yet by destroying itself and 'a society that wallows in stupidity', socialism, even if born of revenge, may yet become a worthy enemy. Nietzsche concludes that resistance to socialism may prove 'useful and therapeutic' in forcing noble Europeans 'to retain spirit' and vigilance in the face of their resentful enemy.

We may now ask Marx the Nietzschean question: what is the genealogy of the Commune, was it noble or was it born of *ressentiment*? This specific question implies the broader one of whether resistance can ever be noble or if it is always reactive and tainted by *ressentiment*? Put even more starkly: is Marx's text driven by a desire for revenge? One of Marx's voices *is* certainly the voice of vengeance; it is the voice of violent satire, the voice that proclaims the lost battle but not the lost war, the voice that closes *The Civil War in France* prophesying the vengeance of history on the 'exterminators' of the Paris Commune: 'history has already nailed them to that eternal pillory from which all the prayers of their priests will not avail to redeem them' (Marx 1974, 233). The evocation of the judgement of history and the verdict of eternal calumny on the victors over the Commune is the Communist equivalent to Tertullian's joy at the sufferings of the damned. This voice of *ressentiment* is closely linked with another, more subtle timbre, that of sacrifice, one later adopted by Lenin with respect to the Paris Commune. The Communards are described as the 'self-sacrificing champions of a new and better society' and 'working men's Paris, in the act of its heroic self-holocaust, involved in its flames buildings and monuments' (Marx 1974, 228). This praise of suicidal sacrifice is almost a textbook verification of Nietzsche's suspicion that 'in a socialist society life negates itself, cuts off its own roots' (Nietzsche 1968, § 125). Marx, in other words, resists the calumnies of the Commune by the Party of Order (Marx 1974, 230) by resorting to discourses of self-sacrifice and final, eternal revenge that are rooted in *ressentiment*. The rulers 'tearing apart the living body of the proletariat cannot expect to return triumphantly into the intact architecture of their abodes' (Marx 1974, 228).

Yet there is another voice in Marx's Address which is much stronger, and of unquestionable nobility. It is the voice of the coming new world, the International Working Men's Association which speaks through Marx. For the Civil War in France is not just the French Civil War, but the latest manifestation on French soil of a global civil war between Empire and Commune. The specific empire in contention is the French Second Empire of Louis Napoleon, but globally the empire at issue is the state form in general that uses its monopoly of violence, concentration of wealth and bureaucratic domination to repress the insurgent working class. The Commune is the emergent political form in which the means of violence are democratically distributed in militias, ownership of the means of production held in common and bureaucratic domination replaced by democratic self-determination. For Marx, global civil war is the conflict between Empire and Commune, the old world with the new, the slaveholders against the slaves, a conflict driven by the desire for vengeance, only not where Nietzsche saw it, but in the masters, in 'this civilisation and justice (that) stand forth as undisguised savagery and lawless revenge'

(Marx 1974, 226). In the face of repression and vengeance, the resistance of the Commune to Empire takes on a noble and affirmative character, creating a new democratic world beyond resisting the old.

The affirmation of the Paris Commune sounds through and beyond the voices of negation and dialectical opposition that Marx adopts when describing it as '[t]he true antithesis to the *Empire itself* – that is to the state power, the centralized executive of which the Second Empire is only the exhausting formula…' (Marx 1974, 248). The First Draft also speaks of the '[t]he Second Empire [as] the final form of this state usurpation. The Commune was its definite negation, and therefore, the initiation of the social revolution of the nineteenth century. Whatever therefore its fate in Paris, it will make its way round the world' (Marx 1974, 249). Yet something else emerges from this language of negation: the Commune does not merely reactively resist or 'revolt against' Empire but, more importantly, affirms itself and its own good: the Commune, in the words of the First Address, 'sprung up', was a 'positive form' or something new and historically unprecedented.

The affirmative character of the Commune is expressed by Marx in terms of its expansive rather than repressive character. In the First Draft of the Address, Marx noted that '*It was only the working class that* could formulate by the word "Commune" – and initiate by the fighting Commune of Paris – this new aspiration' (Marx 1974, 249). The Commune raised the revaluation of values that was the social revolution of the nineteenth century to a new level and intensity. Marx recognizes its nobility in a remarkable passage on the riddle of the Commune in the Third Address:

> The multiplicity of interpretations to which the Commune has been subjected, and the multiplicity of interests that have construed it in their favour, show that it was a thoroughly expansive political form, while all previous forms of government had been emphatically repressive. Its true secret was this. It was essentially a working-class government, the produce of the struggle of the producing against the appropriating class, the political form at last discovered under which to work out the economical emancipation of labour. (Marx 1974, 212)

This passage introduces the notion of an 'expansive political form', one that is entirely new, and a break with the 'repressive' state form adopted by all previous forms of government.[29] It is, in short, not a reactive/repressive, but an affirmative/expansive political form. It has generated a worldwide movement and with it a multiplicity of interpretations that testify to it being an event resisting subsumption under existing, repressive political concepts such as the state. It becomes less the spectre haunting the old capitalist world than a sphinx inhabiting the borderlands of the new. Yet its true secret was that, while emerging from the reactive predicament of a struggle *against* Empire, it was nevertheless capable of creating a new political form *for* the emancipation of labour or 'Commune'.

Marx's emphasis on the affirmative character of the Commune places the purity of Nietzsche's genealogy of *ressentiment* into question. There is never a pure noble morality free of *ressentiment*, nobility consists not in innocent creation but in overcoming a predicament of *ressentiment*. In Marx's scenario, the proletariat in its struggle *against* Empire finds affirmation in the *struggle for* a new political form. By resisting Empire, the proletariat defies an already reactive and poisonously vengeful political logic of repression. In section IV of the Third Address Marx establishes a parallel between France and the slave society of the American South and thus between the French and the American civil wars. Both, he suggests, are revolts against the Republic mounted by slave-owners, literally in the case of the American and metaphorically in the case of the French Civil War.[30] Far from being a 'slave revolt in morals', the Commune marked a noble resistance to the 'slave-masters revolt in morals' (see Marx 1974, 253, 263), affirming the future in a critical citation of the past political form of the 'commune'.

By emphasizing the slave revolt in morals against Empire, seeing in it a reactive desire for revenge, Nietzsche did not understand that this revolt was directed not against any 'noble morality' of Empire, but against the *ressentiment* of an existing slave*holders* revolt in morals. By not seeing what was new and expansive in the Commune, seeing it only as regression, Nietzsche misunderstood its fusion of resistance and affirmation as well as its politics of citation: 'Who can say whether modern democracy, even more modern anarchism and especially that inclination for *commune* for the most primitive form of society which is shared by all the socialists of Europe, does not signify in the main a massive *counterattack* (Nietzsche 1969, 1, 5). His model of socialism was the atavistic anti-Semitic Christian Socialism of Dühring, itself a precursor of German National Socialism also criticised at length by Engels: he was unable to see what distinguished the Commune from Christian Socialism, regarding both as manifestations of the same regression. In a rare moment of philological weakness, Nietzsche did not see that the word 'commune' was itself a citation combining archaic and new, a pre- and a post-state political form. As Marx noted

It is generally the fate of completely new historical creations to be mistaken for the counterpart of older and even defunct forms of social life, to which they may bear a certain likeness. Thus, this new Commune, which breaks the modern state power, has been mistaken for a reproduction of the medieval communes, which first preceded, and afterwards became the substratum of, that very state power. (Marx 1974, 211)

Marx's care for this new 'expansive political form' combined resistance in the present with an orientation towards the future. In the celebrated letters to Kugelmann of 12 and 17 April 1871 Marx emphasizes the initiative of the Communards in terms that both exceed and confirm sacrificial discourse: 'what elasticity, what historical initiative, what capacity for sacrifice in these Parisians!' (Marx 2008, 86). The seizure of initiative and the flexibility or elasticity of response to difficult circumstances exceed any logic of reaction or *ressentiment*, even if this reappears in the 'capacity for sacrifice' and Marx's search for 'who is to blame' for its failure. For Marx it was the Communards themselves who were to blame for not being sufficiently affirmative in seizing the opportune moment, or *kairos*, by taking the initiative in the civil war. The right moment was missed because of moral and political scruples: 'They did not *want to start the civil war*, as if that mischievous *abortion* Thiers had not already started the civil war with his attempt to disarm Paris' (Marx and Lenin 2008, 86). By renouncing the initiative and lapsing into a reactive posture, the Commune compromised its own invention of an 'expansive political form'.

With these reflections on the civil war, Marx reorients the vector of resistance, seeing the government of Thiers as resisting the insurgent future 'positive form' of the Commune. Lenin in his citations of the Paris Commune was sensitive to this initiative, the opening to a new future. In his comment on Marx's reference to a 'positive form' in *State and Revolution* Lenin asks 'What was the state it was beginning to create' (Lenin 2008, 110). He understood the new form in terms of a 'gigantic replacement' of state institutions by others (perhaps no longer even 'institutions') of a 'fundamentally different order'. Although he resorts to the dialectical rhetoric of a transformation of quantity into quality, he is clearly referring to something entirely new, even if its novelty is compromised by the necessity of resistance; the reactive posture of 'suppressing the bourgeoisie and its resistance' could only compromise the creative, futural gesture that was and will be the Commune. Lenin followed Marx in scrutinizing the Commune for the new 'political forms it had *disclosed*' (28, 123, Lenin's emphasis). The disclosure of a new 'expansive form' was compromised but not entirely suppressed by the need to resist a prior resistance, by the necessity of being an episode in a global civil war at the same time as taking care for a future world peace.

Marx's text on the Paris Commune speaks in many voices: in the voice of vengeance and sacrifice that makes *The Civil War in France* a classic of socialist *ressentiment*, but also in the voice of invention, affirmation and the welcoming of the new. The latter voice proclaims the Paris Commune's challenge to all existing categories of political constitution by announcing the emergence of a new, expansive political form opposed to the repressive form hitherto adopted by the state. While Nietzsche was able to diagnose the Commune's *ressentiment*, he was not capable of appreciating this affirmative moment, perhaps because he too, in the end, looked at it through the lens of *ressentiment*. One voice that is strikingly absent from all of these proceedings, however, is the voice of consciousness: at no point in any of his Addresses on the Commune does Marx emphasise the term *consciousness*, nor does he show any sign of organizing his reflections in terms of it. This is, of course, ironic given the subsequent obsession of Marxist theorists and militants with the philosophy of consciousness and the single-minded application of its protocols to the problem of revolutionary action. Instead Marx's Addresses evoke the actuality of the Commune, the opening achieved in this event that, despite all repression, could not subsequently be closed.

Resistant and Political Consciousness

Lenin's *What is to be Done* (1901) has also been rediscovered as a text of many voices (Budgen 2007; Lih 2008; Lih 2011) but one in which the voice of consciousness prevails. Lenin's care for the Communist future focused on ensuring correct class-consciousness. Yet this embrace of the philosophy of consciousness is not innocent of the Nietzschean trope of reactive and affirmative moralities, as becomes evident in Lenin's distinction between reactive or resistant, trade union consciousness and affirmative revolutionary party consciousness. The importance of Nietzsche for late nineteenth-century social democracy and especially for the Russian Bolshevik faction is a matter of historical record,[31] including Lenin, whose copy of *Also Sprach Zarathustra* was found in the Kremlin book cabinet after his death (Service 2000, 203).

However, the theoretical significance of this historical proximity has only recently begun to be appreciated. A striking example is Alain Badiou's essay 'One Divides itself into Two', which employs Nietzschean categories in what amounts to reading Lenin and Mao as the fulfillers of Nietzsche's *grosse Politik*. In understanding their work and practice he cites Nietzsche's destruction of metaphysics, the transvaluation of all values and the distinction between active and passive nihilism. Yet he does not explicitly declare the implied conclusion that Leninism is a Nietzschean politics grafted onto Marxist economics; his allusions to the presence of Nietzschean concepts in Lenin are not spelt out. His reluctance is shared by Lars L. Lih, whose research has done much to trouble the clichés surrounding Lenin but who does not openly confront the possibility of Leninism as a Nietzschean politics. The idea that Nietzsche might be an important and catalytic figure in the complex articulation of classical and modern philosophical texts that make up Lenin's philosophy is still not on the political or philosophical agenda.

The importance of Lenin's philosophical reflection to his political practice was already acknowledged in Lukács' pioneering study of 1924 *Lenin* and subsequently in Althusser's *Lenin and Philosophy* and Antonio Negri's *Trentatre lezioni su Lenin* from the early 1970s. The inquiry into Lenin and philosophy focuses less on his explicitly philosophical texts such as *Materialism and Empirio-Criticism* than on *What is to be Done* and selectively edited extracts from the notebooks of his Bern exile during the First World War when he closely studied Hegel's *Logic*, Aristotle's *Metaphysics* and Clausewitz's *On War*. The war and his philosophical studies radicalized Lenin's views on revolutionary action, leading to the well-known *April Theses* and *State and Revolution* where, citing the Paris Commune, he came close to anarchistic positions on the abolition of the state (see Balibar in Budgen, 207–21). What is at issue in this philosophical politics can be summed up in his famous aphorism from the notebooks of 1917:

> *Aphorism*: it is impossible to obtain a complete understanding of Marx's *Das Kapital* and especially its first chapter without first having made a thorough study and acquired an understanding of the *whole* of Hegel's *Logic*. Consequently not one Marxist in the past half century has completely understood Marx.

This call for a radical reading of Hegel has continued to trouble many philosophical readers of Lenin, above all Althusser, and especially with respect to the travails of consciousness. Such readers will be troubled even further by the claim that understanding Lenin in turn requires that Hegel be supplemented by Clausewitz. Lenin read Clausewitz as part of the same study programme that included Hegel, and his interest, as shown in his notes, fell on three themes in Clausewitz: the dialectic, the continuation of politics as war, and the movement between attack and defence (or the problem of resistance).[32] So as Lenin insisted in 'The Bankruptcy of the Second International'

The fundamental thesis of the dialectic ... is that war is a simple continuation of policy by other means (more precisely, by violence). Such is the formula of Clausewitz, one of the greatest writers on the history of war, and whose thought was inspired by Hegel. This was also the viewpoint of Marx and Engels who regarded any war as the continuation of the policy of enemy powers – and different classes within these countries in a defined period. (cited Heuser, 19)

This recognition of the centrality of the theme of resistance to Clausewitz supports the view of readers such as Negri who argue that Lenin's philosophical positions were already in place in *What is to be Done* and were only refined and developed in the philosophical notebooks.[33]

The importance given to consciousness in Lenin's political philosophy forces us to ask: is Lenin a political Cartesian, and is *What is to be Done?* his discourse on method? For contrary to Marx, Lenin's text is obsessed with the philosophy of consciousness – it is the *quality* of consciousness that distinguishes mere resistance to capitalism from its revolutionary overthrow. And, consistent with the philosophy of consciousness inaugurated by Descartes, not only the quality but also the subject of consciousness is important. In place of the consciousness of the philosopher, Lenin's subject of consciousness is a social class, one paradoxically constituted by its consciousness of itself and its historic vocation. Lenin's philosophy and political practice is defined by consciousness, and even a sophisticated and critical reader such as Negri (also and not coincidentally a close reader of Descartes) is forced to remain within its terms. Negri reads Lenin's philosophy as an account of the formation of a subject – one emerging from resistance to the ambient forces of production and reproduction to the attainment of full political subjectivity through consciousness. Yet intrinsic to any account of the emergence of consciousness – from Descartes' *Discourse on the Method* to Hegel's *Phenomenology of Spirit* – is an understanding first of time and then of the struggle between the emergent clarity of consciousness and the obscure promptings of force.

The political strategy elaborated in Lenin's 1901–2 text has profound philosophical investments. *What is to be Done: Burning Questions of Our Movement* addresses debates within the Russian Social Democratic Party concerning the role of the party and party organization. It recognizes that the existence of autocratic government places the party in a posture of resistance, but argues that this defensive posture may be transformed through clear theoretical consciousness into a revolutionary initiative. Its five chapters propose a phenomenology of revolutionary consciousness, moving from simple consciousness emerging from resistance to specific injustices up to the reception of Marxist theory and with it full revolutionary class-consciousness. The account of the formation of consciousness, as in Descartes, is also an account of the formation of the subject of consciousness, in this case the class-conscious proletariat. This subject, however, is not one, but a combination of what Hegel called 'natural' and 'philosophical' consciousness. (Lenin 1975, 36)

Lenin's second chapter on the 'Spontaneity of the Masses and the Consciousness of the Social-Democrats' gives a synoptic account of his entire position. Section A 'The Beginnings of the Spontaneous Upsurge' describes the emergence of an understanding of Marxism among the Russian intelligentsia during the 1890s alongside the 'spontaneous' resistance of the workers to their conditions. He insists on a difference between two kinds of spontaneity, distinguishing them above all in terms of their degree and quality of *consciousness*:

> Strikes occurred in Russia in the 'seventies and 'sixties (and even in the first half of the nineteenth century), and were accompanied by the "spontaneous" destruction of machinery etc. Compared with these "riots" the strikes of the 'nineties might even be described as 'conscious', to such an extent that they mark the progress the working-class movement had made in that period. This shows that the "spontaneous element," in essence, represents nothing more nor less than consciousness in an *embryonic form*. Even the primitive riots expressed the awakening of consciousness to a certain extent: the workers were losing their age long faith in the permanence of the system which oppressed them. They began ... I shall not say to understand, but to sense the necessity for collective resistance, and definitely abandoned their slavish submission to their superiors. (Lenin 1975, 35–6)[34]

This remarkable passage combines a history of strikes in nineteenth-century Russia with a phenomenology of consciousness. The consciousness accompanying spontaneous acts of resistance such as riot and sabotage – 'embryonic' consciousness – is succeeded by a 'sensed' consciousness that undermines faith in the *permanence* of oppressive conditions; with this emerges a 'sense' (but not understanding) of the necessity for collective struggle. Spontaneous individual resistance in the face of oppressive necessity is succeeded by a sense of the necessity of collective resistance. So far Lenin's historical narrative maps itself onto the stages of Hegel's phenomenological unfolding of consciousness – moving experimentally from the embryonic to the level of sense certainty and then rising to the level of full consciousness with the possibility of arriving at absolute knowledge where consciousness constitutes its own subject and object.

Yet this is not a continuous process, since Lenin's grammar mobilizes the Nietzschean ellipsis (Derrida's teleiopoetic …) to signify the open-ended and indeterminate character of resistance. The ellipses mark the break with history and the advent of the time of revolution, an event described by Derrida in his reading of *What is to be Done* as: 'The revolution, that is not only the seizure of power by a new governing class according to this or that model, it is above all an absolute break with the historical concatenation, an irremediable tear, the interruption of the wholly other in the fabric or chain of politics' (Derrida 2007, 31). Yet these interruptions of the process of emergent consciousness discerned by Derrida in Lenin's text tend to be gathered by Lenin into the full light of revolutionary consciousness. The spontaneous beginnings of resistance are flickerings of a consciousness that emerges from the reactive and defensive postures of riot and sabotage. For Lenin these flashes of resistance ('rudiments of purposiveness' Lih, 701) were 'more in the nature of outbursts of desperation and vengeance than of *struggle*. The strikes of the 'nineties revealed far greater flashes of consciousness' (Lenin 1975, 36). The early acts of resistance were motivated by *ressentiment* or by the spirit of revenge in defying or saying no! to an oppressive world; for Lenin they were but the spontaneous prelude to conscious and affirmative struggle. Against Lenin's resolution of the flashes of resistance into the blazing light of revolutionary class-consciousness, subsequent Marxism (Benjamin, Bensäid) has seen in the flashes and intermittencies of resistance an index of its messianic, irruptive character. Indeed, we shall see that for Georges Didi-Huberman in *Survivances des lucioles,* the flashes of resistance in the night of history are all we can have – yet for Lenin these are but the faltering beginnings of revolutionary consciousness. They must rise to the full illumination, glare or glory, of consciousness, a trope of elevation Didi-Huberman identifies and criticizes in the late work of Pasolini and in the recent work of Agamben.

For Lenin, political consciousness as full illumination must inform revolutionary action, but it does not arise spontaneously from individual or collective acts of resistance. Resistance is not the path to absolute knowledge; it cannot in Lenin's terms constitute a revolutionary subject, but is always flickering out, always beginning again – consequently the light must come from elsewhere: 'We have said *there could not yet be* Social Democratic consciousness among the workers. It could only be brought to them from without.' (Lenin 1975, 37) The positive construal of the bringing of light to the Platonic cave is inflected with a definite Nietzschean accent.

The light of affirmative political consciousness must expose the *ressentiment* or reformism that issues from spontaneous reactive resistance. Lenin claims that consciousness can be 'overwhelmed by spontaneity', that workers' resistance is reactive in responding to a predicament and risks having the predicament define the character of its resistance. There is no break in the Derridean sense of an interruption with prior history, but the inverted inscription of that history in the resistance itself. The struggle for more wages accepts the wage form, the struggle for better working conditions accepts the discipline of factory production – resistance, in short, tends towards reform rather than revolution. Lenin prompts his reader to ask the question 'why does the spontaneous movement, the movement along the line of least resistance, lead to the domination of bourgeois ideology?' (Lenin 1975, 51) and answers: because it is older and stronger and that 'trade union consciousness' is a reactive *ressentiment* resistance – it says no to particular injustices while affirming the institutional structure of capitalism; it does not yet say yes in the name of something new, as in Marx's affirmation of the Paris Commune.

In section E of the third chapter of *What is to be Done,* 'The Working Class as Vanguard Fighter for Democracy', Lenin ironically assumes the following consensus: '"everyone agrees" that it is necessary to develop the political consciousness of the working class' and goes on to criticize 'the conviction that it is possible to develop the class political consciousness of the workers *from within*, so to speak, their economic struggle' (Lenin 1975, 97). The latter as a reactive struggle must be supplemented by an affirmative moment brought from 'outside' – the Social Democratic party will bring this consciousness of the actuality of Communism to the working class mired in the *ressentiment* of reactive struggles.

The subsumption of resistance under the protocols of the philosophy of consciousness would have enormous consequences for subsequent Marxism and its understanding of revolt. Resistance is a condition of the possibility of its own overcoming in the revolutionary consciousness of the proletariat – in Hegelian terms it is a 'vanishing moment' that emerges from the clash between the repressive force of the autocracy and the emergent force of the proletariat. But it leaves open the question of whether organized resistance remains simply 'resistance' or whether it can metamorphose into something new without the intervention of consciousness from without. The response to this question may be framed in terms of organization: is resistance opposed to organization, or does it point to another form of organization than one understood in terms of unification under consciousness. With the theory of Rosa Luxemburg another thought of organization enters Marxist theory and the theory of resistance, one indebted to the later Kant as refracted through the texts of Goethe and one whose model is not consciousness but biological metamorphosis, a position already anticipated in Lenin's consistent use of metaphors drawn from embryology.

As a near contemporary of Lenin and a leading theoretician of the Polish section of the German Social Democratic party, Rosa Luxemburg's thought marks a clear break with the prevailing effort to subsume resistance under the paradigm of consciousness. Her text *The Mass Strike, the Political Party and the Trade Unions* openly confronts Lenin's *What is to be Done?* on the terrain of consciousness and temporality. Luxemburg insists that acts of resistance and insurrection do not fit into the kind of continuous logical and temporal narrative contrived by Lenin. His emphasis on the gathering of the flashes of resistance into the steady light of consciousness (or the movement from awareness to purposiveness in Lih's version) embodied in revolutionary theory is decisively challenged by Luxemburg. Her immanent materialism refused to accept the distinction between the episodic spontaneity of resistance and the constant self-correcting presence of revolutionary consciousness. In a reflection on the unfolding of the 1905 Revolution in Russia, Luxemburg noted

> [...] there was no predetermined plan, no organised action, because the appeals of the parties could scarcely keep pace with the spontaneous risings of the masses: the leaders scarcely had time to formulate the watchwords of the onrushing crowd of the proletariat. Further, the earlier mass and general strikes had originated from individual coalescing wage struggles which in the general temper of the revolutionary situation and under the influence of the social democratic agitation, rapidly became political demonstrations: the economic factor and the scattered condition of trade unionism were the starting point; all embracing class action and political direction the result. (Luxemburg 1970, 170)

In a deliberate inversion of Lenin's privileging of consciousness, Luxemburg claimed '[t]he movement was reversed' – consciousness *followed* the movement and metamorphoses of resistance, it did not direct it.

Luxemburg figures the passage from resistance to revolution not in terms of the clash of solids, as in Lenin's view of integrated and conscious class subjects, but as the movements of fluid forces made up of diverse currents moving at different velocities. Between them Lenin and Luxemburg repeat Clausewitz's view of the transition from the *ancien* solid to the revolutionary regime of liquid warfare; strikingly neither arrive at the vaporization and condensation of violence that defined Clausewitz's view of war of the resistance. Luxemburg nevertheless grants resistance greater dignity than serving as a vanishing moment for the imputation of consciousness; for her resistant interruptions of the course of the world constitute their own intricate rhythmic flow:

> Political and economic strikes, mass strikes and partial strikes, demonstrative strikes and fighting strikes, general strikes of individual branches of industry and general strikes in individual towns, peaceful wage struggles and street massacres, barricade fighting – all these run through one another, run side by side, cross one another, flow in and over one another – it is a ceaselessly moving sea of phenomena. And the law of motion of these phenomena is clear; it does not lie in the mass strike itself nor in its technical details, but in the social and political proportions of the forces of the revolution. (Luxemburg 1970, 182)

The revolution is an internally differentiated vital phenomenon, a fundamental disproportion of forces that manifests itself in tiny events – influencing action 'in a thousand invisible and scarcely controllable ways. But strike action does not cease for a single moment. It merely alters its forms, its dimensions, its effects. It is the living pulsebeat of the revolution and at the same time its most powerful driving wheel' (Luxemburg 1975, 182). The lesson Luxemburg drew from the Russian Revolution was that arresting the motion of capitalist production and reproduction in the mass strike (mass interruption) was itself the 'method of motion of the proletarian mass' (Luxemburg 1970, 182). Organization is understood in terms of an autopoietic process of correction and challenge expressed in a dynamic response to an environment; the sum of infinitesimally small acts of resistance ensures that there is no single reactive response but a continuous process of testing and transformation in which resistance is crucial:

> With the spreading, clarifying and involution of the political struggle, the economic struggle not only does not recede, but extends, organises and becomes involved in equal measure. Between the two there is the most complete reciprocal action. (Luxemburg 1970, 185)

There is no question of a synthesis of consciousness, but instead a dynamic conflict and expansion of forces whose actions produce involutions, leave traces and, as in this beautiful figure of the wave of resistance leaving traces of its passage in the sand, changing the environment of future struggle. The flashes of resistance are not lost in the darkness of repression nor raised to the light of consciousness, but are eddies in the stream of becoming that leave traces: 'After every foaming wave of political action a fructifying deposit remains behind from which a thousand stalks of economic struggle shoot forth. And conversely. The workers condition of ceaseless economic struggle with the capitalists keeps their fighting energy alive in every political interval...'. (Luxemburg 1970, 185).

Luxemburg's break with the model of consciousness liberated resistance from the tutelary role given it in Lenin's theory. The consistency or coherence of individual acts of resistance is not produced by a conscious synthesis but emerges through a process of metamorphosis. The testing of the hostile environment through resistance leaves an archive of traces inscribed on both the capitalist environment and the emergent organization of the revolutionary proletariat. The history of such acts of resistance has its own consistency, which is not that of consciousness but retains experience of past struggles while remaining oriented towards the future.

Luxemburg's work has not enjoyed the same philosophical attention as Lenin's, with the notable exception of its elaboration in the political philosophy of Hannah Arendt. Yet it is an important critique of the philosophical assumptions of Lenin's *What is to be Done?* and its understanding of resistance. It too is fundamentally influenced by Marx's *The Civil War in France* but draws from it different conclusions, emphasizing the political invention of the Commune, its courage and making explicit the biopolitical discourse of vitality and health that occupied the margins of the Addresses and other texts by Marx. It also drew inspiration from Marx's affirmative understanding of the *nobility* of the Paris Commune and his appreciation of its anomalous temporality; its break with the history of the state and empire came too early, it was the future breaking into the continuum of the present and the past. Yet what was important for Luxemburg was the opening of this interval and the indelible trace that it left in the memory of working class resistance.

Unconscious Resistance

The break with the model of consciousness and the discovery of unconscious resistance intimated by Luxemburg was consolidated in two bodies of work produced independently in Vienna during the first half of the 1920s: Georg Lukács' *History and Class Consciousness: Studies in Marxist Dialectic* of 1923 and Sigmund Freud's *Inhibitions, Symptoms and Anxiety* and *The Question of Lay Analysis* both of 1926. Emerging from very different milieus, the two texts share an impatience with the philosophy of consciousness and a critical approach to resistance. For both authors the rethinking of political action and psychic wellbeing was inseparable from the rethinking of resistance.

For Lenin, resistance expressed a low level of reactive consciousness, while for Luxemburg it was the means by which the workings of vital force could be inscribed in the archive of class struggle. Lukács' response to this fundamental difference with respect to the assessment of resistance in Marxist theory and practice was to inquire into the philosophical origins of the problem of consciousness in German Idealism. This took him to the limits of the philosophy of consciousness and beyond. For Lenin, the explosions of resistance were destined either to fade and disappear into the darkness of repression or be carried up into the light of full revolutionary consciousness. Luxemburg's critique forced Lukács into a philosophical and political confrontation with the problem of consciousness which led beyond consciousness towards a theory of affirmative or inventive resistance.

The central chapter of *History and Class Consciousness*, 'Reification and the Consciousness of the Proletariat', examines the emergence of reified consciousness in classical German philosophy. Weaving together Marx's critique of the commodity form, Simmel's theory of reification and Weber's rationalization thesis, Lukács proposes that 'Reification requires that a society should learn to satisfy all its needs in terms of commodity exchange...' and that the 'principle of rational mechanisation and calcu-lability must embrace every aspect of life' (Lukács 1971, 91). Lukács sees this embrace as extending extensively and intensively, colonizing not only the world but also consciousness itself: 'Just as the capitalist system continuously produces and reproduces itself economically on higher and higher levels, the structure of reification progressively sinks more deeply, more fatefully and more definitively into the consciousness of man' (Lukács 1971, 93). The reification of consciousness is seen as an historical process tending to the limit of total reification embracing not only the world but also 'man's physical and psychic nature.' (Lukács 1971, 101). In so identifying an historical tendency towards the reification of life and consciousness, Lukács makes the theory of resistance crucial to any attempt to defy the tendency.

One response to the predicament of reification proposed by Lukács is to see the worker as the commodity that has become self-conscious of its commodity status, a change at the level of consciousness that has immediate consequences for action (see Lukács 1971, 208). This response is modulated into the Leninist solution of importing self- or revolutionary consciousness from the outside that is to say, the consciousness of totality denied the reified consciousness of the worker which is partial and reactive. In his essay on 'Class Consciousness' Lukács acknowledges that reactive consciousness tends towards empiricist and utopian 'extremes': 'In the one case, consciousness becomes a completely passive observer moving in obedience to laws it can never control. In the other it regards itself as a power which is able of its own-subjective-volition to master the essentially meaningless motion of objects' (Lukács 1971, 77). The latter position is elaborated in his critique of Rosa Luxemburg, who for him overestimates '*the spontaneous, elemental forces of the Revolution*' (Lukács 1971, 279). Yet alongside these efforts to resolve the problem of reification through a philosophy of consciousness emerges a different kind of response that looks beyond the confines of the theatre of consciousness.

This response, departing from the analysis of reification, looks less to the possibility of changing consciousness than to identifying the sites, places or moments where resistance to reification can emerge. These are the moments of invention that explode in a culture dedicated to calculation – whether political invention in the Workers Councils or Soviets advocated by Luxemburg or by leaps of artistic imagination beyond reification. Lukács can still describe this response in the closing essay of the collection 'Towards a Methodology of the Problem of Organisation' in terms of the problem of the 'interaction of spontaneity and conscious control' (Lukács 1971, 317), which he linked to the organizational form of the 'communist party', but it is clear that this resistance can be found elsewhere. It can be found in the works of art and philosophy which point to potential sites of resistance to reified culture and consciousness. It was this possibility of forms and sites of resistance beyond the philosophy of consciousness that stimulated the thought of Adorno, Benjamin and the Frankfurt school. Their work elaborated Lukács' intuition of non-conscious sites of resistance into a meditation upon aesthetic resistance, messianic/prophetic resistance, even the resistance of the concept – in short, a universe of resistances no longer tied to the discourses of consciousness and force.

The members of the Frankfurt school saw very clearly the affinity between those moments of Lukács' work that exceed the discourse of consciousness and the clinical practice of psychoanalysis pioneered by Freud. Freud's analysis of the tactics of resistance, while fusing the discourses of force and invention with biomedical considerations, also questioned the assumed affinity between resistance and revolution by showing its complicity with repression and suppression. In some respects it might be said that the entire psychoanalytic project is a meditation upon resistance, and perhaps not just a meditation but the invention of a way of working against the grain of resistance.

Already in the *Studies in Hysteria* of 1896 Freud reported encounters with resistance on the part of his patients, notably in resistance to hypnosis. He describes it topologically as a diagnostic sign of proximity to the pathological core of a neurosis, understanding it as an immunological defence mechanism preventing the passage of unconscious pathologies to conscious scrutiny – with the difference that, contrary to emergent immunological discourses, it is not the organism defending itself against a pathogen, but the pathogen defending itself against the organism. Thus Freud understands resistance in terms of the prevention of access, with the guarding of secrets, and casts the psychoanalyst as one who works with resistance in order to allow access to the concealed. There is a strong parallel with Lukács, who not only speaks of a 'political unconscious' but also considered the exploitation of the working class – the extraction of surplus value under the form of the equal exchange of the wage contract – as a secret whose exposure capitalism resisted at all costs. What emerges in both is a certain ambivalence with respect to resistance, as much a force of repression as of liberation. It is an ambivalence that belongs to the dynamic character of resistance, its at-once active and reactive quality as a force.

Freud's work with resistance is guided by the subtle intuition of its devastatingly fugitive character as that which 'fully brings work to a halt', not just through strikes, sabotage and demonstrations but by means of intricate displacements, condensations, figurations and transferences. Working with what brings work to a halt is the effort to resist resistance, appreciating the reflective character of resistance as always already a counter-resistance. It is work that requires tactical cunning, indirect confrontation and the ability to exploit the ambivalences of resistances in overcoming them, a work that conforms in other words to the strategic profile of guerrilla warfare. Indeed Freud even describes his work in terms of 'Our fight against resistance in analysis...' (Freud 2001, 159). The experience of the campaigns of resistance to resistance recounted in Freud's case studies, above all Dora and the Rat Man, is systematized in the strategic classification of resistances in Appendix A of *Inhibitions, Symptoms and Anxiety* of 1926. There Freud extends one of Nietzsche's more disquieting insights, that we want to be ill, that we resist being healthy by preferring to will nothingness rather than not will at all, into the five actualizations of resistance. Three of these are close to what we think we know to be consciousness, the ego resistances, while the other two are of a very different and far more elusive character issuing from the Id and Superego. The first actualization of resistance finds itself in proximity with repression: 'An important element in the theory of repression is the view that repression is not an event that occurs once but that it requires a permanent expenditure (of energy)… This action undertaken to protect repression is observable in analytical treatment as *resistance.*' (Freud 2001, 157). Resistance here assumes the defensive posture of securing of the conditions to repeat and in so doing defends repression. The second of the three 'ego resistances' is transference, or the resistance to the recollection of repression by means of a theatrical displacement that 'succeeds in establishing a relation to the analytic situation of the analyst himself and thus re-animating a repression which should only have been recollected' (Freud 2001, 160). What seems to be resistance to repression is in fact its confirmation by a displacement onto the clinical situation. The third resistance is the gain from illness – the reluctance to be freed from the symptom because of the satisfaction gained from playing the role of the patient.

The fourth and fifth actualizations of resistance are found beyond the scenario of the ego and its vicissitudes. The fourth is manifest in the intractable resistance of the unconscious or id; even if the patient is conscious of their symptoms and their ego resistance has been overcome, the symptoms persist. At this point we encounter the limit of Freud's commitment to the philosophy of consciousness as the move from a passive to an active relationship to repression in which even consciousness is unable to overcome 'the power of the compulsion to repeat'. There is an 'unconscious prototype' which continues to exert attraction 'upon the repressed instinctual process' (Freud 2001, 159). Freud now contemplates a closure of the possibility of the future – the inhibition of desire – that operates at a level of resistance far beyond the reach of consciousness. This fatal resistance is succeeded by a fifth or 'superego' resistance that is for Freud 'the most obscure if not always the least powerful one. It seems to originate from the sense of guilt or the need for punishment' and is a tactic employed to 'oppose every move towards success, including, therefore, the patient's own recovery through analysis' (Freud 2001, 160). With this Freud completes his strategic assessment of the capacity to resist of his enemy, revealed as the capacity to resist itself.

In the contemporary 'On the Question of Lay Analysis' (1926) Freud moves from strategy to tactics, writing a 'What is to be Done' for the aspirant analyst. Emerging from the wars of resistance *to* psychoanalysis whose features and aetiology were diagnosed in 'Resistances to Psychoanalysis' (1924), 'On the Question of Lay Analysis' offers tactical advice for the conduct of the guerrilla war engaged by the analyst against the analysand's 'capacity to resist'. When the guerrilla or lay analyst has found a plausible interpretation of the analysand's symptoms, they must adopt a politics or therapy of time, engaging a protracted war against resistance. Simply to place the interpretation before the consciousness of the patient can only reinforce the resistance; everything becomes a question of choosing the right moment and the correct, usually indirect, approach. The appropriate choice of time and disposition requires what Freud, echoing Clausewitz, regards as strategic 'tact':

> You will be making a bad mistake if, in an effort, perhaps, at shortening the analysis, you throw your interpretations at the patient's head as soon as you have found them. In that way you will draw expressions of resistance, rejection and indignation from him; but you will not enable his ego to master the repressed material. The formula is: to wait till he has come so near to the repressed material that he has only a few more steps to take under the lead of the interpretation you propose. (Freud 2001, 220)

The leading role of the analyst in drawing the analysand to the point of being able themselves to overcome resistance entails the dissemblance of the interpretation; a strategy of taking one step back to secure two steps forward cast in terms analogous to the political work prescribed in Lenin's *What is to be Done*. It is axiomatic that the *ressentiment* of the patient – their investment in guilt and self-punishment – entails that they have 'no wish whatever to be cured' and that their resistances are reactive. The analysand occupies a fortress of resistances 'that oppose the work of recovery' – sheltering behind the ramparts of gain from illness, guilt, fear, and the insecurity provoked by facing the need to break with history and to abandon an 'instinctual process which has been going along a particular path for decades' – and rendering the analysand reluctant suddenly to 'take a new path that has just been made open to it' (Freud 2001, 224).

The military undertone of Freud's texts – the examples drawn from war neurosis and the sense of a duel between analyst and analysand – suddenly becomes explicit as he describes 'all the forces that oppose the work of recovery as the patients's "resistances"'. (Freud 2001, 223). Indeed Freud describes the process of analysis in terms of a guerrilla war, with the struggle between analyst and analysand to overcome or preserve the capacity to resist cast in terms that recall *On War*.[35] The 'struggle against all these resistances...' (Freud at this point focuses on the plurality of resistances in the place of Clausewitz's single capacity to resist) '...is our main work during an analytic treatment' (Freud 2001, 224) and this struggle requires time – analysis is the protracted war of resistance against resistance – with the analyst adopting the long-term strategic posture of the guerrilla against the resistance of an occupying army. The length of the struggle between the adversaries depends less on the terrain than on the strength of the enemy's resistance: 'An army can be held up for weeks on a stretch of country which in peace time an express train crosses in a couple of hours – if the army has to overcome the enemy's resistance there. Such battles call for time in mental life too.' (Freud 2001, 224). The object, however, is not to overcome the analysand's resistances but to teach them through struggle to constitute their own affirmative and actively resistant subjectivity, for it is 'as this struggle and of the overcoming of the resistances, (that) the patient's ego is so much altered and strengthened that we can look forward calmly to his future behaviour when the treatment is over' (Freud 2001, 224). The vanguard analyst no longer wages a war on the terrain of consciousness – the 'task of making interpretations is nothing' (Freud 2001, 224) compared to the war with resistance – but seeks to clear paths, secure terrain and overcome sites of resistance in order to open new and more inventive futures. Paradoxically the analyst must disable the analysand's existing capacity to resist in order to permit its more effective reconfiguration. It is a work that calls on the analyst's 'courage' and fortitude – even when entering the transference the analyst cannot be 'cowardly' – once more echoing the theme of war neurosis.

Freud invites us to consider that resistance to repression is a resistance to counter-resistance, situating us in a terrain of opposed forces in which each force can switch from possessing the initiative to resisting it. Yet resistance can also exceed the theatre of force – as we saw in Sartre's reflections on 27 October 1960 – and become a subtle and cunning disposition, mobilizing resistance in order to confirm its own repression. There is almost a Kierkegaardian opposition between this Freud and the work of Luxemburg and moments in the work of Lukács. For Luxemburg, all resistance and the traces it leaves point to a working through of the revolution, to an opening of the future in the release of desire, while for Freud resistance and its ruses can fatally confirm repression. Perhaps it is necessary to maintain both positions, especially when considering the work of the historical resistance raised against the claims to total domination mounted by Colonialism, Fascism and Nazism. As Marx, Nietzsche and psychoanalysis taught us, resistance is always directed against a prior resistance – Fascism and Nazism are acts of resistance to modernity and to the threat of Communism – a conscious and protracted resistance in the face of insecurity and the uncertain future which dedicated itself to freezing social identities and political forms for a thousand years. How is it possible then to resist this resistance? Once again psychoanalysis shows decisively that confrontation at the level of consciousness will not suffice, but that resistance has at once to counter resistances and to engage with the invention of an affirmative, resistant subjectivity. But this project in its turn exceeds the clinical context and recalls the central Clausewitzian concern with the role played by violence in sustaining and attempting to overcome the capacity to resist.

2 VIOLENT RESISTANCE

The Logic of Escalation

Clausewitz's equation of war and resistance was an answer to the question of how to resist the new fluid warfare of the Napoleonic armies. But the question had implications that ranged beyond the historic circumstances of resisting French imperialism to the very possibility of resistance at all. Clausewitz's logic seemed to point inexorably to the violent resolution of the question. Yet it was a resolution without dialectic, since the violence unleashed by the war of resistance was as likely to provoke the mutual ruin of the adversaries' than any *Aufhebung* of their enmity. *On War's* Kantian critique of escalation or the passage to absolute war or pure resistance presented a political and strategic dilemma. Was this passage to be pursued – indeed, intensified – as we saw Clausewitz suggesting in the *Bekenntnisdenkschrift*, or was it to be deferred or otherwise diverted into politics and diplomacy as argued in certain sections of *On War*? And what was the role of violence in this intensification or deferral? Mao Zedong's strategic doctrine of the violent revolutionary war of resistance provides one answer to this question, Ghandi's non-violent strategy of *Satyagraha* another; both were elaborated as strategies for resistance to colonial domination. Another approach adopted in post-war French philosophy, in the context of a successful historical experience of resistance, was to question the very terms of the Clausewitzian scenario. The working through of the Clausewitzian legacy marked an important current of post-war French philosophy, surfacing explicitly in the work of Raymond Aron, Eric Weil, Emmanuel Levinas and, most recently, René Girard.

Clausewitz's work indeed represents one of the most formidable assaults on Hegelian dialectic. It is perhaps surprising that his devastation of dialectic was not even more important for the powerfully anti-Hegelian, anti-dialectical current of post-war French philosophy. Perhaps this is due to

Clausewitz's willingness to entertain a move towards a destructive extreme, a tendency distinguished from more familiar versions of anti-dialectical thought that tend towards its neutralization. The avoidance of dialectical resolution through diversion or deferral contrasts with Clausewitz's anti-dialectic which tends towards absolute war or the escalation of enmity to the point of mutual destruction.

The theme of violent escalation is central to Clausewitz's thought and prominent in what are widely recognized to be his last thoughts on war in the first book of On War. Yet the close relationship between escalation and the capacity to resist was not fully addressed even by post-war readers of Clausewitz. Thus the importance of the *capacity* to resist in the definition of war is overlooked by both Aron and Girard. Yet Aron's own experience in the French Resistance allowed him to see and to appreciate that Clausewitz was a fellow resistant:

> In order to sympathise with Clausewitz's attitude between 1806 and 1815 a Frenchman need only remember his own experiences between 1940 and 1945. Not that I would want to compare Napoleon to Hitler: the German patriot resisted no less the French domination of Europe. A resistant, Clausewitz refused the peace of abdication with an eloquence that moved the men of my generation. (Aron 1976a, 13)

While acknowledging this affinity, Aron cannot fully appreciate the theoretical role played by the capacity to resist in Clausewitz; he could not see that On War could equally be titled On Resistance. Girard too underestimates this dimension of Clausewitz's thought, although he begins to develop the theme of the capacity for passive resistance as one of the few possible exits from the Clausewitzian logic of the escalation of violence. In his search for such an exit he turns to Pascal and the enmity between truth and violence, to the example of Jesus Christ, and even to the Resistant historian Marc Bloch who called for a justice without vengeance, one that would contain rather than intensify the escalation of enmity.

War – in Clausewitz's clear and unambiguous definition – is dedicated to overcoming the enemy's *capacity to resist*. The reciprocal also holds: war is also the preservation and enhancement of the same capacity against the onslaughts of the enemy. The logic of violence – escalation – essentially concerns the process unleashed by each adversary's attack on the other's capacity to resist at the same time as defending their own. This movement of attack and defence unleashes the possibility of an escalation of violence.

The escalation of violence is described by Clausewitz as the outcome of three reciprocal actions. The first arises from the definition of war as 'an act of violence pushed to its utmost limit; as one side dictates the law to the other, there arises a sort of reciprocal action, which logically must lead to an extreme. This is the first reciprocal action, and the first extreme with which we meet' (Clausewitz 1982, 103). In war, each escalation of violence provokes an escalated response, which in turn provokes a further escalation. Resistance seems wholly implicated in the logic of escalation – attacking the enemy's capacity to resist at the same time as preserving one's own against the attack of the enemy – but there is also the hint of a deeper resistance, that is, a resistance to the logic of escalation itself. This will be developed as the resistance of the theory of non-violence pioneered in Gandhi's anti-colonial struggle, but is already implied in Clausewitz. The second reciprocal action develops this hint more fully, albeit still allusively. In this definition, developed in section 4 of *On War*, 'The aim is to disarm the enemy' (that is to say, minimize the enemy's capacity to resist) either through his being 'positively disarmed or placed in such a position that he is threatened with it' (Clausewitz 1982, 104). It is interesting to note the options of physical or moral force: the enemy can be disarmed either physically through *actual* destruction or morally through the *threatened* destruction of their capacity to resist.

Clausewitz develops this thought further by insisting we recognize that 'war is always the shock of two hostile bodies in collision, not the action of a living power upon an inanimate mass, because the state of non-resistance would be the negation of war which is always the collision of two living forces' (Clausewitz 1982, 104, translation modified). The significance of this passage has not been fully appreciated: at one level it involves a distinction between *war* or the collision of two hostile bodies, and *production* or 'the action of a living power on an inanimate mass'. The act of war does not resemble the exercise of labour power; yet beyond disengagement of production from war (thus ruling out in advance class war), there is the further hint that non-resistance is the enemy of war itself. Non-resistance as a 'living power' can pose a devastating ethical threat to physical war by compromising the adversary's moral capacity to resist. Clausewitz points to this possibility but then quickly moves to a formal statement of the second reciprocal action that fuels the escalation of violence: 'As long as the enemy is not defeated, he may defeat me; then I shall no longer be my own master; he will dictate the law to me as I did to him. This is the second reciprocal action, and leads to a second extreme' (Clausewitz 1982, 104). This almost anticipates Kojève's reading of the master/slave dialectic: the slave refuses the struggle to the death, turns to production and by so doing overthrows the master who, without resistance, withers away. The scenario of war is constant, but the strategic response to it also includes the effective option of non-violent resistance.

The third reciprocal action requires us 'to proportion our efforts to [the enemy's] power of resistance', the latter once again understood in terms of 'two factors which cannot be separated, namely the sum of available *means* and *the strength of the Will*' (Clausewitz 1982, 104) – i.e. physical and moral force. The third reciprocal action is especially significant for emphasizing the role played by consciousness in war, here present in the guise of the mutual estimates of the force of the enemy. I have to become conscious of my enemy's physical and moral strength and then 'review my own means'. But while doing so, while bringing my enemy under surveillance, the enemy is doing the same to me: 'But the adversary does the same; therefore there is a new mutual enhancement, which, in pure conception, must create a fresh effort towards an extreme' (Clausewitz 1982, 105). The possibility of deception here – Mao's 'paper tigers' – is not systematically explored by Clausewitz. At this point he is interested above all in how this and the other two 'reciprocal actions' can escalate a difference to the point of self-destruction. It is an apocalyptic logic that Aron strove to contain at the level of the third reciprocal action through enhancing communication and the exchange of information, that is, through politics and diplomacy. Aron attempts to widen the opening to consciousness in the third reciprocal action by arguing that with it we can contain the escalation of the first two reciprocities. In his passionate critique of Aron, Girard refuses this possibility and argues that we are now fully and irreversibly engaged in an apocalyptic logic of escalation. The differences between the two positions – and of both from our emphasis on the capacity to resist – become absolutely clear in the discussion of the 'trinity' of war that Clausewitz introduces at the end of Book 1, perhaps the most disputed part of Clausewitz's text and legacy.

Departing from the notorious statement in Book I, section 24 of *On War* that 'War is not merely a political act, but also a real political instrument, a continuation of political commerce, a carrying out of the same by other means' (Clausewitz 1982, 119), Clausewitz arrives at the following 'result' for the theory of war: war is composed of three elements, an infernal or – for Clausewitz – 'a wonderful trinity, composed of the original violence of its elements, hatred and animosity, which may be looked upon as blind instinct; of the play of probabilities and chance, which make it a free activity of the soul; and of the subordinate nature of a political instrument, by which it belongs purely to the reason' (Clausewitz 1982, 121). He then maps these three elements – corresponding roughly to the Kantian sensibility, understanding and reason – with three subjectivities: 'the people', the 'general and his army' and 'the government', each shaped respectively by the 'passions', by strategy or the 'realm of probabilities and chance' and by political logic. The theory of war has to 'keep itself poised in a manner between these three tendencies, as between three points of attraction' (Clausewitz 1982, 122), aware that their internal cohesion is unstable and may provoke an escalation tending toward mutual destruction; it must also remain sceptical of any attempt to impose a dialectical logic of *Aufhebung* or resolution onto this logic of escalation.

This balance or poise between the three elements, subjects and tendencies remains a challenge to contemporary philosophy. Aron would put more weight on the third, political logic and government, allying the people with the government in a democratic polity and ensuring the subordination of the military. The government must respect the people's passions while controlling the generals and the army. Girard in deliberate contrast emphasizes the predominance of the second element, arguing that the grammar of the military now dictates the passions of the people who are duped, but also the government which is but a mask for procuring the resources for escalating military violence. But what happens to this trinity if we try and maintain the balance between the elements and try to think of this balance in terms of resistance?

Clausewitz attempts in Chapter 2 to do just this. Looking at the campaign and the objective of 'disarming a nation', that is, compromising its capacity to resist, Clausewitz argues that a military campaign must attack not only military power and government but also the will of the enemy. The first two objectives – the extinction of the physical resistance of the military and the organizational resistance of government – are attainable, while the submission of the people's will is not a realistic war aim: moral resistance can always re-emerge, even if in defeat the greater number 'turn themselves away completely from the road to resistance' (Clausewitz 1982, 123). At this point Clausewitz's treatise turns to the proposition that 'disarming the enemy is rarely attained in practice' and the treatise on war mutates into a treatise on resistance, its preservation and overcoming. How is it possible to smother or to sustain and enhance the 'sparks' of resistance in a people which otherwise may have smouldered on quietly, or not so quietly …?

As a treatise on resistance, *On War* develops some extraordinary propositions. A particularly controversial proposition involves the suspension of the state's monopoly of violence proposed in Book Six Chapter 26 on the arming of the people. This discussion introduces the theme of resistant subjectivity – the subjectivity of the partisan – and the development of the view discussed earlier that the appropriate military strategy for a resistant subject is vaporous as opposed to the movement of solid and liquid masses characteristic of military subjectivity. In words that we saw anticipate some of the positions of Rosa Luxemburg in the *Mass Strike* and those of T. E. Lawrence on the science of guerrilla war, Clausewitz wrote: 'People's War as something vaporous must never be concentrated in a solid body since an enemy would despatch an appropriate force against this and would break it' (Clausewitz 2010, IV, 26). The strategy of resistance maximizes the workings of chance and probability in order to gain time for the preservation and enhancement of the capacity to resist. The command of a partisan army has to intensify the role of chance and probability in its actions through flexibility and the cultivation of a resistant imagination. Both enemies are subject to chance, but while the regular army attempts to reduce its role as far as possible, the guerrilla intensifies it and prepares to grasp the opportunities it affords. In Clausewitz's words, the army must conduct a war of time and not of space or territory; it 'must disperse itself and pursue defence through unexpected attacks rather than concentrating itself and risking confinement in a narrow refuge in a conventional defensive posture' (Clausewitz 2010, IV, 26).

Informing this capacity to fight across time is a strategy of unpredictable manifestation: it is necessary for the resistant to appear and disappear unpredictably, to emerge from out of and then disappear back into the depth of the element of the people. If the people still maintain the capacity to resist, then they can support a partisan army that appears and disappears, provoking its enemy without ever remaining visible long enough to become subject to the grammar of territorial war. Neither Aron nor Girard can see that this alliance between people and a new kind of army – a resistant subjectivity and its armed expression – is precisely the alliance pursued by Clausewitz. It is less the alliance of army and state that engages a logic of escalating violence that interests him than the possibility of resisting this logic through the alliance of the people with a new kind of army that fights in and for time, one which affirms chance instead of trying to minimize it, and one that potentially enhances the existing capacity to resist. It is a model of war and resistance that affirms imagination and the imaginative response to chance over the combination of force and consciousness that characterizes the military posture of the nation state. It is one that refuses to enter the logic of escalation and its tendency to make both enemies increasingly present to each other for the 'decisive blow' or final apocalyptic battle, and one that conducts war by evading escalation while compromising the enemy's capacity to resist in a protracted war in and for time. The most important theoretical expressions of this form of resistant warfare dedicated first of all to the preservation and enhancement of the capacity to resist were subsequently elaborated by Mao Zedong and Gandhi in the context of extended anti-colonial struggles against a materially and organizationally superior enemy.

The 'Protracted War of Resistance'

The object of war is specifically 'to preserve oneself and destroy the enemy' (to destroy the enemy means to disarm him or 'deprive him of the power to resist,' and does not mean to destroy every member of his forces physically).

(MAO, THE PEOPLE'S WAR)

Clausewitz's significance for Marx, Engels and Lenin also extended to one of the most significant revolutionary and military theorists of the twentieth century, Mao Zedong, who refers to him as an esteemed 'foreign military expert'.[1] In a sense Mao represents the development of a particular interpretation of Clausewitz that emphasized the subordination of politics to military action, and the understanding of this action in terms of the violent war for time. In the enormously influential *Little Red Book* (more than a billion copies published during the Cultural Revolution alone) Mao couches his thoughts on revolutionary strategy in terms of the direct citation and commentary on propositions drawn from *On War*.

The citations collected in Books five, eight and nine of the *Little Red Book* under the titles 'War and Peace', 'People's War' and 'People's Army' represent a sustained engagement with the strategic thought of Clausewitz. Book 5 begins with a commentary on the formula 'War is the continuation of politics', offering the chillingly blunt gloss: 'since ancient times there has never been a war that did not have a political character...It can therefore be said that politics is war without bloodshed while war is politics with bloodshed' (Mao 1966, 18). This is a recycled citation from the important 1938 strategic text 'On Protracted War'.[2] It is bleak enough, but its sombre recognition of the predicament of violence is compounded by the biomedical metaphor of catharsis in which violence constitutes a revolutionary subjectivity: 'revolutionary war is an antitoxin that not only eliminates the enemy's poison but also purges us of our own filth' (Mao 1966, 18). The cathartic quality of violence in purifying the violent subject of its compromised history would in certain developments of Maoism become a revolutionary end in itself.[3]

The rigour of Mao's commentary on Clausewitz is hardened by a number of other perspectives, most obviously his immersion in Marxist-Leninism and his commitment to global class war, but also his passion for bandit romances such *The Water Margin* and his familiarity with the classical Chinese tradition – above all, the ancient text on strategy by Sun Tzu, *The Art of War*.[4] It should not be underestimated how far Mao's understanding of Sun Tzu was shaped by the romances and works of fiction influenced by *The Art of War*. These theoretical influences and Mao's practice as a guerrilla leader during the Chinese civil wars and the foundation of the People's Republic of China produced a powerful and influential contribution to the theory of resistance. It is particularly important for its attention to the violent military aspect of resistance and its argument for a continuity between resistance and revolution. The military focus of his theory of resistance distinguishes it from that of Gandhi, but both resistants share the view of a transition from resistance to revolution in anti-colonial struggle. Mao's military theory of the 'war of resistance', although itself only partially successful (the Japanese withdrawal from China was due more to the 'paper tiger' of the nuclear attacks by the USA than the popular war of resistance), nevertheless provided a model that was applied successfully in Vietnam, less successfully in Peru and Northern Ireland, and currently of growing significance in a modified form in Nepal and India.

It is possible to see Mao's thought along with Gandhi's as the entry of non-Western, non-'philosophical' elements (in the sense of not derived from the Greek tradition) into the theory of resistance: in place of the emphasis on consciousness or force the anti-colonial struggles brought to the study of strategy very different conceptions of the relationship between time, space and resistance. In place of the basic intuition of a theatre of opposed active and reactive forces that informs Clausewitz and his successors' theory of resistance, we find in Mao an intuition of mobile shapes in a landscape, an *ecology* of war and resistance expressed in terms of meteorological metaphors absent from the Western discourse, such as the famous phrase from Book 5 of the *Little Red Book*, 'The East wind is prevailing over the west wind', which is by no means a mere metaphor.

A very useful and interesting introduction to what is different about Mao's strategic thinking and its application of Clausewitz can be found in François Jullien's 2005 work *Conference sur l'efficacité*.[5] Jullien directly confronts two different approaches to strategic thinking, one emerging from Machiavelli and Clausewitz, the other from Sun-Tzu, Mencius and Mao. He bases the contrast on the difference between plan and evaluation:

> This art of war thus begins, not with what would become a form of planning, but with an evaluation, which is that of the potential of a situation (it is by the way thus translated with the title 'Of Evaluation' by the first translator Amiot in 1772). (Jullien 2009, 29)

As opposed to the plan of battle central to the Western art of war, consisting in the attempt to plot the disposition of opposed forces with respect to an ideal plan, Jullien sees the Chinese strategist as evaluating the potential of a situation, evaluating the entire ecology of the war. Consistent with Western, Platonic metaphysics to which his thought was indebted, Clausewitz according to Jullien opposes the plan or 'idea' to circumstances: the idea or plan is only imperfectly realized due to 'friction' or other obstacles. As with Plato's artisan realizing through his art the idea of the table, the artisan of war opposes the ideal battle to 'circumstances' – seeing the relationship between them in terms of an ideal plan compromised by the depredations of chance and 'friction'. The Chinese strategist, by contrast, departing from a landscape of war and resistance, does not encounter the problem of participation or the translation of the idea into reality; the strategist is more interested in the potential of a landscape, the adaptation of a shape to a landscape. Jullien describes this potential in terms of the 'potential of a situation':

> For Clausewitz the circumstance was that which would make the course of war deviate, putting a screen between the modelling and its application, and was the source of 'friction' in the manoeuvre. Now Sun Tzu says precisely the opposite, that war, the victory does not deviate because victory is always the result of the potential of a situation, which renew itself in the course of operations. That which takes place at every moment is necessarily the consequence of an implicit relation of forces. The analysis here is rigorous and leaves no place for chance; war at each stage appears always as the product of the potential of a situation for one who knows how to view it under all its aspects and in its evolution. (Jullien 2009, 30)

This view of the potential of a situation intrinsic to Sun Tzu and later Taoism informs much of the bandit and military fictions of which Mao was an avid reader and subsequently his own theorization of the 'war of resistance'. Many of Mao's slogans and tactical innovations are thus drawn directly and indirectly from Sun Tzu, although they are sometimes posed in opposition to Sun Tzu's aphorisms. When theorizing the People's War and its tactics of mobile and guerrilla warfare (*Yundong Zhan* and *Youji Zhan*) he repeatedly cites the following aphorism:

> When Sun Wu Tzu said in discussing military science, 'know your enemy and know yourself and you can fight a hundred battles without danger of defeat', he was referring to the two sides in a battle. (Mao, 52)

This aphorism underlines one of the salient differences between the Greek Western and the Chinese tradition: Apollo's oracle 'know thyself' adopted by Socrates must be complemented in the Chinese tradition by knowing one's enemy – perhaps Socrates went to his death precisely because he knew only himself and did not sufficiently know his enemy? What Sun Tzu meant by 'knowing', however, is not the Cartesian consciousness of an extended object but awareness of shape – shape is constantly in motion, changing over time, capable of assuming illusory forms. It is important for Sun Tzu both to know the shape of the enemy and to be able to mislead the enemy as to his own shape – as important as knowing the enemy is ensuring that one is not known *by* the enemy. War becomes theatrical: the enemy will employ 'paper tigers' which must be known for what they are. The constant changes of shape are also linked to force (*chi*), but not in the Newtonian sense of opposed forces adopted by Clausewitz and the Western tradition. Mao insists that an effective resistance involves misleading the enemy about the disposition of forces; in *Basic Tactics* he cites Sun Tzu to this effect:

> The redoubtable force of a guerilla unit definitely does not depend exclusively on its own numerical strength, but on its use of sudden attacks and ambushes so as to 'cause an uproar in the east and strike in the west,' appearing now here and now there, using false banners and making empty demonstrations, propagating rumours about one's own strength, etc. in order to shatter the enemy's morale and create in him a boundless terror. (Mao 1966a, 84)

These instructions for deception and theatre – shape-changing – feed into the theory of guerrilla war and are absolutely consistent with the axioms of Sun Tzu's art of war, which is to win wars by avoiding battles. For Sun Tzu, the war is lost if a battle has to take place. Instead of an emphasis on confrontation and the concentration of time in a 'decisive blow', Sun Tzu and Mao advise evasion, illusion and the tactic of exasperating the enemy and inducing them to err, Mao making explicit what remained in the margins of Clausewitz's text.

The mutual implication of knowing oneself and one's enemy informs Mao's strategy of mobile and guerrilla warfare. Mao's conception of mobile warfare is contained in the slogans: '1. When the enemy advances, we retreat!' '2. When the enemy retreats, we pursue.' '3. When the enemy halts, we harrass him.' (Mao 1966a, section 16: 'Meeting a superior enemy,' 61–5).[6] In each of these, the secret of resistance consists in refusing to concede any initiative to the enemy. The avoidance of confrontation, the absolute avoidance of reactive action is fundamental to this view of resistance: it is vital never to surrender the initiative; indeed, it is even strategically advisable to give the enemy the illusion that *they* have the initiative. This is above all the case with the kind of guerrilla warfare advocated by Mao. In his instructions for waging guerrilla war in both 'On Proctracted War' and

'Basic Tactics' Mao emphasizes suppleness and flexibility over the amassing of mobile forces central to Napoleonic doctrine. What is absolutely crucial, once again, is the ability to seize the initiative – understood in terms of affirmative rather than reactive action – but with the Taoist virtue of flexibility modulating the Nietzschean affirmation adopted by Lenin. In the section on 'Initiative, Flexibility, Planning' that follows Mao's Clausewitzian analysis of the 'specific strategy of the War of Resistance Against Japan,' initiative is contrasted as affirmation to reactive passivity:

> Initiative is inserable from superiority in capacity to wage war, while passivity is inseparable from inferiority in capacity to wage war. Such superiority or inferiority is the objective basis of initiative or passivity... to maintain the initiative always and everywhere, that is, to have the absolute initiative, is possible only when there is absolute superiority matched against absolute inferiority. (Mao 1967, Vol. II 163)

Even though 'absolute initiative' or pure affirmation is impossible, it is crucial to avoid lapsing into a reactive posture: this is to expose vulnerability and to allow one's shape to be known by the enemy. Flexibility of shape, the ability rapidly to change and dissemble is above all a question of good timing or the ability to create surprise through deception:

> deliberately creating misconceptions for the enemy and then springing surprise attacks upon him are two ways – indeed two important means – of achieving superiority and seizing the initiative. What are misconceptions? "To see every bush and tree on Mount Pakung as an enemy soldier" is an example of misconception...it is often possible by various ruses to succeed in leading the enemy into a morass of wrong judgements and actions so that he loses his superiority and the initiative. (Mao 1967, 166)

Co-ordinated timing and deception in tune with the ecology of forces, with the potential offered by a landscape (that intangible potential pursued by Chinese landscape painting) is the central strategic intuition of Mao's theory of resistance and the key to its affirmation of initiative and through it the achievement of victory.

In a sense, the entire focus on initiative and the pursuit of affirmative in place of reactive action shifts the emphasis of resistance from decision and the Clausewitzian model of the duel or decisive battle to deferral of battle and the prolongation of the war. Resistance involves refusing the initiatives of the enemy, above all the initiative of deciding when and where the war will begin and end. This position and its novel politics of time was most clearly expressed in Mao's theorization in the late 1930s of the 'Protracted War of Resistance'. Mao might seem to diverge from Sun Tzu at this point, who recommended that a 'protracted war' be avoided at all costs: 'there has never been a case of protracted war from which a kingdom has benefitted'. But this forgets that Sun Tzu was dedicated to preserving the kingdom, recommending a strategy to a ruler who wishes to maintain his rule; Mao, however, sought to overthrow the kingdom, and in calling for a prolonged war of resistance was trying to entice the enemy into precisely the unwinnable scenario recognized by Sun Tzu. In his 1937 operational call for a 'war of resistance' against the Japanese occupation of parts of China, 'On the Operational Principles of the Red Army', Mao urged that 'we must carry out independent, self-reliant and dispersed guerrilla warfare and not positional warfare, nor should we concentrate our forces for a campaign' (Mao 2004, 6) – tactics conducive to a protracted war. Yet this strategic recommendation also implied broader political objectives, since Mao wanted to move from the war of resistance to revolutionary war – a transition that we have seen is by no means automatic or self-explanatory.

We encounter here – as almost everywhere in Mao's thought – the problem of resistant subjectivity. This is not understood in Cartesian terms as the bearer of a clear and distinct class-consciousness, as with Lenin, nor in terms of the emergent historical consciousness of Luxemburg. It is helpful here to return to the notion of a 'shape' in a landscape undergoing a process of transformation, a cloud for example. In Mao's strategic thought there is a drama of stasis and movement, between the fixity and the mobility of shape, and in both cases it is power that is decisive for establishing the final shape of things. The experience of the anti-colonial war of resistance sketches the outline of a potential revolutionary subjectivity inhabiting the ecology of global class war. During the 1920s Mao first pursued and then grew wary of the Comintern assumption that a defined revolutionary subject, the proletariat, potentially existed and needed to be supported by a military supplement. In the 1930s he pursued instead the notion that subjectivity is shaped by resistance, with mobile resistance gradually consolidating itself into revolutionary subjectivity, territorial gain and subsequently the creation of the conditions for the extension and intensification of revolutionary subjectivity. This movement from enhancing the capacity to resist to affirming revolutionary war was described in the important text 'Strive to Establish a Key Strategic Fulcrum for Engaging a Prolonged War of Resistance'. The establishment of fulcrums followed three stages: creation of revolutionary base areas, introduction of land reform, and finally the encirclement of cities. Resistance moves into the interstices of the shape of the enemy and grows, breaking down and disaggregating the forces and contours of the adversary and reorganizing the terrain so gained from the enemy.

Mao's view of resistance formed in the anti-colonial wars of the 1930s was not only an effective strategy for a peasant-led revolution. It was certainly adopted as such by many Asian revolutionary movements, and the contemporary Maoist movement in India is in many respects (but not all) almost a textbook version of Mao's strategic doctrine, pursuing the passage from indigenous resistance to multinational domination and the Indian State through regional control and revolutionary base areas to, in the last instance, world revolution. But it was also extended to a broader terrain of struggle in the Cultural Revolution. Here the enemy was the bureaucracy of the revolutionary state itself – the PRC – and the strategy and tactics of the guerrilla and mobile wars of the 1930s were brought into the institutions of the Communist State that it created. Here we encounter the idea of resistance to a bureaucracy that proved so enticing for radical thought in the West, especially France in the late 1960s, but which was not really what it seemed, a political movement. It confirmed in many ways Girard's view of Clausewitz as the theorist of the military suppression of politics. Mao, always the military commander, never a statesman or politician, used his influence in the Peoples Liberation Army to create paramilitary groups controlled by the army – the Red Guards – that attacked the bureaucracy and indeed the very notion of politics. When the forces unleashed took a revolutionary turn not foreseen by the military or Mao – as in the Shanghai citation of the Paris Commune – Mao moved to arrest it by all means. The grammar of military resistance and revolutionary war remained the only way in which he could conceive of political change. The primacy of military action and the almost cathartic significance lent to violence would have devastating consequences in other revolutions as well as in China. The model of violent resistance and revolutionary war threatened to undermine the formation and enhancement of the very capacity to resist itself. This distinguishes Mao's military theory of resistance from that of Gandhi, which with the doctrine of *ahimsa* self-consciously renounced violence and concentrated on enhancing the overall capacity to resist.

Gandhian Resistance: *Ahimsa* and *Satyagraha*

Mao's theory of resistance brought together Clausewitz, Marxist-Leninism and the *Art of War* of Sun Tzu. War and politics are inseparable, but war is understood in terms of the prescriptions of Sun Tzu dedicated to pursuing the pure goal of victory, one achieved not by frontal battle and the expenditure of force and violence but by deception, protraction and the avoidance of battle. To know yourself requires first of all knowing your enemy, but also ensuring that your enemy does not know you: it is strategically important and ethically permissible to deceive the enemy in the name of victory, to create illusions and to resist indirectly and obliquely. With the appeal to Sun Tzu, Mao was able to make an important contribution to the theory and practice of resistance that developed aspects of Clausewitz's thought that had otherwise not been noticed let alone appreciated. He lent great significance to retaining the initiative, even if this meant giving the enemy the illusion that it is they who possess it. This notion of indirect resistance was fully compatible with violence, indeed with a cathartic view of violence in which bloodshed was crucial to the formation of a resistant subjectivity. In an intensification of the Clausewitzian element in Mao's strategic thought, knowledge of the self and the quality of one's revolutionary morale became inseparable from the murder of the enemy.

The emphasis on victory and with it the licence to deceive the enemy seems to challenge the emphasis placed by Greek philosophy on the values of truth, justice and the good. Yet Mao and Sun Tzu force this self-perception of Western philosophy to be examined a little more critically. Recent scholarship on the core values of Greek philosophy, beginning with the work of the resistant Jean-Pierre Vernant, have shown the centrality of conflict, cunning, warfare and victory not only in Greek culture but also in its philosophy (see also Lloyd & Sivin 2002). Already Nietzsche had understood that the values of truth, goodness and justice ostensibly pursued in Greek philosophy might be feigned weapons dedicated to ensuring victory in argument or 'dialectic'. Yet the value of truth over victory was central to the theory and practice of the Indian struggle for independence from British colonial rule and the role played in it by the theories and the example of Gandhi.[7]

Gandhi's views on non-violent resistance become most clear when they are contrasted with the violent resistance of his contemporary Mao. Placed beside one another the similarities and differences between the two anti-colonial theories of resistance are very striking. While Mao focused on violence, Gandhi attempted to theorize a non-violent resistance; while Mao followed Sun Tzu in the rejection of considerations such as truth and ethical consistency in the pursuit of victory, Gandhi insisted that 'truth' was the supreme political value, and ethical consistency preferable to military victory. While Mao dedicated his efforts to building up a military power with the capacity to deliver military violence in the name of resistance and revolution, Gandhi rejected military violence, indeed any exercise of violence. And finally, both Mao and Gandhi brought to the Western theory of resistance – Clausewitz for Mao, Christ and Tolstoy for Gandhi – the insights and intuitions of non-Western bodies of thought – Sun Tzu and Taoism for Mao, the Ramayana and Bhagavad Gita for Gandhi. Gandhi especially admired Jesus' Sermon on the Mount for its statement of the doctrine of non-resistance and the recommendation to turn the other cheek, but he also admired writings inspired by this Christian tradition such as Tolstoy and Ruskin. This openness would earn him the derision of conservative thinkers such as Blanchot, who sustained a persistent and almost personal attack on Gandhi in the early 1930s, but it also disquieted Christian imperialists who were resisted in the name of their own religion, and the radicalization of Christ's sermon on non-violence.[8]

There are considerable obstacles to a philosophical discussion of Gandhi's theory of resistance, stemming from the fact that he and his tradition did not value the role of detached theory. While Mao inherited the prestige of theory from the Marxist tradition, Gandhi showed modest theoretical aspirations. His thinking was more oriented towards the practice of resistance – one that was theoretically informed but which did not call for sustained abstract reflection nor for philosophical justification. This practice of resistance began during his work in South Africa after 1893 against extreme and violent colonial discrimination in terms of 'race'. His resistance took various forms, focusing on the defence of the legal rights of Indians in South Africa and resistance to discriminatory legislation and practices. The experience of colonial oppression in South Africa served as a laboratory for the invention and testing of tactics of resistance, ranging from resisting in the courts on the basis of legality, publishing newspapers (*Indian Opinion* in 1903), founding a political organization (the Natal Indian Congress in 1894 based on the model of the 1886 Indian Congress), developing political theatre such as the taking of public vows of fasting and chastity, and in 1906 calling for a campaign of civil disobedience against racial legislation. We can see in Gandhi's work up to this time an attempt to constitute a resistant subjectivity not, as with Mao, through violence, but through information, example, provocation and non-violence.

In 1908 the various practices of resistance pursued by Gandhi and his allies were given the name '*Satyagraha*', meaning firmness in the commitment to truth. It combines an ethic of truth with a commitment to its resolute pursuit. Very far from Mao and Sun Tzu, *Satyagraha* nevertheless became an effective strategy for anti-colonial resistance. It was linked from the start with another term and value – *ahimsa* or non-violence. The link between truth and non-violence became axiomatic for Gandhi and guided his practice of resistance, first in South Africa and then in India. An early action of *Satyagraha* was the mass burning of identity cards (1908) and the acceptance of mass imprisonment. In the context of these actions Gandhi composed his first sustained theoretical reflection: the *Hind Swaraj* of 1909, written during the voyage from London to South Africa. It introduces another term, already current in debates around the tactics for Indian Independence, namely *Swaraj* or 'self-rule, self-government'. The ethical and political value of *Swaraj* is defined in terms of the truth of conscience, lending an importance to the self and knowledge of the self far removed from Sun Tzu and Mao's view that the self cannot be known apart from knowledge of the enemy, that enmity is an essential element of identity.

After proclaiming the strategy of *Satyagraha* in 1908, Gandhi began to explore a number of further dimensions of resistance. One was to withdraw from direct confrontation with the oppressor by founding communities such as the Tolstoy Farm near Johannesburg, founded in 1910, and the Ashrams founded subsequently in India. He also developed the tactic of the 'great march', mobilizing the population not in a military column as in Mao's Long March but in peaceful and demonstrative protest. Gandhi reflected on his experience of resistance in South Africa in two texts published after his return to India in 1915 and a difficult decade of resistance: the autobiography *Story of My Experiments with Truth* published in two parts in 1927 and 1929 and *Satyagraha in South Africa* in 1928. In these texts he sets out to show that the essentials of his theory and practice of resistance were already in place by 1915 when they were brought to bear on the Indian struggle for independence from British colonial rule. Gandhi applied the tactics of *Satyagraha* in 1917 and 1918 to settle agrarian and industrial disputes and then extended it to resist repressive acts of colonial legislation. Yet he consistently withdrew from confrontation when the peaceful protest provoked violence, whether on the part of the colonial power or by the resistance, thus refusing to engage in any escalation of violence. Repeatedly in prison and refusing to defend himself against charges of sedition, Gandhi subsequently led marches, such as the salt march in 1930, attended negotiations with the Imperial power and launched the Quit India movement in 1942. All these actions testify to important common ground between Mao and Gandhi regarding, first, the strategy of prolonged struggle or protraction that employed the *longue durée* of resistance to wear down the morale or capacity to resist of the oppressor, and then the importance of the constitution of a resistant subjectivity whether through violent or non-violent defiance. Both shared an implacable commitment to struggle, motivated in Mao by the pursuit of victory and in Gandhi by the moral certainty of a just cause supported by the truth.

The emergence of Gandhi's theory and practice of resistance is narrated in his autobiography and *Satyagraha in South Africa*, to which we will return in the next chapter, but it is the *Hind Swaraj* that is the essential text for understanding the political strategy of non-violent resistance and justifying the renunciation of physical force. Indeed Gandhi republished it in 1919 as a call to resistance, declaring his aspirations for Indian independence and laying out his strategy and tactics for achieving it. It is written in the form of a dialogue and is thus Socratic in its commitment to the pursuit of truth through discussion. *Hind Swaraj* begins by situating itself with respect to an important event in the colonial history of India and the formation of a resistant subjectivity. The British partition of Bengal deliberately planned to compromise the nationalist movement by dividing Muslims and Hindus and prompted a movement of resistance, the Swadeshi movement, which mobilized various forms of resistance – including, towards the end, terrorist tactics of assassination and violence.[9] The Swadeshi struggle eventually divided the Congress into moderate and extreme factions, leading to the intended breakdown of unity in the ranks of the anti-colonial resistance.

Gandhi responded to the political and tactical differences exposed by the Swadeshi movement with an analysis of the kind of independence he wished to see for India and the strategy and tactics necessary for achieving it. He explains what he means by *Swaraj* through a seemingly traditional reflection on the aims of life. He organizes this part of the discussion around the traditional division of the four aims of life or *purashatras*: *dharma, artha, kama* and *moksha*. Each is given, in varying degrees, a modern inflection, with *dharma* or duty extended to the Western notion of rights and responsibilities, *artha* taken to mean wealth or power, which Gandhi believes has been put out of balance by 'civilization' or societies such as those of the West that concentrate them in the hands of the few, while *kama* concerns pleasure and *moksha* salvation. Gandhi believes that *Swaraj* consists in the proper balance between these four aims of life, allowing none to dominate the others.

Inseparable from any philosophical interest in the nature of *Swaraj* is the issue of how to achieve it, and Gandhi carefully introduces his view of the appropriate tactics of resistance in Chapters 15, 16 and 17 of his text. The first, Chapter 15, is dedicated to the example of the Italian wars of national unification which Gandhi interprets as an elite struggle which left the population unmoved. Gramsci would later return the compliment of this analysis in his discussion of India in the *Prison Notebooks*, which set Gandhi's form of non-violent resistance within a wider context of violent and guerrilla forms of resistance that for him characterized the broader

Indian anti-colonial struggle. Yet in this chapter and throughout *Hind Swaraj* Gandhi is careful to distance himself categorically from violent forms of resistance. Much of the discussion of Italy is dedicated to questioning the necessity and value of violence and political murder. The voice of Gandhi in the dialogue insists that any freedom gained through violence will be compromised and that 'those who will rise to power by murder will certainly not make the nation happy' (Gandhi 1997, 77). This position is elaborated in Chapter 16 on 'brute force', which takes the example of the 1857 Indian mutiny as an occasion to reflect on the role of violence. The mutiny was much discussed in this period, but Gandhi reflects on it in order to develop a critique of violence. He argues that responding to colonial force by means of force means that 'we can only get the same thing they got' (Gandhi 1997, 81), for violent resistance can only lead to a violently secured result, in the process producing violent subjectivities incapable of living in peace after the conclusion of the struggle. He also adds the pragmatic, Clauswitzian consideration that the tactic of individual terror, theorized and practised by young Bengalis, would prove no match in any contest of forces with the well-armed colonial power, and would even be welcomed by it as a pretext for compromising the movement's moral and physical capacity to resist.

In Chapter 17 on 'Passive Resistance' Gandhi moves to a statement of the strategy and tactics of resistance. The advocate of violence in the dialogue – 'The Reader' – claims there is no evidence 'for any nation having risen through soul force' – through love and the force of truth. The voice of Gandhi replies:

> Thousands, indeed tens of thousands, depend for their existence on a very active working of this force. Little quarrels of millions of families in their daily lives disappear before the exercise of this force. Hundreds of nations live in peace. History does not, and cannot, take note of this fact. History is really a record of every interruption of the even working of the force of love or of the soul. (Gandhi 1997, 90)

Anthony J. Parel notes in his edition of *Hind Swaraj* that in the Gujarati original of the text Gandhi describes this 'exercise of force' as *Satyagraha*. Having established the normality of peace – which Gandhi insists is 'natural, not rooted in history' – the argument moves to the discussion of the theory of passive resistance. Gandhi writes:

> Passive resistance is a method of securing rights by personal suffering; it is the reverse of resistance by arms. When I refuse to do a thing that is repugnant to my conscience, I use soul force. (Gandhi 1997, 90)

Once again, in the Gujarati version Gandhi refers to *Satyagraha*, giving it the gloss:

> Satyagraha or soul-force is called passive resistance in English. That word is applicable to a method by which men, enduring pain, secure their rights. Its purpose is the opposite of the purpose of using force of arms (labaidal). When something is not acceptable to me I do not do that work. In so acting I use satyagraha or soul force. (Gandhi 1997, 90)

The debt to Thoreau is evident here; 'passive resistance' is not only the preferred translation for *Satyagraha*, but the very formulation of the strategy of resistant *Satyagraha* was to some degree shaped by Gandhi's reading of 'On Civil Disobedience' in 1906.[10]

Gandhi gives an example of *Satyagraha* whose spirit and phrasing is at first sight close to Thoreau's 'On Civil Disobedience' but quickly becomes something very different:

> the government has passed a law which is applicable to me. I do not like it. If, by using violence, I force the government to repeal the law, I am employing what may be termed body-force. If I do not obey the law, and accept the penalty for its breach, I use soul force (satyagraha). It involves sacrifice of self. (Gandhi 1997, 91)

On this basis Gandhi overturns many of the premises of Western political theory in which the self of the political actor is the main locus of action and the reason for action: 'The real meaning of the statement that we are a law-abiding nation is that we are passive resisters. When we do not like certain laws, we do not break the heads of the law-givers, but we suffer and do not submit to the laws' (Gandhi 1997, 91). Here Gandhi makes the important discovery that legitimacy is correlated to resistance, and imagining the constitution of a subjectivity that by refusing to 'obey laws that are unjust, no man's tyranny will enslave him'.

At this point Gandhi develops a critique of the Clausewitzian logic of escalation that anticipates the position recently defended by René Girard that violence always escalates to the point of disaster:

> To use brute force…is contrary to passive resistance. For it means that we want our opponent to do by force that which we desire but he does not. And, if such a use of force is justifiable, surely he is entitled to do likewise by us. And we should never come to an agreement…[it] must lead to disaster. (Gandhi 1997, 93)

Passive resistance, as we shall see in the following chapter, creates a formidable subjectivity, one which is 'free like the king of the forest, and his very glance withers the enemy' (Gandhi 1997, 94). The resistant subject described by Gandhi in *Hind Swaraj* ('after a great deal of experience') is one that observes 'perfect chastity, adopt(s) poverty, follows truth and cultivates fearlessness' (Gandhi 1997, 96), the first of the many catalogues of the qualities of a satyagrahist that Gandhi would compile over the coming decades. Here the theory of *Satyagraha* re-enters the wider theory of resistance: the resistant subjectivity must be concentrated; it must have control over its desire; it must abandon the distraction of wealth; it must be dedicated to an absolute commitment to truth; and ultimately, and underlying them all, it must subscribe to the virtue of courage – 'Those alone can follow the path of passive resistance who are free from fear, whether as to their possessions, false honour, their relatives, the government, bodily injuries, death' (Gandhi 1997, 98). The rigour of this vision of a militant, resistant subjectivity exceeds even that of the Leninist professional revolutionary; its emphasis on the ineluctable and inescapable life of resistance in which individual needs and desires are irrelevant draws close to the revolutionary subjectivity of Mao.

Gandhi's insight into the disastrous outcome of the escalation of violence joined with the equally radical view that even the smallest violence was intrinsically prone to escalate. He did not see any place for, or any possibility of, a controlled use of violence. He also believed that the exercise of violence corrupted resistant subjectivity which through it became physically and morally vulnerable to complicity with the violence of the adversary. However, it must be remembered that Gandhi's strategy of non-violence, while also a philosophy and a way of life, was primarily a strategic option in a war of anti-colonial resistance. This understanding of non-violent war proved difficult to grasp for European thinkers for whom, following Clausewitz, war was always violent but diplomacy and politics not necessarily so. In the eyes of Western readers, non-violence as an anti-colonial strategy was very quickly translated into an abstract ethical stance that globally opposed war and struggle, becoming a form of renunciation indifferent to the pursuit of political goals. This was very far from Gandhi's view and practice of the war of non-violent resistance. The strange under-estimation of the militancy of non-violent resistance led to some even stranger distortions in its European reception, with the development on the one hand of the view that violence was apocalyptic and on the other that non-violence was at best an individual ethical stance with few implications for organized political resistance.

Resisting Apocalypse

The prominence of the theme of violence in post-war French thought emerged from the historical matrix of resistance. This comprised the experience of the French Resistance to Nazi occupation and Petainist collaboration, the anti-colonial wars of liberation against French colonial rule in Vietnam and Algeria, as well as the apocalyptic potential for absolute violence unleashed by the nuclear attacks on Hiroshima and Nagasaki in 1945. In Clausewitzian terms the nuclear attacks destroyed the Japanese moral and physical capacity to resist and, with the ensuing Japanese withdrawal from China, also contributed indirectly to Chinese victory in their local war of resistance. Mao's protracted war of resistance was concluded by the escalation of violence by the United States. Unlike Gandhi, Mao did not win the war of anti-colonial resistance as a result of his own strategic and political initiative, but was awarded it by the 'paper tiger' of the United States' nuclear weaponry; he was at best the victor in the civil war that followed the withdrawal of the Japanese colonial power. With the nuclear arming of the USSR in 1949, the Cold War would be conducted in terms of a Clausewitzian duel, with both adversaries poised on the brink of a literally apocalyptic escalation. The potential for local or limited resistance within such a scenario and the threat of the absolute escalation of local anti-colonial and civil violence to an apocalyptic extreme became one of the main preoccupations of post-war French philosophy.

The return to Clausewitz and the study of his dilemmas became one of the major ways of exploring the potential link between resistant and escalating absolute violence. It provided the occasion for a rethinking of violence and its relationship to the war and politics of resistance. The shadowy figure of Clausewitz implicitly qualified the glaring presence of Hegel in post-war France, inspired by the influential but idiosyncratic commentary on the *Phenomenology of Spirit* pursued by Alexandre Kojève during the 1930s and published by Raymond Queneau as *Introduction à la lecture de Hegel* in 1947. The citation of Clausewitz served as an antidote to the statist, if not imperialist, tendency of Kojève's reading of Hegel, with Clausewitz assuming his proper place as a theorist of resistance.

Perhaps the most questionable aspect of Kojève's passionate commentary was his view of Hegel's philosophical endorsement of Napoleonic Empire. Hegel is cast as an advocate of Revolutionary Imperialism, even as its philosophical conscience; Kojève goes so far as to emphasize Hegel's christological view of Napoleon as the literal incarnation of the universal state or Empire. What is equally striking in this philosophical apology for Empire is the suppression of the theme of violence and the absence of Hegel's contemporary Clausewitz. Not only does Kojève restrict the military adventures of Empire to the level of 'struggle' and 'work', thus overlooking the centrality of absolute violence in the imperial project, but he also excludes Clausewitz from his discussion of the German opponents of Napoleon against whom he favourably contrasts Hegel: 'the adversaries of Napoleon do not *act* against him, they do not destroy him; their judgement is thus pure vanity, loquaciousness' (Kojève, 153). Clausewitz is the great and staring exception to this judgement, yet Kojève does not allow this to trouble his view that 'Hegel recognised and revealed Napoleon to Germany. He thought to save Germany (through his phenomenology) to conserve it in sublimated form [*aufgehoben*] within the Napoleonic Empire' (Kojève, 153). Napoleon in this reading is 'the "perfect" man…and if Napoleon is the revealed God (the appearing God) it is Hegel who reveals him' (Kojève, 153). The christological imperialism induced by Kojève in Hegel accompanies the reduction of the role played by violence in imperial history to its inaugural phase, preparatory to the age of imperial and philosophical perpetual peace.

For Kojève, Hegel is the philosopher of work; accordingly, politics – even Napoleonic imperial politics – is understood in terms of work, pointedly not, as with Clausewitz, in terms of violence. Kojève's reading of the master/slave dialectic from the *Phenomenology of Spirit* is framed in terms of the battle or 'labours' of Jena. Kojève understands the dialectic in terms of a movement between struggle and work that issues in a history: 'taken together, the history of struggles and of work which arrive finally at the Napoleonic wars and the table on which Hegel writes the *Phenomenology* in order to understand these wars and this table' (Kojève, 171). Kojève moves through a vocabulary of struggle, war, work, domination and freedom, all the time avoiding the word 'violence'. Yet the slave's strategy in the struggle of recognition, one of secession that moves from struggle to work, implies the renunciation of any capacity to resist. The slave does not resist the master/adversary but turns away and sets themself to work. But while Kojève has Hegel setting the slaves to peaceful transformative work in and for the new Empire, Clausewitz sees the subjected as developing new potentials and strategies for violent, political resistance to imperial domination itself. For Kojève's Hegel the vanquished become serfs and slaves, while for Clausewitz they become guerrillas and partisans. The parallels between Kojève's view of the Empire of work and the contemporary USSR are unavoidable, and perhaps for this reason his idiosyncratic view of the relationship between the philosopher and the imperial military dictator – cast in terms of an understanding of history as a process of labour – provoked a negative reaction in some of his listeners at *L'école pratique des hautes études* in the mid–1930s who understood the contemporary parallel only too well. Eric Weil and Raymond Aron reacted to this view of history with a sustained attempt to restore the thinking of violence, and – in Weil's case, at least – to bring it to reason.

Clausewitz's thought was central to the thinking of violence and its control pursued by Weil and Aron in the immediate post-war years and the beginnings of the Cold War. The Clausewitzian insight that violence escapes any dialectical logic, opening realms of risk, danger and chance that seemed closed by the incarnation of Napoleon, the perpetual peace of universal world Empire and the transformation of war into work informed their critiques of Kojève and his view of the imperial end of history.[11] Against this closure, Clausewitz taught the risks and dangers attending the exercise of violence, the inextricability of violence and politics, and the intrinsic instability of violence and its tendency to escalate. Weil and Aron in their post-war and post-Kojèvean reflections on Clausewitz nevertheless engage with the question of the possible control of violence. Their view, completely opposed to that of Gandhi, is that it can be controlled, while after them Girard will differ radically by developing an apocalyptic reading of Clausewitz that sees violence as catastrophic not only for the future of politics but more broadly for the future of the world. What is at stake in resisting or succumbing to the apocalypse is the scope allowed to the development of the capacity to resist. It does not only consist in the vanquished setting themselves to work and, by some ruse of history, unconsciously resisting through the creation of a world of work, as Kojève seemed to suggest, but also in acknowledging a flight from violence.

One of the earliest appearances of Clausewitz in French post-war philosophy occurs ten years after the war with an article by Eric Weil that was continuous with his attempt to revise the reading of Hegelian politics in *Hegel and the State* (1998). In 'Guerre et Politique selon Clausewitz' (1955) Weil introduces Clausewitz to a new audience, presenting his basic positions but in a way that emphasizes his stature as a thinker of resistance as well as one sensitive to the dangers inherent in the resort to violence. The task of the theoretician of war consists in helping the statesman understand the 'the conditions for the correct use of the political instrument that is war' (Weil 1955, 297). Yet he is immediately sensitive to the disparity between the ends pursued by war and politics: 'war, considered in itself, is pure violence, and its inherent goal is the destruction of the adversary while politics finds its field of operation in the commerce of nations' (Weil 1955, 297). Weil discerns an apparent 'flagrant contradiction' between the view of war as an instrument of politics, limited to achieving specific political goals, and as 'total, unlimited, absolutely destructive violence' (Weil 1955, 297). However, his citation of the definition of the aim of war as the destruction of the capacity to resist puts this contradiction into perspective. In a thoughtful footnote to this citation Weil observes that the definition 'shows that Clausewitz did not think of the material destruction of the forces of the adversary, but aimed to break their will to resist – thus introducing the political motif into the very definition of the goal of war' (Weil 1955, 297). Unfortunately he does not pursue the question of the political constitution of the capacity to resist and how it can be compromised, but nevertheless the remainder of his article remains sensitive to the threat that, along with the capacity to resist, war might destroy the very possibility of politics itself.

Politics becomes for Weil the realm in which the exercise of practical reason is at least possible, and reason takes its place within politics as a means of overcoming, or at least avoiding, the resort to violence. Yet on occasion, such as the French Revolution but revolutions in general, politics can free itself from reason and unleash internal and externally directed violence. In a long concluding paragraph Weil sums up his reading of Clausewitz by claiming that

> …[t]he degree of (war's) violence will be consequently a function of the intra-national tensions on one side and international tensions on the other. The high tensions between nations are, however, normally functions of the revolutionary tensions within different communities… (Weil 1955, 313)

War is the outcome not of reason's march through history, but of the breakdown of the alliance between reason and politics: 'Pure violence will thus only be unleashed in moments when the fall of potential politics (internal politics) becomes sufficiently great between states' (Weil 1955, 314). The primacy of internal politics or the management of violence within a state is given predominance. At the moment of revolution the controlled, instrumental use of violence can escalate to absolute violence, inadvertently releasing imperial adventures such as that of Napoleon. The implication is clear: Weil deflates Kojève's reading of Hegelian reason into imperial history by regarding imperialism as the result of the breakdown of politics and reason and not as their culmination in a universal state. At this point Weil redefines reason (or 'sound' politics) by aligning it with the democratic control of the escalation of violence. In periods of non-revolutionary war, when ' the [existence of the state] is not in danger, neither heads of state nor the people can accept under these conditions

the highest sacrifice, which is to deploy and suffer absolute violence'
(Weil, 314). Yet Weil concludes on the grounds of the experience of the
democratic revolutions that 'it is not violence but reason which judges in
the last instance, and the violence which claims to be revolutionary must
justify itself before the tribunal (of reason)' (Weil 1955, 314).

Aron dissents from Weil's formalistic account of Clausewitz's logic of
war and politics, remaining unconvinced that the equation of democratic
will and reason is capable of judging or containing violence. Aron's confrontation of reason and violence through the close reading of Clausewitz in
his study *Penser la Guerre* confronts the experience of resistance with the
predicament of nuclear war. His experience as a resistant enabled him not
only to read Clausewitz as a thinker of resistance, implacable enemy of the
Napoleonic Empire and theorist of guerrilla war, but also to appreciate that
his emphasis on defence inaugurates the wider project of the protracted war
of resistance. His discussions of Lenin and Mao in the second volume of
Penser la Guerre along with shorter, more explicit essays such as 'Clausewitz,
stratège et patriote' and especially 'Clausewitz et la guerre populaire'[12]
present a coherent account of Clausewitz as the philosopher of the global
war of resistance. But this insight sits uncomfortably with perhaps the
major motivation of his reading, which is the problem of the control of the
escalation of violence posed by the predicament of nuclear war.

As a thinker of the Cold War, Aron finds in the political control of the
escalation of violence the 'confirmation and completion' of Clausewitzian
thought. His analysis, however, is conducted at a less abstract level than
Weil's equation of democracy and reason. Aron focuses on the tension
between political control of the means of violence and the inherent
tendency of violence to escalate beyond such control. In a 1975 essay
'La société des Etats et la Guerre' Aron summarizes his attempt to adjust
Clausewitz to late twentieth-century conditions in Volume Two of *Penser
la Guerre*. The political context is now global, and the existence of nuclear
weapons makes absolute war no longer a hypothetical limit condition but
a militarily feasible objective. In this case:

If escalation signifies in our epoch an escalation towards nuclear war, the
sense of the two Clausewitzian movements changes radically. Escalation
leads either to the battle of annihilation or in a more general sense, to
decision: the defeated enemy consents to discussion and accepts the
conditions of the victor... [the existence of nuclear weapons] forces
a choice between the two Clausewitzian principles: annihilation and
decision on one part and the supremacy of the political on the other'
(Aron 2005, 106).

For Aron, the existence of nuclear arms in many ways completes Clausewitz's thought by allying the real threat of escalation with a renewed primacy of the political. The threat of mutual destruction

> [...] fills, to put it thus, a gap of which the Clausewitzian concep-
> tualisation was aware, but left empty due to the limits of historical
> experience; the diplomatic use of arms in view of effective prevention of
> their use. The strategy called dissuasion may be precisely defined as the
> use of the nuclear menace in view of avoiding its putting into execution.
> (Aron 2005, 106)

In his attention to the Clausewitzian trinity Aron plays down the role of the people and the commander in favour of the politician and the diplomat. Unlike Weil, Aron is not terribly convinced that escalation may be controlled through the use of democratic reason on the part of the people, or that it may be entrusted to the military judgement of the commander. He sees politics as most effective when conducted at the level of diplomacy and according to the 'unwritten alliance of the two great powers against total war' (Aron 2005, 111). Beyond the opposition of politics and military, a politico-strategic decision has been taken and an unwritten pact agreed concerning the primacy of the political. It is thus diplomatic reason that now defines international politics and war. Aron is well aware that little wars risk provoking escalation, but goes to considerable lengths to show how all parties to warfare are now attentive to this threat, not only the great powers with their unwritten pact to avoid it, but even the partisans who are under an ideological and political discipline that is attentive to the potential for escalation.

Yet there is a tension between Aron's view of a diplomatic reason working to defer escalation to a point where every capacity to resist is minimized and his view of the emergence of small wars of resistance capable of provoking escalation. Alongside global society and nuclear weaponry, Aron sees a third change since the period of Clausewitz, namely the emergence of the institution of the armed people prepared to wage guerrilla wars of resistance. While for Clausewitz '[t]he arming of the people figured during the wars of the Empire as one of the last resources of an oppressed people and counted among the advantages of a militarily and politically defensive war' (Aron 2005, 118), it was not pursued lightly, since its detractors feared it would create a 'revolutionary potential' among the people. Aron comments that in the last analysis they were not deceived, but he quickly moves to contain the threat posed by armed movements of resistance to the escalation of violence. Clausewitz envisaged the Prussian armed people as a supplement to the regular army; Aron grasps this to argue that contemporary movements of armed resistance – China, Cuba, Vietnam – are the products either of a fused regular and people's army, or the bringing of the armed people under military discipline: 'The partisan is already a semi-regular insofar as he submits himself to the imperative command of even distant officers or sub-officers' (Aron 2005, 119). The discipline of the partisan along with diplomatic reason of state serves to check any escalation of violence and, for Aron, mark the completion of Clausewitz's thinking of war initiated at the outset of the revolutionary period. In effect, Aron has adapted Clausewitz's grammar of war to the thesis of the end of history proposed by his teacher Kojève.

René Girard took issue with Aron's views of the political and diplomatic control of escalation. The title of his extended discussion with Benoît Chantre, *Achever Clausewitz*,[13] suggests that Aron's claim to complete Clausewitz, or to see his completion in diplomatic reason, was premature. Instead his discussion of Clausewitz is dedicated to the proposition that an apocalyptic escalation of violence is not only possible but is already in course. It is a reading directly addressed to Aron and against the positions of *Penser la Guerre*. In his postface, Chantre describes how he arrived at his discussions with Girard 'full of Aronian assurance and certain of being able to extract from my teacher and friend some reasons for still believing in politics' (Girard 2011, 374), a confidence quickly shaken by Girard's apocalyptic reading of *On War*. For Girard believes that escalation is already engaged and that any capacity to resist it has already been fatally and irreversibly compromised.

In *Achever Clausewitz* Girard discovers in escalation an apocalyptic logic that is far removed from the convictions of Weil and Aron – that it was possible politically to contain the escalation of violence. Girard's position follows from his earlier reflections on scapegoat, mimesis and his complex view of the historical and contemporary significance of Christianity. By refusing to resist violence by violence, by turning the other cheek, by 'allowing himself to be crucified', Christ makes explicit what is for Girard the sacrificial foundation of human society. The crucifixion removes the 'dissimulation' of violence in sacrifice and ritual at the same time as dismantling the barriers 'which thus protected human societies from their own violence' (Girard 2011, 16). The death of God and the dearth of 'new festivals' lamented by Nietzsche's madman in *The Gay Science* initiates for Girard a logic of escalating violence driven by the mimesis discerned in the hostile postures of the adversaries analysed by Clausewitz in Book One of *On War*. Girard imagines two possible responses to the predicament of escalation that has in his view been unleashed by Christian revelation. The first adverts to the Christian roots of Gandhian *ahimsa*, the second to the faith in the power of the political advocated by Aron.

In the first case, the escalation of violence may be contained by the renunciation of violent resistance. In Girard's words, 'To make the revelation entirely good, not at all menacing, it would be enough for humans to adopt the comportment recommended by Christ: the complete abstention from reprisals, the renouncing of escalation' (Girard 2011, 18). This response to the threat of escalation entails in the final analysis the renunciation of resistance rather than its continuance by other-than-violent means. The absence of a sustained reading of Gandhi in Girard leads to an underestimation of the power of non-violent resistance. Without the adoption of Christian non-resistance Girard sees the imminent and present threat of 'the extinction of all life on the planet' (Girard 2011, 18). He cannot accept Aron's hope for a political solution to the apocalypse provoked by the escalation of violence:

> It is this possibility that Raymond Aron saw when reading Clausewitz. He thus wrote a forceful *summa* in order to exorcise the spirit of the apocalyptic logic, to persuade himself at all costs that the worst will be avoided, that 'dissuasion' will always triumph. (Girard 2011, 18)

While Girard opposes his 'completing' of Clausewitz to Aron's hopes for political and diplomatic reason in *Penser la guerre*, he nevertheless presents *Achever Clausewitz* as 'radicalising Aron's gesture' (Girard 2011, 65). Aron is 'the first to have the merit of extending (Clausewitz) out of the strict military context. It is the vicious circle of violence which he has to be able to renounce, that eternal return of the sacred less and less contained by rites and which now confounds itself with violence' (Girard 2011, 65). Aron's faith in political and diplomatic reason assumes the existence of a dialectic of violence; Girard on the other hand argues that the grammar of violence identified by Clausewitz in the escalation towards absolute war leaves no dialectical result, but eventually consumes itself.

Aron and Girard's readings of Clausewitz emerge from a shared obsession with the general question of violence, Girard in a number of books from *La Violence et le sacré* (1972), *Des choses cachées depuis la fondation du Monde* (1978), *De la violence à la divinité* (2007), and Aron in an even greater number of contributions, most prominently *Paix et Guerre entre les Nations* (1962) and *Le grand Débat. Initiation à la stratégie atomique* (1963) that make up his 'transcendental dialectic' of absolute war and those writings emerging from the Resistance and La France Libre, such as *De l'Armistice à l'Insurrection nationale* (1945). The shared fascination with violence led to a shared concern with the possibility of its management. And it is at this point that the paths of Aron and Girard diverge so markedly. Aron is convinced that limited violence *can* make sense politically, that violence, war, can have a positive dialectical outcome. Even nuclear war or its threat can prove an incitement to politics – at bottom, violence can indeed be managed politically. This conviction that violence can have a positive political outcome testifies to Aron's Hegelianism and once again to his being the heir of Kojève. Girard on the other hand has a wholly apocalyptic understanding of violence; for him the end of the world, its violent self-destruction is already happening: violence is not only consuming politics but in absolute war will eventually consume itself.

In taking a distance from Aron, *Achever Clausewitz* also distances itself from Hegel and the Kojèvian reading of Hegel never far from Aron's thought. Emphasizing the enormous distance between Hegel and Clausewitz is one of the structural features of Girard's book; they are one of the few pairs in his work who do not enter into a mimetic relationship. In close readings of Hegel's writings on Christianity and on Napoleon – precisely Kojève's chosen terrain[14] – Girard shows that Hegel cannot think apocalyptically, cannot think escalation: 'What Hegel cannot see… *is that the oscillation of contrary positions, become equivalent, may just as well escalate…*' (Girard 2011, 70). Hegel's thought is at best tragic, at worst an imperial theodicy, but for Girard his ambition to think the absolute disqualifies him from thinking the apocalypse:

> Hegelian thought has its tragic aspects, but it is not catastrophic. It confidently passes through the dialectic to reconciliation, from reciprocity to relation, and gives the impression indeed of forgetting where it came from. (Girard 2011, 70)

In a phrase from later in the book, where Hegel is placed alongside Dante as one of the two great thinkers of Empire, Girard observes that Hegel 'lacked lucidity into the ravaging consequences of violence' (Girard 2011, 346). Clausewitz, on the other hand, had no illusions about Empire and no illusions about the disasters of war; dialectic had no place in his sombre vision of the dreadful consequences of the escalation of violence.

Girard introduces Clausewitz as an apocalyptic thinker able to theorize catastrophe, but at the same time considers him to be a realist. Convinced that apocalypse is in course, he sees no paradox in these positions. The comforting illusions of Hegel's dialectical results and resolutions and his eschatology of a coming philosophical Empire of peace contrast with Clausewitz 'who observes, with a terrible lucidity, the accelerated movement of history, this history that loses reason, becomes mad' (Girard 2011, 84). Yet Girard, after distinguishing and continuing to insist on the distinction of Hegel and Clausewitz, nevertheless recognizes that they must be read together. It is the lack of lucidity into the causes and consequences of violence, the 'lack of a radical concept of violence', that makes Hegelian thought a 'danger' (Girard 2011, 75). It is necessary to read both Hegel and Clausewitz, not in order to reconcile them but in order to make their division stark and unnegotiable: 'One sees immediately that the unity of the real and the concept leads to peace with Hegel, to escalation with Clausewitz' (Girard 2011, 75). The escalation has no internal means of arrest, and the possibility of resistance to it seems highly attenuated; there is certainly no easy passage from it to a post-historical reign of perpetual peace when the real is finally rational.

Girard pursues the question of 'ideological war' or a war that disowns its own violence in the name of ultimate ends through the example of Leninism. He adopts Aron's description of Leninism as 'military Hegelianism' and describes it as mounting an absolute war against class enemies in which reason is of no assistance: 'Incapable of resisting force, reason instead opens a boulevard for it and justifies it' (Girard 2011, 86). Girard describes ideological war, or reason's inability to resist force, in terms of a metaphor drawn from Haussman's Paris and the iconography of the Paris Commune. Reason has no *barricades* to erect against violence, so instead it opens the boulevard and celebrates it. With ideological war, we seem to have arrived at the end of resistance, but we shall see that Girard's views on the question of resistance are more complex and tormented. The military and ideological revolutions realize the 'meaning of history' through their violent actions, but instead of arriving at the Hegelian result of a world socialist society, the war with the class enemy escalates and 'civil war replaces national wars. This inflection of the definition of war accomplished by Leninism contributes to the spread of war: very quickly civil war becomes European war and then world war' (Girard 2011, 86).[15] Girard closes his reading of Clausewitz and of European history since the French Revolution by pointing to the steady escalation of violence and voicing the presentiment that violence has now attained an apocalyptic level. He concludes with these words, which reprise his differences with Aron:

Clausewitz testifies in a way more realist than Hegel to the fundamental incapacity of politics to contain escalation. The ideological wars, monstrous justifications of violence, have in effect carried humanity to that beyond of war where we are today. The West will exhaust itself in a conflict with Islamic terrorism which it has itself incontestably ignited. It was in the inter-state conflicts of the nineteenth century that Clausewitz saw the upsurge of violence. The nations were there to contain the revolutionary contagion. The French campaign was terminated by the Congress of Vienna in 1815. That epoch is now complete, at the moment when violence no longer knows the least restraint. It may be said, from this point of view, that the apocalypse has begun. (Girard 2011, 352)

With the announcement of an apocalyptic escalation of violence that can no longer be contained politically – even the *catechon* or restrainer has left in despair – Girard returns to the theological sources of his thinking. The ambivalence of Christianity noted above – its release of unrestrained and undissimulated violence as well as the antidote to it – is reaffirmed in the final lines, and especially in the startling but not unexpected claim that 'Satan is another name for escalation' (Girard 2011, 362). The desired 'completion' of Clausewitz consists in showing that *On War* (like his earlier *Bekenntnisdenkschrift*) is a profession of faith in the satanic character of violence. The antidote for Girard seems to consist in non-resistance and the acceptance of violence; there seems no other possible place from which resistance to escalation can depart. Yet with this, with the choice between the worst – the end of life in the escalation of violence – and the call to awaken sleeping consciences, we arrive at the question of how far the apparent absence of resistance in Girard's completion of Clausewitz has contributed to the apocalyptic terminus of his thinking.

The word 'resistance' does not appear in the admirably full and detailed index to *Achever Clausewitz*, but there is nevertheless an extended, if subterranean, meditation on resistance running through the text. Girard's critique of revolution and ideological war is wholly unambiguous, but his position with respect to resistance is more fugitive and difficult to grasp. We have seen that, for Girard, politics is unable to resist escalation and violence only intensifies it, while reason explicitly renounces any possibility of arresting its passage to the extreme. Where, then, is it possible to locate resistance to escalation? Girard located resistance – without naming it – in the example of Christ's non-reprisal and renunciation of violence in the Sermon on the Mount that was one of the sources of Gandhi's strategy of *Satyagraha*. Yet if never openly addressed, the meditation on resistance winds its way between and across the lines of his text, occasionally intensifying but never attaining full expression.

At one point Benoît Chantre asked Girard the simple but devastating question: 'The law of escalation is thus ineluctable?' Girard understood immediately that this was a question addressed not so much to the necessity of the law of escalation as to the possibility of resisting it. He begins by reiterating the contemporary significance of Clausewitz, the differences between his own and Aron's Hegelian reading and the importance of the relationship to Christianity. Girard very beautifully observes that 'the future of the world escapes us and yet is in our hands' and from this predicament turns personally to the revelation of the New Testament. In an allusive passage, he describes his 'astonishment' and 'fascination' with 'the formidable passive resistance that this message encounters…', especially in the wake of Hegelianism. It is this 'revelation' that he turns to – one close to passive resistance – which 'tells us that reconciliation is not immanent to the movement of history' (Girard 2011, 102), which for him makes Pascal and not Hegel our contemporary. Yet while this revelation is central – and with it in some way 'passive resistance' – its character remains obscure. Nevertheless the theme of resistance returns in another aside which turns out to be crucial, this time at the end of the section on 'The Duel and Reciprocity' which reflects on the example of Dreyfus and the Dreyfusards. Girard describes the Affair as 'typically Clausewitzian' in that the perceived needs of military command assumed precedence over those of the political and the state. As if still replying to Chantre's earlier question, he endorses the opposition of the Dreyfusards to patent injustice using the name of resistance:

The Dreyfusards resisted, they did not think that the condemnation was the end of it, that they were committed to a necessity which must see itself through to its end, that the rehabilitation of the Captain would come in its own good time! Because I am apocalyptic, I refuse all forms of providentialism. It is necessary to fight until the end, even if one thinks that one acts in vain (Girard, 2011).

The refusal to accept providentialism or any Hegelian resolution also holds for satanic escalation; it should be resisted until the end. Yet once again, even after this passionate profession of resistance, the theme itself once more submerges.

Resistance resurfaces for the last time in a number of powerful pages on the experience of the French Resistance in the section on 'France and Germany'. Chantre once again asks a pointed question, all the more powerful given the context of the French resistance to National Socialist Germany:

Doesn't your reasoning in terms of 'great masses' in which you can envisage history in terms of the longue durée and in an apocalyptic perspective minimise the ethic of the Resistance which was essential to the revival of the European idea? (Girard 2011, 321)

Girard's improvised reply is at once direct and evasive, beginning with the figure of De Gaulle and his admiration for the General's 'having gloriously escaped that spirit of resignation' (Girard 2011, 322). By the spirit of resignation, however, it turns out that Girard is not referring to the France of the early 1940s but to France during the 1930s, that 'force of inertia' which, far from being a capacity to resist violence, contributed to its return with the defeatist view that 'The French knew that they could not resist a German attack' (Girard 2011, 320). And yet, Girard also cites De Gaulle as 'saying himself that France had not followed the Resistance, or that the Resistance could not have brought together the French' (Girard 2011, 322). This apparent minimizing of the role of the Resistance is followed by a digression on Jacques Maritain in which Girard claims: 'This is why I do not at all minimise that which you call the "ethic of the Resistance"' (2011, 323). Yet immediately afterwards we return to the General who 'did not make any illusions about the Resistance' (2011, 323), but nevertheless in his call for resistance placed the political above the military, soliciting the careful comment from Girard that '[i]t is this that makes the utopia of the Resistance, whose grandeur I do not at all wish to minimise' (Girard 2011, 324). After citing Bloch and Cavaillès, Girard finally arrives at a definition of resistance via a citation from Pascal: 'Not being able to strengthen justice, they justified force.' The first observation by Girard is that '[a]rms should only be a means to "strengthen justice" against those who justify force' (2011, 326) – a view which seems to admit the justification of armed resistance. This is followed by a puzzling passage:

> Note that we find once again the reciprocal intensification of violence and truth, a truth that reinforces a violence that can do nothing, by contrast, against the truth. In my view there is no other definition of resistance. It holds for every one of us today. (Girard 2011, 326)

This definition of resistance – close to Gandhi's in emphasizing the power of truth to interrupt the cycle of escalation – nevertheless remains very tentative and underdeveloped. The discussion ends with an example – those who risked their lives and their children in order to save persecuted Jews – but it is introduced in terms of a critique of any notion of pure resistance: 'Thinking in terms of Resistance and Collaboration is to remain in a mythical framework, to hold on to differences that were more fluid than one might think' (2011, 327). It would seems as if Girard believes that the Just who saved Jews – while acting according to truth and conscience – were not necessarily resisting, or that their actions should not be considered as a resistance that might be opposed to collaboration.

The conclusion seems inevitable that Girard sees little place for resistance in the completion of Clausewitz. The escalation of violence has seemingly left no resources for resistance. The apocalyptic end of any capacity to resist is the victory of Satan, with but the faint hope of a Christian revival of conscience. Yet even this is not necessarily to be counted as resistance. The violent consumption of any capacity to resist was also adopted, as we shall see, by Chamouray in the explicitly post-Clausewitzian *The Man Hunt*. Yet this ignores the historical experience of non-violent resistance, especially Gandhi and its discussion. Gandhi remains a slight presence in the work of Girard and the suffocating proximity of apocalypse throughout his thought is the consequence of the absence of a constructive principle of non-violent resistance or, perhaps, of any developed view of what Clausewitz meant by the capacity to resist.

Non-Violence and the Capacity to Resist

The ontology of war also arrives at peace, but the peace of empire, at totality. (Levinas)

In an essay on the resistant Jacob Gordin published in *Difficult Freedom*, Levinas confidently asserted that 'Our age certainly no longer needs to be convinced of the value of non-violence' (Levinas 1990, 171). This prompted the reply from Jean-Marie Muller that, on the contrary, '[i]t seems rather that we still have everything to learn about non-violence' (Muller, 54). Muller's work on the philosophy of peace, *Le principe de non-violence. Parcours philosophique* (1996), draws largely on Gandhi and, along with Jacques Semelin's historical and theoretical analyses of 'civil resistance', proposes a constructive philosophy of non-violence. Both are convinced that is it necessary to replace the opposition of violence and counter-violence with one of violence and non-violence, not solely in order to escape the predicament of escalation described by Clausewitz, but also because of the ethical primacy of a non-violent morality and subjectivity. Beyond Girard's violent apocalypse Muller sees the potential emergence of a 'civility of non-violence' (Muller, 305), while Semelin describes a dual resistance with a negative defiant pole that refuses servitude and an affirmative 'cultural resistance' 'founded on an identity and a legitimacy different from that of the adversary' (Semelin, 41). Yet these assertions of a principle and a culture of non-violent resistance defined against Clausewitz and Girard do not fully appreciate the force of Levinas's reflection on violent and non-violent resistance, his warning against being 'duped by morality' and his insistence that we reflect on the sombre gravity of what it means to be a subject of resistance.[16]

Levinas's assertion regarding the value of non-violence was part of a broader critique of the 'humanist ideal' of Western history and philosophy for 'ignoring the vanquished, the victims and the persecuted, as if they were of no significance' (Levinas 1990, 170). He regards the calls for non-violence issued on the basis of this humanism as a disavowal of 'the violence through which this history was none the less achieved' and thus an example of the non-violence of the 'victors' that Clausewitz claimed was always desired the day after a violent victory. Regarding such pacified non-violence, Levinas continued implacably:

> The denunciation of violence risks turning into the installation of a violence and an arrogance: an alienation a Stalinism. The war against war perpetuates war by ridding itself of all bad conscience. (Levinas 1990, 171)

While the experience of the twentieth century shows the 'value of non-violence', the latter needs to be more closely investigated, and supplemented by a 'new reflection on passivity' and on suffering. Without this, the philosophy of non-violent resistance was in danger of becoming a moralism that superficially negated the symptoms of violence without recognizing how its non-violence remained implicated in violence and war. As such it would always be vulnerable to apocalyptic arguments such as Girard's or to the return of a greater violence.[17] For Levinas, the value of non-violence has to be proven against the strongest claims of war.

Levinas himself had already embarked on this project in *Totality and Infinity*, which is a sustained reflection on war with its origins in the author's experience as a prisoner of war. The work begins with a warning against being 'duped by morality', seeking lucidity in this and every other respect in 'the mind's openness to truth' or in 'catching sight of the permanent possibility of war' (Levinas, 21). Levinas's point of departure in *Totality and Infinity* is Clausewitzian: war 'suspends morality', 'divests eternal institutions and obligations of their eternity' and strips 'unconditional imperatives' of their necessity. Radicalizing Clausewitz in a way that anticipates Foucault, Levinas defines politics as 'the art of foreseeing war and of winning it by every means' (Levinas, 21). The first page of *Totality and Infinity* continues implacably: war is the revelation of being, the truth of the real, it rends dissemblance, it burns the drapings of illusion, it forces into movement 'beings hitherto anchored in their identity' (Levinas, 21). The violence of war described by Levinas consists

> [...] not so much in injuring and annihilating persons as in interrupting their continuity. Making them play roles in which they no longer recognise themselves, making them betray not only commitments but their own substance, making them carry out actions that will destroy every possibility for action. (Levinas, 21)

War continues even when there seems to be peace – 'The peace of empires issued from war rests on war' (Levinas, 22) – leaving violence at the heart of pacified non-violence. Non-violence from this perspective is imperial pacification, the province of the Hegelian 'beautiful soul' who does not want to recognize that their enjoyment of peace in non-violence is thoroughly implicated in a prior and subsisting violence.

Nevertheless Levinas does point to an outside of war, in his claim that the face of war is totality. Against this totality he poses a 'prophetic eschatology' not, as Girard, an apocalypse of escalation, but a break 'with the totality of wars and empires in which one does not speak' (Levinas, 23). This mute resistance is not that of 'an impotent subjectivism cut off from being' (the beautiful soul), but is infinity. With this the introduction to *Totality and Infinity* seems to open itself to the possibility of an end to war through non-violence expressed in terms of alterity and the advent of the other. Yet this is only a momentary alleviation, for later in the text, especially in the section 'The Ethical Relation and Time', alterity and infinity are themselves implicated in war which in its turn is recognized as presupposing 'beings structured otherwise than as parts of a totality' (Levinas, 222). This latter section is one of the oldest passages in *Totality and Infinity* dating back to themes addressed in Levinas's prisoner-of-war notebooks under the title of the 'dialectic of violence' and thus identifiable as one of the origins of Levinasian ethics, or rather 'strategy'.

Part 1, 'Subjectivity and Pluralism' of 'The Ethical Relation and Time' in *Totality and Infinity* offers a rigorous description of a resistant subjectivity emerging from the Clausewitzian premise of the primacy of the enemy. Levinas's objective is eschatological peace, not the imperial pacification of totality, for '[o]nly beings capable of war can rise to peace. War like peace presupposes beings structured otherwise than as parts of a totality' (Levinas, 222). Thus war and violence are distinguished from 'limitation' or competition for the scarce resources of a totality, or even from 'the logical opposition of the *one* and the *other* by which both are defined within a totality open to a panoramic view, to which they would owe their opposition' (Levinas, 222). In contrast to this understanding of war and violence as ultimately contained as the negotiation of a relation within a totality, Levinas states a clear commitment to Clausewitz's concept of absolute war, of a war that transcends and is even directed against imperial totality and its peace:

> In war, beings refuse to belong to a totality, refuse community, refuse law; no frontier stops one being by another, nor defines them. They affirm themselves by transcending the totality, each identifying itself not by its place in the whole, but by its *self*. (Levinas, 222)

Moralistic readings of Levinas at this point move quickly to a critique of self in the name of the infinity of the face of the other. Levinas, too, seems to license too quick a passage to ethics, but on the ultimately disquieting Clausewitzian premise that the other is the *enemy*.

Levinas pursues the thought of alterity as enmity to the point of constituting an implacable vision of resistant subjectivity. The self that affirms itself can only do so before an enemy, a view expressed by Levinas in the thought that 'War presupposes the transcendence of the antagonist' (Levinas, 222). The enemy is 'a presence that always comes from elsewhere, a being that appears in a face. It is neither the hunt nor struggle with an element' (Levinas, 222).[18] As in Clausewitz, the encounter with the enemy is characterized by chance and risk; for Levinas the 'breach of totality' takes place because of 'the possibility, retained by the adversary of thwarting the best laid calculations... The calculations that make possible the determination of the outcome of a play of forces within a totality do not decide war' (Levinas, 223). Affirmation of self outside of the terms supplied by a totality depends on the enemy, and for this reason 'adversaries seek out one another' (Levinas, 223). The possibility of war outside of totality is also the possibility of peace, but one which rests on a very different understanding of community, subjectivity and relation than the exchanges between the pacified beautiful souls of imperial totality.

Such a view of peace requires a different understanding of freedom with respect to such inimical subjectivities. Levinas begins by showing the self-contradiction in the notion of freedom as autonomy, that 'freedom' proposed by Rousseau and Kant in which freedom gives itself law – founding a totality – to which it then freely submits itself. Levinas refuses to take his part in rehearsing the aporias of autonomy in what he describes as 'the great drama of contemporary thought' (Levinas, 223), since – and again here he is close to Clausewitz – such a concept of freedom 'can not describe beings in the relation that does not constitute totality, beings in war' (Levinas, 224). In its place he attempts to think through a freedom of resistance, an other, anarchic freedom. The argument he provides takes the form of a sombre leave-taking from Heidegger and his view of freedom as being for death in Chapter 2, Division 2 of *Being and Time*. A being at war, a subject exposed to its enemy, is 'a being independent of and yet at the same time exposed to the other… a temporal being; to the inevitable violence of death it opposes its time, which is postponement itself' (Levinas, 224). The resistant subject is always subject to death at the hands of the enemy, in a sense it has already been killed by the enemy, and consequently any time it enjoys has been won from the enemy in a war for time:

> Time is precisely the fact that the whole existence of the mortal being – exposed to violence – is not being for death, but the 'not yet' which is a way of being against death, a retreat before death in the face of its inexorable approach. (Levinas, 224)

Thus Heideggerian being for death is for Levinas mere sentimentality; what is required is being for life in the face of imminent and ineluctable death at the hands of the enemy.

It is enmity and war that shapes a resistant subjectivity and ensures that it is not duped by morality:

> In war death is brought to what is moving back, to what *for the moment* exists completely. Thus in war the reality of the time that separates a being from its death, the reality of a being taking up a position with regard to death, that is, the reality of a conscious being and its interiority, is recognised. (Levinas, 224)

War tears back the curtains, revealing that life is not a gift but has been won and must continually be secured under conditions of risk and enmity. Peace and security – the luxury of Heidegger's *Das Mann* – cannot be taken for granted; the enemy must always be expected and the subject in order to survive must conduct a perpetual guerrilla war:

> The adversary's skill, which cannot be summed up in forces, has to be taken into account – but how to take it into account? My skill postpones the inevitable. To hit, the blow must be struck there where the adversary has absented himself; to be parried, I have to pull back from the point at which he touches me. Ruse and ambush – Ulysses' craft – constitute the essence of war. (Levinas, 224–5)

As with the resistant commander Vernant, life as resistance involves ruse and attack, Clausewitz's tact and Mao's flexibility, which find their equivalent in Levinas's 'suppleness' of the body and of discourse.

Levinas's emergent and still-tentative notion of resistant freedom involves a complex and ambivalent relationship to violence. The being who lives in resisting their enemy 'is exposed but also opposed to violence. Violence does not befall it as an accident befalls a sovereign freedom' (Levinas, 224). Violence does not simply happen by chance to a free being secured by its own laws, but is for Levinas 'the primordial fact'. It has a 'hold over' this being, it is its predicament. Freedom itself is but 'its adjournment by time' (Levinas, 224). The resistant subject is in a sense already killed, its freedom is

> [...] originally null, offered in death to the other, but in which time arises as a détente...It is détente or distension-postponement by virtue of which nothing is definitive yet, nothing consummated, skill which finds for itself a dimension of retreat there where the inexorable is imminent. (Levinas, 224)

Yet the exposure to violence is also opposition to violence and thus an intimation of a peace or non-violence beyond pacification and its illusory security.

Levinas ends this crucial section of *Totality and Infinity* by reflecting further on the exposure and opposition to violence. He does so by reorienting the terms of self and enemy, reflecting on the fact that I am the enemy to my enemy's self, that everything my enemy is to me I am to them. Consequently '[w]ar can be produced only when a being postponing its death is exposed to violence' (Levinas, 225), which is a claim for mutual exposure: I as myself and as my enemy's enemy, joins the enemy whose self is as my enemy in a shared predicament of violence. Furthermore, this posture is open to escalation or, in Levinas's terms, 'unlimited negation' or mutual destruction. Even if the enemy is in 'the field of my powers', this may be ruse and thus the risk of exposure is high; the enemy is thus to be considered infinite and consequently '[v]iolence can aim only at a face' (Levinas, 225). It is this predicament that for Levinas is the proper point of departure for thinking peace and non-violence. Levinas moves very quickly to asserting that the negative transcendence of the enemy is but an aspect of the transcendence of the Other in general, one that has an affirmative instance in 'the moral resistance of the face to the violence of murder' (Levinas, 225). This non-violent resistance is held to 'subtend war' as a resistance to violence in the shape of an 'asymmetrical relation with the other who, as infinity, opens time, transcends and dominates the subjectivity' and in so doing 'solicits a response' (Levinas, 225) which does not necessarily have to be war.

Levinas's subsequent work sought to fill out this intuition of a non-violent relation to the Other, but it is important to remember that from the outset it is identified with a predicament of resistance, whether to the Other as enemy or to the predicament in which the Other appears as an enemy.[19] What emerges is an implacable description of resistant subjectivity, one which does not enjoy freedom as autonomy but which finds itself in a predicament of survival. Such subjectivity is suspended between violence and non-violence and lives a life whose time is not secure and guaranteed but is only provisionally won or secured against chance and adversity.

3 RESISTANT SUBJECTIVITIES

Modes of Resistance

The resistant subject does not enjoy freedom; on the contrary, the resistant subject finds itself in a predicament that does not admit the luxury of possibility. In this sense, and as Levinas showed us, resistant subjectivities deviate from the modern, revolutionary adventure of the pursuit of freedom through autonomy inaugurated by Rousseau and Kant. Their resistance may be grafted onto revolutionary possibility – the workers' movement is one history of this difficult grafting and we shall see that there have been others – but resistance and the pursuit of freedom do not enjoy a pre-established harmony. Resistance is closer to the pre-modern doctrine of the virtues than to the modern value of freedom: it responds to an implacable demand for *justice* with actions characterized by *fortitude* or the ability to sustain courage over a long period of time without any certainty of outcome, along with *prudence* in the choice and deployment of limited means.

Clausewitz had little patience for the rhetoric of freedom, whose truth he saw realized in Napoleonic Empire. His reading of Kant did not privilege the modal category of possibility and with it the freedom of the subject with respect to the sum of appearances, but rather the category of actuality. The relationship of a *resistant* subject to appearances was defiant, governed by chance and enmity and dedicated to the actualization of a capacity to resist in the face of this predicament. Such actualization might take place under the sign of possibility as the revolutionary actualization of freedom, but it can also resort to the third modal category of necessity in which there is no choice but to resist. This resistant subject facing chance and violence, suffering the 'slings and arrows of outrageous fortune', is bereft of the luxury of choice between possible outcomes. If the time was out of joint, then it was 'cursed spite' that the resistant subject had to put it right, and the appropriate modalities for 'putting right', as Hamlet learnt to his cost, are actuality and necessity.

Resistant subjectivities, then, do not enjoy the freedom of possibility, but only a bare capacity to resist enmity and chance. The modal category of actuality corresponds to this capacity and is expressed in terms of the distension of the event: the capacity to resist does not occupy a punctual present, but is strung between past and future. Resistant subjectivity is in a sense already dead, a posthumous subjectivity evoked by Bakunin in the *Revolutionary Catechism* and echoed in the declaration before a court of martial law by the German revolutionary Levine that Communists are the dead on leave:[1] they must live as if their death has already been decreed by the enemy; they have no right to life, their survival a matter of chance.[2] It is the sheer necessity of resisting that intensifies their capacity for resistance. Mao, Fanon and the Zapatistas occupy this dead present with varying degrees of affirmation; theirs is the resistant subjectivity described by Clausewitz in terms of the *aktus* of resistance.

The capacity to resist occupies a subject that *must* resist. The classic expression of necessary resistance is the Gandhian vow, formulated in the *Satyagraha* struggles in South Africa, given preliminary expression in *Hindi Swaraj* and expounded at length in the prison writings of the mid–1920s, above all in the diptych *Satyagraha in South Africa* and *An Autobiography or the Story of my Experiments with Truth*. A striking common feature of Gandhi's various canons of rules for the constitution of the *Satyagrahist* or non-violent resistant is the scorn for possibility. In the *aktus* of resistance, the resistant subject responds to a predicament of necessity by actualizing necessity in their subjectivity; intolerable, repressive conditions provoke a response which irreversibly breaks with these conditions. Yet this break assumes various forms, reactive and/or affirmative, expressed in violent action, vengeance or the vow and invention of community.[3]

The formation of the capacity to resist in a subject can take place in various ways, whether through discrete acts, discussion and communication, or through the creation of military and civil institutions. The capacity to resist may emerge reactively in response to a predicament of oppression, manifesting itself in spontaneous acts of violence that defy insufferable conditions. Yet the specific subjectivity of the violent resistant lashing out at repression remains shaped by the enemy and is initially a resistance of *ressentiment*. We shall see how Fanon diagnosed this subjectivity in *The Cursed of the Earth*. Yet this moment of reactive resistance is volatile and vulnerable and needs in some way to metamorphose into an affirmative, inventive resistance that does not just react to an intolerable predicament but transforms itself and its condition through the work of resistance, the actualizing of its capacity to resist.[4] The exit from a logic of *ressentiment* and the invention of new forms of resistant subjectivity is achieved in the Marxist tradition through consciousness, but other routes are also possible. One is the consecration of violence, the creation of subjectivities through the exercise of extreme violence, a path fraught with the risk of lapsing into *ressentiment* and entering a self-defeating escalation of violence. Another is through the invention of new forms of solidarity and subjectivity – the formation of new capacities to resist – through attempts to escape oppositional logics and the trap of escalation on the enemy's terms. Exits from the course of the world through vows and communities and the invention of new capacities and subjects characterize these affirmative resistant subjectivities.

The chapter begins with an analysis of the actuality of violence in resistant subjectivity forged during violent, anti-colonial struggle, focusing on the work of Frantz Fanon. Then we shall analyse the return to Clausewitzian formulations of the resistant subject proposed by Schmitt and Jünger in the figure of the partisan. Following this we shall consider the variants of non-violent, necessary resistance pioneered by Gandhi, one based on the vow of the subject devoting itself to *Satyagraha* and another in the affirmative women's resistance to the logic and institutions of war in the occupation of Greenham Common. The invention of a hybrid capacity to resist pioneered by the indigenous resistance of the Zapatistas precedes a reading of Genet as the figure of a total resistant subject affirming the capacity to resist in the arenas of sexual, racial and military oppression.

Anti-Colonial Resistance

The work of Frantz Fanon (1925–61) constitutes one of the most sophisticated and unflinching analyses of the constitution of a violent resistant subjectivity. An active combatant in the *Forces françaises libres* after 1943, he was decorated with the *Croix de Guerre*, but had few illusions about the 'false ideology' for which he was fighting. His experience of combat left him with what Magali Bessone has aptly described as 'le sentiment d'une mort en suspens' (Fanon 2011, 25), the sense of already being dead – that is, devoid of possibility – that characterizes many expressions of resistant subjectivity. His medical and philosophical studies led him to qualify as a psychiatrist with a thesis that became *Black Skin, White Masks* published in 1952 while he was working at the hospital of Saint-Alban under the direction of François Tosquelles. His thesis was the last of a remarkable trilogy of theses in medicine produced in the ambience of Saint-Alban, taking its place alongside Tosquelles's *The Lived Experience of the End of the World* of 1947 and Jean Oury's *Essay on Aesthetic Connotation* of 1950 that together contributed to the theory and practice of a resistant psychiatry.

Tosquelles's thesis proposed an aetiology of psychosis in the 'lived experience of the end of the world', seeing in mental illness both a resistance to this experience and the beginnings of salvation in a reconstruction of the world. While Oury in his thesis focused on creativity and reconstruction, Fanon pursued the inquiry into violent resistance at the end of the world and the difficulties encountered by a resistant subject before arriving at the 'site' or 'open' where creativity became possible. Along with Tosquelles and Oury, Fanon was convinced that mental 'alienation' was inseparable from social, economic and cultural alienation and with this insight commenced the inquiry into the pathologies of colonial subjectivity that would culminate in *The Cursed of the Earth* (1961). After three years as *médicin-chef* at the hospital of Blida-Joinville in Algeria, Fanon resigned in 1956 to become active in the Algerian resistance to French colonial rule.

Fanon's diagnosis of the resort to violence as a reactive expression of the capacity to resist has been widely mistaken as an advocacy of violence. Sartre's preface to *The Cursed of the Earth* is a subtle version of this line of interpretation, situating violence within the context of a colonial neurosis. For Sartre, violence is therapeutic, it serves to 'recompose' the afflicted subjectivity; it is a form of creativity, explicitly distinguished (in Fanon's name) from 'an absurd storm, a resurrection of savage instincts or even the effect of ressentiment' (Fanon, 441); it is even compared to the 'lance of Achilles that can heal the wounds that it makes' (Fanon, 448). These views are consistent with a particular interpretation of Tosquelles's view of psychosis and the reconstruction of an injured subjectivity, but do not do justice to the complexity of Fanon's diagnosis of the role of violence in colonial neurosis.

The fate of Fanon's thought resembles in many ways that of Clausewitz; in both, the diagnosis of a predicament of violence has been mistaken for its advocacy; in both, a reflection on the complexity of resistance has been simplified into a Manichean opposition. The drive to the escalation of violence analysed by Clausewitz is the logical extreme of abstract enmity, but is also a historically specific predicament. A similar position informs Fanon's powerful analysis of the colonial relation in the chapter 'On Violence' that opens *The Cursed of the Earth*. From the outset the colonial scenario described by Fanon seems in many respects classically Clausewitzian: there are two antagonists – the colonizer and the colonized – who confront each other in postures approaching absolute enmity. The struggle for decolonization is more than reminiscent of Clausewitzian absolute war: in a declaration that echoes some of the formulations of *On War* as much in its crisp articulation as in its content, Fanon wrote:

> Decolonisation is the meeting of two congenitally antagonistic forces who precisely draw their originality from the kind of substantification which is secreted by and feeds the colonial situation. Their first confrontation takes place under the sign of violence and their cohabitation – more precisely the exploitation of the colonised by the coloniser – is carried out under the cover of bayonets and cannons. (Fanon, 452)

The scenes of *ressentiment* and violence described by Fanon take place within and are aggravated by this scenario of escalating colonial enmity.

Fanon, however, also emphasizes that this abstraction, this 'alienation' – to use the term in the psychiatric sense used in *Black Skin, White Masks* – is a product of specific historic processes. This is affirmed repeatedly throughout 'On Violence', perhaps most graphically in the expression that 'colonialism, as we have seen, is the organisation of a Manichean world, of a compartmentalised world' (Fanon, 488). The Manichean world, created by a mad God and policed by demonic forces, is the theatre of struggle between light and dark; it is the world whose apocalyptic logic Girard subsequently uncovered in Clausewitz's *On War*. Yet for Fanon, it is a world of alienation (in all senses of the word) created by colonial violence, an abstract violence that provokes responses which initiate a mutually destructive escalation.

Fanon's analysis of this process is close to Tosquelles's understanding of the aetiology of psychosis in the 'lived experience of the end of the world'. Colonial violence is experienced by the colonized as the end of the world and their response is apocalyptic. Colonial violence is the 'peaceful violence in which the contemporary world is bathed' – that peace, as Clausewitz cynically observed, desired above all by the victor. But the pacification that has destroyed the world of the colonized provokes a violent response.[5] In the epoch of anti-colonial struggles, '[t]he colonised are persuaded that their destiny is now. They live an atmosphere of the end of the world and they judge that nothing must escape them' (Fanon, 485). Fanon describes the various methods by which the violent end of the world was suffered – religion, magic – before the adoption of the solution of direct counter-violence. The delirium provoked by the end of the pre-colonial world is met with the cathartic truth of violence: 'After the years of unreality, after having wallowed in the most astonishing fantasms, the colonised, machine gun in hand, confronts at last the only forces that contest his being: those of colonialism' (Fanon, 468). Yet this therapeutic violence is itself ambiguous, for as Clausewitz showed, enmity feeds on escalating violence; colonialism is '[v]iolence in the state of nature and will not bow except before a greater violence' (Fanon, 470) – an intransigent posture that can only issue in a process of escalation.

Before the ambiguity of violence – its character as a solicited reaction masquerading as autonomy – Fanon asks the question 'What is the reality of this violence?' and the answer takes him into a harsh reflection on the constitution of resistant subjectivity. The reality of this violence is the 'intuition of the colonised masses that they must achieve their liberation and that they can only do so by means of force' (Fanon, 480). The modal alliance of necessity – 'they *must*' – with the actuality of resisting a predicament of intolerable oppression moves in the direction of violence, a response Fanon approaches in terms of an understandable impatience, but one that can prove vulnerable and dangerous to itself, a potential failure figured in the precedent of the Spartacist slave revolt against the Roman Empire: 'The colonised, these slaves of modernity, are impatient. They know that only this madness can remove them from colonial oppression' (Fanon, 480). The danger, however, in opposing mad resistance to delirious oppression is one of strategic miscalculation, of entering the struggle on the terrain of violence where, in the case of escalation, chance will always favour the colonial enemy.

Fanon judges this impatience strategically, without adopting the view that the 'colonised want to go too fast' (Fanon, 481); nevertheless his text warns against the strategic risks of surrendering initiative (and thus time) to the enemy. Here, as earlier in *Black Skin, White Masks*, he offers a 'clinical analysis' of the effects of alienation on subjectivity. His analysis of the resistant subject's 'impatient' reactive response through violence to a violent predicament understands it as a means of 'reconstructing the world' (Fanon, 125), but one fraught with strategic and therapeutic danger. Above all he sees the resistant subject as driven by necessity, first to resist colonization by all means and then by seeking strategically to counter oppression by creating the necessary capacity to resist. *The Cursed of the Earth* anatomizes the *ressentiment* of violence, which, as Nietzsche insisted, is in its own way creative, as the attempt through violence to actualize a necessary resistance.

Towards the end of the chapter 'On Violence' Fanon describes in Clausewitzian terms the mutual complicity of enemies in a scenario of reciprocal and escalating violence:

The violence of the colonial regime and the counter violence of the colonised come into equilibrium and respond in an extraordinary reciprocal homogeneity... The development of violence in the colonised people will be proportional to the violence exercised by the contested colonial regime. (Fanon 492)[6]

The implications for resistant subjectivity are twofold: violence is at once irreversible, that is, it creates necessity, as well as cathartic. The resistant subject does not discover possibility and freedom, but their own necessity to resist. Fanon describes this process of discovery as 'absolute practice', which is the entry of a subject into the realm of necessity, into the realm of the dead. He illustrates it with an example from the Kenyan anti-colonial resistance:

A new militant was assured when he could no longer return into the colonial system. This mechanism, it seems, existed in Kenya with the Mau-Mau who demanded that each member of a group strike the victim. Each had thus to be personally responsible for the death of that victim. To work meant to work on the death of the coloniser. This adopted responsibility for violence permitted in one stroke the confused and the excluded of a group to return and find again their place, to re-integrate. Violence is thus understood as a royal pardon. The colonised man liberates himself in and through violence. (Fanon, 489)

Violence draws the militant into a new necessity, subjects them to a new implacable law which is (paradoxically) experienced as a liberation from the old necessity of colonial oppression. Such violence is cathartic, but perhaps not strategically effective; it risks leaving severe consequences for the liberated, who may be liberated *from* the colonial past, but not *for* a post-colonial future:

At the individual level, violence de-intoxicates. It relieves the colonised of their inferiority complex, of their contemplative or desperate attitudes. It makes them brave, and rehabilitates them in their own eyes. (Fanon, 496)

Yet the consequences of such violent liberation for life after resistance can be devastating and contradictory. This was the case with Fanon and the French Resistance, which, given that '[n]ot long ago Nazism converted the whole of Europe into a true colony' (Fanon, 502), was itself a form of anti-colonial struggle that all too quickly metamorphosed into implacable colonial repression. Fanon's insight into the dangers of a reactive resistance issues from this experience of the French Resistance and accounts for the subtlety with which he analysed (in all senses of the word) resistant subjectivity. This is far from the celebration of violence for its own sake that Arendt later read into his work, closer indeed to her view that resistance is always close to *ressentiment* and, with this, to a subjectivity at risk of adopting the qualities of its oppressor. Fanon's intimation of an affirmative, Nietzschean resistance declared explicitly at the end of *Black Skin, White Masks* was the invention of a life no longer shaped by responding to the initiatives of oppression and the enemy.

The Figure of the Partisan

In 1906 Lenin published an article on 'Partisan War', which describes this kind of warfare using the modal terms 'unavoidable' and 'obligatory'. For him the Marxist 'bases himself on the ground of class conflict, and not social peace', or more specifically 'the Marxist is *obliged* to take the stand of civil war' (Lenin 1962, 219–20). He thus locates the resistance of the partisan at both local and universal levels: the partisan responds to a specific enemy but on the basis of global class war. Lenin's partisan resistance marks an intermediate phase between local struggle and world revolution. The object of his politics, as seen above, was to transform spontaneous, local resistance into planned, world revolution by means of consciousness, or in this case to transform local partisan resistance through conscious global class war into world revolution. This position was adopted and modified by Mao Zedong, but later criticised by Carl Schmitt who, in an attempt to affirm a theory of world resistance rather than world revolution, transformed what was for Lenin the intermediate military/political figure of the partisan into the harbinger of an epoch beyond sovereignty.

The thought of world resistance and revolution is tied to the fate of European colonial domination, but unlike Arendt in *The Origins of Totalitarianism* Schmitt gives full and explicit recognition to the importance of resistance in the global history of anti-colonialism. This is most evident in an interview Schmitt gave to the Maoist Joachim Schickel in 1968, in which he situates Mao in a context of global resistance or what he calls the war of the partisan:

Yes, this theme takes us repeatedly back to the figure of Mao Tse-toung and infinitely more so today than seven years ago, at the time I wrote my text on the partisan. In it I spoke of Mao as the end point and culmination of a certain development that went from Clausewitz to Mao passing through Lenin. But at the time, I was not in a position to predict that Mao would have such significance for the entire world, a global significance, as much theoretical as practical. (Schmitt 2007, 117)

Here Schmitt places Mao in the familiar line of descent passing from Clausewitz through Lenin,[7] but emphasizing the 'global significance' of Mao's theory and practice of resistance. In fact *Theory of the Partisan* was more prescient than Schmitt allowed, since in it he described Mao as the 'new Clausewitz' and with this insight embarked on the reading of Clausewitz as a theorist of resistance that would culminate in his 1967 essay. He also described Mao's significance in terms of a 'new law of the earth', seeing his theory and practice as inaugurating the epoch of global resistance, in many ways regarding him as the *catechon* within Marxism capable of holding back the escalation of world revolution or the global class/civil war of Leninism. For Schmitt, in short, the post-war epoch is no longer the epoch of sovereignty, but the epoch of total resistance.

Schmitt's interest in the figure of the Partisan and its implications for the political has its sources not only in Lenin and Mao's own writings, but also in the work of Rolf Schroers inspired by Ernst Jünger and the emergent new understanding of the work of Clausewitz pioneered in the interpretation and editions of Hahlweg with its focus on Clausewitz's theory of guerrilla warfare.[8] *Theory of the Partisan* accordingly departs from 'the guerrilla war the Spanish people waged against the army of a foreign conqueror from 1808–1813' (Schmitt 2007, 3) so important for Clausewitz. Schmitt saw the Spanish guerrilla war as producing an historical effect 'whose continuation today in the second half of the twentieth century changed the face of the earth and its inhabitants. It brought about a *theory* of war and enmity that logically culminated in the theory of the partisan' (Schmitt 2007, 5). Schmitt understood that the Spanish war provoked Clausewitz's formulation that 'war is the continuation of politics', which itself 'is the theory of the partisan in a nutshell. This logic will be taken to its limit by Lenin and Mao Tse-toung' (Schmitt 2007, 8). The new alignment of politics and violence intuited by Clausewitz has for Schmitt fundamentally changed our notion of politics and even of humanity itself.

The fixation of the philosophical reading of Schmitt on his writings from the period of the Weimar Republic, above all the *Political Theology* and *Concept of the Political* from the early 1920s, has diverted attention from this fundamental change in his stance. In the early writings we find Schmitt's inquiries into the origins and definition of sovereignty

– its origins in the European wars of religion – and its characteristics of definition of enmity and of the state of emergency. In these writings Schmitt saw sovereignty as the answer to the question posed by the European religious civil war of the early modern period. He later returned to revise these texts in the light of post-war developments, producing a revised *Political Theology* and a revised *Concept of the Political* under the title of *Theory of the Partisan*.

The latter publication registers the radical change Schmitt's thought had undergone since the publication of his theory of global order in *Der Nomos der Erde*. He now proposes that the civil war at the origins of sovereignty he originally located in the religious wars of Europe has become a global civil war, bringing to an end the epoch of sovereignty and the sovereign state. In their place, emerging obscurely, Schmitt glimpsed the nascent epoch of total resistance and the partisan. As we have seen, in *Theory of the Partisan* the beginnings of this development are located in the Spanish resistance to Napoleon, while in *Law of the Earth* they are located in the Greek war of Independence. This understanding of the passing of the epoch of sovereignty brought with it an appreciation of the decline of the conceptual framework that emerged with it: the nexus of sovereignty, friend/enemy, and the state of emergency. These are concepts whose historical moment has now passed for Schmitt. In place of legally regulated war between states conducted by regular armies Schmitt now looks to the emergence of the partisan pursuing a hybrid of civil, class and anti-colonial warfare.

Much of the conceptual rigour of Schmitt's move away from his positions of the 1920s may be traced to a debate in the early 1950s between two of his contemporaries, Heidegger and Jünger, on the question of nihilism. Heidegger closely followed Jünger's work and in the mid–1930s dedicated a seminar to his 1932 book *Der Arbeiter;* in 1955 he returned to Jünger in 'On the Line', replying to a 1950 article by Jünger and implicitly to his political text *Der Waldgang* (1951). In this characteristically equivocal text on resistance and the figure of the resistant, referring also to the experience of Spanish guerrilla warfare, Jünger examines the limits of resistance – going to the wood entails a total resistance.[9] The impact of Jünger's text on Schmitt was compounded by a now unjustly forgotten book inspired by Jünger along with Celan and Char: Rolf Schroer's *Der Partisan. Ein Beitrag zur politischen Anthropologie* (1961), that Schmitt refers to constantly and described as an 'especially important book'. Schroer sees in resistance and the partisan/resistant the figure of a defence and defender of humanity against the oppressive effects of technology. While Schmitt adheres to Schroer's identification of the partisan as the 'resistance fighter in general', accepting the latter's view that 'the illegal resistance fighter and underground activist are the prototype of the partisan' (Schmitt 2007, 128) he disagrees with Schroer's assumption that the partisan posture is essentially defensive and reactive and disengaged from conventional military forces.

Another important but underestimated source for Schmitt's revision of current concepts of the political emerged from Swiss military doctrine. Schmitt was impressed by Hans von Dach's *Total Resistance,* a manual produced for Swiss non-commissioned officers, describing it as 'an impressive document of the will to total resistance', and not only the will, but also detailed orders for its concrete execution.[10] As a state of exception to the modern doctrine of sovereignty, Switzerland became important for Schmitt as a means of understanding global developments beyond sovereignty. Von Dach's handbook is at once a distillation of the historical experience of guerrilla warfare and its application to the Swiss defensive doctrine of 'total resistance' and Schmitt is properly sceptical of its attempt to limit 'resistance to the very end' by reference to the Geneva conventions. Yet it is the work of Mao and the discovery of Lenin and Mao's admiration for Clausewitz that was crucial for Schmitt in developing his new concepts of the political in which sovereignty is replaced by resistance.

In *Theory of the Partisan* Schmitt moves between the intellectual lineage of Clausewitz, Lenin, Mao and the wars of the twentieth century, beginning with the conflict between the USSR and Nazi Germany.[11] Through an allusion to Tolstoy's *War and Peace* he describes the emergence of a myth of Russian nationalist partisan warfare subsequently mobilized by Stalin:

> During World War II, Stalin adapted this myth of the indigenous, national partisan against Germany, and put it very concretely in the service of his communist world politics. This constituted an essentially new stage of partisan warfare one at whose beginnings we find the name of Mao Tse-tung. (Schmitt 2007, 8)

Schmitt situates Stalin's Great Patriotic War within the emergent form of global partisan warfare whose beginnings he dates to 1927 and the beginnings of Mao's guerrilla campaigns in China. He provides a long list of anti-colonial theorists and proponents of partisan war ranging from Ho Chi Minh and Nguyen Giap in Vietnam to Castro and Guevara in Cuba, all to show the global reach of partisan warfare.

As a student of Weber, Schmitt proceeds by sketching an ideal type of the partisan; he proposes four criteria for describing the phenomenon of this new politico-military figure. The first is irregularity: partisans do not respect the rights nor enjoy the protection of the rules of warfare established by sovereign states; they operate outside the lines and legality established by the laws of war between states.[12] The second is the partisan's high degree of mobility, understood by Schmitt in Maoist terms of unexpected movements and attacks, while the third is a high degree of political engagement and motivation – the partisan fights in the name of ideology, whether of the nation, class or revolution. Finally the partisan is 'telluric', by which Schmitt means he is rooted in a territory. By the latter, Schmitt understands not only literal territory, but also territories such as the sea, the air, to which we might now add the digital environment of the internet. The four features combine in a new kind of warfare and a new kind of politics that is strikingly close to Mao's politicized vision of guerrilla warfare.

For Schmitt, Mao's anti-colonial struggle combined all four aspects of the partisan war, adopting features of, while also limiting the reach of the Marxist-Leninist extension of class war to a global civil war. Schmitt contrasts Lenin and Mao, regarding Lenin as the theorist of world civil/class war and his notes on Clausewitz (whom he now recognizes as above all a theorist of resistance) as one of the most significant texts of twentieth-century political theory.[13] Schmitt traces the 'spark' ignited by the Spanish guerrillas through Clausewitz to Marx and Engels and finally Lenin. For him 'Lenin was the first who consciously conceived of the partisan as a significant figure of national and international civil war, and tried to make him into an effective instrument of central Communist Party leadership' (Schmitt 2007, 34). Schmitt refers to Lenin's article 'On the Partisan Struggle' and notes its links with *What is to be Done*, but mistakes Lenin in identifying the partisan with the professional revolutionary. This would later prove a complication in his understanding of the partisan, since he read Lenin, and especially the notes on Clausewitz, as maintaining that 'only revolutionary war is true war for Lenin, because it derives from absolute enmity. Everything else is a conventional game' (Schmitt 2007, 35). Identifying the partisan with the revolutionary weakens the link between the partisan and defensive warfare or resistance and prepares the ground for recognizing the revolutionary as a terrorist. In terms of the narrative of *Theory of the Partisan*, Lenin's interpretation of Clausewitz's absolute war issued in the hybrid partisan/terrorist that history remembers under the pseudonym of Stalin, who, for Schmitt

[…] succeeded in linking the strong potential of national and homeland resistance – the essentially defensive, telluric power of patriotic self-defence against a foreign invader – with the aggressive character of the international communist world revolution. The connection of these two heterogenous movements dominate partisan struggle around the world today. (Schmitt 2007, 38)

The reading of Stalin's fusion of national defence and global class war prepared Schmitt for his appreciation of Mao, whose view of the partisan is subtly distinguished from that of Lenin and Stalin. He argues 'in short' that 'Mao's revolution is fundamentally more telluric than Lenin's' (Schmitt 2007, 40), emphasizing the intensification of Stalin's territorial war in Mao's doctrine. While Lenin and Stalin move from a national to an international class enemy, Mao, in Schmitt's reading, moved in the opposite direction linking 'a global-universal, absolute, world enemy lacking any territorial space – the Marxist class enemy – with a territorially specific real enemy of the Chinese-Asiatic defence against capitalistic colonialism' (Schmitt 2007, 41).[14] This reversal of orientation contained an internal limitation to the reach of apocalyptic global class war. For Schmitt, Mao was the Marxist *catechon*, 'the opposition of *One World*, of a political unity of the earth and its humanity, to a plurality of *Grossräumen* which are rationally balanced internally and in relation to one another' (Schmitt 2007, 41). As a theorist and strategist of partisan class war, Mao for Schmitt 'depicted the pluralistic image of a new *nomos* of the earth' (Schmitt 2007, 59) that could hold back the apocalypse of global civil war (still feared as we saw by Girard), thus serving both as *catechon* and legislator of a new global order. Mao for Schmitt saves politics from the threat of apocalyptic global class war; he and not Lenin was for Schmitt the true heir to Clausewitz.

A final element of Schmitt's vision of a global partisan war that recurs throughout *Theory of the Partisan* is the technological character of this war. This becomes an important parallel theme to the contrast between Lenin/Stalin and Mao that runs throughout his meditation. It is based on the question – present throughout *Theory of the Partisan* – of whether technology will achieve the mutation of partisan warfare from resistance into terrorism that Schmitt saw prepared politically by Lenin and accomplished by Stalin. Early in his discussion Schmitt entertained the possibility of the technological mutation of the partisan into a terrorist:

Even the autochthonous partisan of agrarian origin is being drawn into the force field of irresistible, technical-industrial progress. His mobility is so increased by motorisation that he runs the risk of complete dislocation... A motorised partisan loses his tellurian character. All that's left is a transportable and exchangeable cog in the wheel of a world political machine, which deploys him in overt and covert war, and deactivates him as the situation demands. (Schmitt 2007, 14)

What is essential in the transition from partisan to terrorist is the transformation of the real concrete enemy into the absolute and abstract enemy.[15] Absolute enmity provokes a war of annihilation in which any political negotiated peace is ruled out, since absolute enmity and its correlate absolute war entails the dissolution of politics into war.

In his closing comments of the book, Schmitt reflects on the role of the partisan with respect to global technology. One scenario, not Schmitt's, sees the partisan disappearing or remaining but as an 'irritant'. Another is the emergence of what Schmitt calls 'the technical-industrial partisan' (Schmitt 2007, 56). What is left in question here is whether this mutation will lead to an offensive terrorism that will devastate the earth (followed by a low-technology partisan war among the survivors) or to the emergence of a new technological partisan dedicated to resistance, a figure whom Schmitt names, not entirely tongue-in-cheek and anticipating the figure of the hacker, the 'cosmo-pirates or even cosmo-partisans' (Schmitt 2007, 57), fighting from a global base against the new law of the earth. Nuclear warfare is identified by Schmitt as an example of the former – 'such absolute weapons of mass destruction require an absolute enemy' (Schmitt 2007, 66) – with the implication that opponents of nuclear war can be cosmopartisans. Schmitt ends with a plea for the recognition of real enmity and a stepping back from absolute enmity. This entails a defence of the partisan and finally of global resistance as a defence of politics and the hope for a 'new nomos of the earth' (Schmitt 2007, 95) whose promise seemed incarnated in the figure and thought of Mao Zedong.

The Gandhian Vow

During the 1920s, between jail and intense political work, Gandhi dedicated himself to a work of memory and strategic reflection. The report on his life as an 'experiment with truth' began as a 'jail diary' and developed into a series of weekly articles published episodically from 1923 to 1928 and collected in the two complementary volumes *Satyagraha in South Africa* (Gujarati 1924–5; English 1928) and *An Autobiography or the Story of My Experiments with Truth* (Gujarati 1927–9; English 1928–9). Together they form an exemplary meditation upon the formation of a non-violent resistant subjectivity. At the heart of Gandhi's description of the non-violent resistant subject or *Satyagrahi* is the notion of the *vow* or the commitment to a way of life removed from the course of the world, its *himsa* or violence and any compromise with it.

Although Gandhi gave precedence in his account of the invention of the *Satyagraha* strategy of resistance during the struggles in South Africa, it was clear that this was inseparable from his autobiographical account of how he became a *Satyagrahist*. In the preface to *Satyagraha in South Africa* he introduces himself as a 'general' reporting on the conduct of a campaign, one which for the first time 'invented and employed' the strategy of *Satyagraha* to 'politics on a large scale' (Gandhi 1928, 2). The narration is thus both a scientific report on an experiment – the *invention* of a new form of resistance – and the strategic assessment of its conduct, a military report on the effectiveness of a new tactic. The urgency that surrounds the writing of the report is prompted by Gandhi's conviction that *Satyagraha* will prove an effective strategy in the anti-colonial struggle in India. In addition he must resolve for himself the tension between *Satyagraha* understood as a technique of resistance and his conviction that it is a form of life or resistant subjectivity that envelops all aspects of a militant existence.

Satyagraha in South Africa is also the vindication of the theses advanced in *Hind Swaraj*, a text considered by many contemporaries in India as utopian and unrealistic.[16] Gandhi continues his preface with examples of the successful application of the *Satyagraha* tactic to the resistance struggles in India, but with doubts about the 'purity' of the struggle. He recognizes the effectiveness of 'non-violence in deed' as a tactic, but is concerned that 'superficial non-violence' is volatile and vulnerable to provocation. He insists that it must become the constitutive principle of a resistant subjectivity, and proposes to illustrate how this is possible through an account of the origins of *Satyagraha* in the initial resistance to colonial rule and legislation[17] and its successful development in the prefiguration of a liberated form of life:

> My object in writing the present volume is that the nation might know how satyagraha, for which I live, for which I desire to live and for which I believe I am equally prepared to die, originated and how it was practiced on a large scale; and knowing this, it may understand and carry it out to the extent that it is willing and able to do so. (Gandhi 1928, 80)

The commitment of Gandhi's resistance to the value of truth and the understanding of *Satyagraha* in terms of steadfastness in truth were discussed in Chapter 2. Here the focus falls on the notion of 'steadfastness' and the formation of the kind of subject that is able to become 'steadfast'. In the extraordinary Chapter XI of *Satyagraha in South Africa*, 'The Reward of Gentleness – the Black Act', Gandhi describes how the publication of the 'Draft Asiatic Law Amendment Ordinance' coincided with his service in the Medical Corps in the repression of the Zulu resistance to the colonial power. Since European medical orderlies refused to tend wounded Zulus, the responsibility was assumed by the Indian orderlies. It is in this context that Gandhi began the formalization of the qualities of the *Satyagrahist* or resistant subject that would occupy him for the rest of his life: 'While I was working with the Corps, two ideas which had long been floating in my mind became firmly fixed' (Gandhi 1928, 84). These were the qualities of chastity and poverty prominent in the character of the *Satyagrahist* already sketched out in *Hind Swaraj*. This discovery of qualities necessary to become a resistant subject is interrupted by Gandhi's reading of the Ordinance in which he saw 'nothing except hatred of Indians' (Gandhi 1928, 84). Having witnessed the consequences of such hatred in the denial of medical care to wounded Zulus, he had no illusions about the consequences of this Ordinance: it posed a question of life or death for the Indian community.

The Ordinance served as the catalyst for the invention of *Satyagraha*. If the tactics of resistance used up to now – memorials, representations, petitions – failed, then 'the community must not sit with folded hands. Better die than submit to such a law. But how were we to die? What should we dare and do so that there would be nothing before us except the choice of victory or death' (Gandhi 1928, 84). Here Gandhi describes the modal necessity of resistance: the community *must not* submit to this law; but in order not to submit, in order to resist,[18] it was necessary not only to face the choice of life or death, which is to remain within the realm of possibility, but to accept the choice of *what* death awaits the resistant: not should we die but how must we die? The steadfastness lent by chastity and poverty is augmented by the conviction of the necessary death, indeed of already being dead. The question for the resistant or *Satyagrahist* is: what kind of death? Is it to be the 'useless death', to use the Zapatistas' term, the 'reactionary suicide' described by Huey Newton, or the resistant death?

A crucial moment in the passage to a resistant subjectivity occurs in the passing of the 'Fourth Resolution' at the 11 September 1906 meeting at the 'Jewish Theatre' that Gandhi describes as 'The Advent of Satyagraha'. As befits a moment of political invention, Gandhi observed: 'I must confess that even I myself had not then understood all the implications of the resolutions I had helped to frame; nor had I gauged all the possible conclusions to which they might lead' (Gandhi 1928, 87). The unforeseen consequence of the passing of the Fourth Resolution – 'not to submit to the Ordinance in the event of its becoming law in the teeth of their opposition and to suffer all the penalties attaching to such non-submission' (Gandhi 1928, 87) – was the invention of *Satyagraha* itself. In an enthusiastic seconding of the resolution Sheth Haji Habib, 'deeply moved', 'went so far as to say that we must pass this resolution with God as witness', declaring 'in the name of God that he would never submit to that law, and advised all present to do likewise' (Gandhi 1928, 87). Startled and on his guard, Gandhi immediately sensed that the distinction between a resolution and a vow or oath was enormous, but then 'perplexity gave way to enthusiasm' and Gandhi spoke of the implications of taking an oath to resist. On the best construal

[…] if a majority of the Indians pledge themselves to resistance and if all who take the pledge prove true to themselves, the Ordinance may not be passed and, if passed, may soon be repealed… [but] it is not at all impossible that we may have to endure every hardship that we can imagine, and wisdom lies in pledging ourselves on the understanding that we shall have to suffer all that and worse. (Gandhi 1928, 90)

This was to be a pledge unto death, 'to die but not to submit to the law' (Gandhi 1928, 91) and with it Gandhi knew that 'some new principle had come into being'; while initially using Thoreau's term 'passive resistance' he subsequently adopted, following a competition in *Indian Opinion,* the term *Satyagraha*:

Truth (*satya*) implies love, and firmness (*agraha*) engenders and therefore serves as a synonym for force. I thus began to call the Indian movement 'Satyagraha', that is to say, the force which is born of Truth and Love or non-violence, and gave up the use of the phrase 'passive resistance' in connection with it…(Gandhi 1928, 93)

In the face of well-meaning interpretations of *Satyagraha* as 'passive resistance', Gandhi began to articulate what distinguished his practice from Thoreau. It is distinguished from 'armed resistance' through its non-violence as it is distinguished from passive resistance or 'the weapon of the weak' by virtue of its constituting a powerful resistant subjectivity. Gandhi begins: 'If we continue to believe ourselves and let others believe we are weak and therefore offer passive resistance, our resistance will never make us strong, and at the earliest opportunity we will give up passive resistance as a weapon of the weak' (Gandhi 1928, 96). *Satyagraha* contributes to the formation of a strong, resistant subjectivity that enhances its own capacity to resist through acts of resistance:

> Fostering the idea of strength, we grow stronger and stronger every day. With the increase in our strength, our satyagraha too becomes more effective and we would never be casting about for an opportunity to give it up. (Gandhi 1928, 96)

As expansive and affirmative, *Satyagraha* affirms love while avoiding hatred, and is consistent in its commitment to non-violence: 'While in passive resistance there is a scope for the use of arms when a suitable occasion arrives, in satyagraha physical force is forbidden…' (Gandhi 1928, 96–7). Passive resistance still operates within a Clausewitzian concept of the battle and the 'idea of harassing the other party…while in satyagraha there is not the remotest idea of injuring the opponent' (Gandhi 1928, 97). As Gandhi saw in the declaration of an oath, the *Satyagrahist* has put at stake their very subjectivity, and with this conviction he began his extended interest in detailing the 'the characteristics of satyagrahis as they ought to be' (Gandhi 1928, 98). The main difference consisted in the distance between a political tactic or 'weapon of the weak' and the formation of a resistant subject through an oath.[19] The oath could be used to test the strength and quality of the resistance, as Gandhi described later: 'it was found necessary to re-administer the oath of resistance for safety's sake just to reinforce the awakening of the community and to probe the extent of its weakness if any' (Gandhi 1928, 110). He continued, anticipating Subcomandante Marcos's later play with the term 'weapon of resistance', that 'We are fearless and free, so long as we have the weapon of satyagraha in our hands' (Gandhi 1928, 134). Once again however, this fearlessness issues from an embrace of death – as Gandhi described it later: 'For many years I have accorded intellectual assent to the proposition that death is only a big change in life and nothing more, and should be welcome whenever it arrives' (Gandhi 1928, 155) The strength of the resistant subject comes from the courage produced by being vowed to death. The *Satyagrahist* or resistant subject is dead to the world, but by stepping outside of the temporality of the world, the resistant becomes open to an extended duration of struggle: 'as a satyagraha struggle is prolonged, that is to say by the adversary, it is the adversary who stands to lose from his own standpoint, and it is the satytagrahi who stands to gain' (Gandhi 1928, 174). The vow of the *Satyagrahist* frees the resistant from time and allows them to pursue a protracted and patient struggle against an impatient and limited enemy.

In *An Autobiography* Gandhi situates the extraordinary significance placed on the vow in the invention of *Satyagraha* in the context of his personal vow of chastity and continence, for which 'the final resolution could only be made as late as 1906. Satyagraha had not then been started. I had not the least notion of its coming' (Gandhi 2010, 159). The vow to take responsibility for his sexual, corporeal and spiritual subjectivity slightly preceded and flowed into the moment of invention of *Satyagraha* at the Jewish Theatre. Gandhi noted the confluence, commenting:

> As though unknown to me, the *brahmacharya* vow had been preparing me for it. Satyagraha had not been a preconceived plan. It came on spontaneously without my having willed it. (Gandhi 2010, 160)

It consisted in applying the power of the vow or the 'control of the senses in thought, word and deed' to resistance against unjust laws. Yet this confluence of an ascetic renunciatory vow with resistant subjectivity could not be achieved in one blow, but was the outcome of experiment and invention. It was one that in practice enhanced itself, became exemplary and, when practiced by others, finally came to constitute a formidable capacity to resist. At the end of *An Autobiography* Gandhi reflects on the link between individual renunciation and politics in terms of purification, which 'being highly infectious, purification of oneself necessarily leads to the purification of one's surroundings' (Gandhi 2010, 372). When the principle of ascetic subjectivity 'to become absolutely passion-free in thought, speech and action' (Gandhi 2010, 372) is carried over into politics, it is transformed into the principle of *Satyagraha* or the constitution of resistant subjectivity.

'Resist the Military'

'*Resist the Military*' was a call to resistance issued by the Greenham Common Women's Peace Camp Yellow Gate on the tenth anniversary of the NATO decision to site cruise missiles in Europe.[20] It distils the experience of almost a decade of non-violent resistance to state and military violence. Although the resistance of the Women's Peace Camp was directed specifically against the deployment of cruise nuclear missiles from USAF Greenham Common, the broader objective was resistance to the logic of military violence itself. As a document of resistance to the neo-Clausewitzian doctrine of nuclear deterrence,[21] '*Resist the Military*' testifies to the formation of a non-violent capacity to resist in the face of the military activities of states committed to absolute war. It is a call to resist that combines a philosophical meditation on genocide and non-violence with strategic reflection on the objective of ending military violence accompanied by tactical advice to resistants on how to attain this end. Central to the document is the idea of a resistant subjectivity possessing the capacity to stage a protracted non-violent resistance, in this case of almost twenty years, against a repressive adversary.[22] It is also significant for its refinement of the tactic of occupation, providing a number of important lessons that do not seem to have been heeded by recent occupations and the Occupy movement.

A number of elements contributed to the formation of a resistant subjectivity capable of sustaining long-term opposition to state violence at Greenham Common. These emerge in the first collective text *Greenham Common: Women at the Wire* (1984), published at what would prove still an early stage of the resistance but one at which it was already clear that the purpose of the occupation was not only a discrete act of resistance but also part of the development of a broader capacity to resist:

> The initial purpose of the camp was to protest against Cruise, but its role soon extended to include the preparation of women to bring about such changes. Now the emphasis has moved further towards preparing and politicising women and it would be more accurate to describe Greenham as a 'women's resistance camp'. (Harford and Hopkins, 6)

Among the elements that contributed to the invention of a resistant subjectivity at Greenham were the constitution of a specifically feminine capacity to resist[23] and, linked with this, extreme strategic clarity concerning the practice of non-violent resistance and its place within feminist politics. At a strategic level, the tactic of occupation and encircling the military camp was situated within the invention and cultivation of a broader *network* of resistance. The occupation became a counter-camp, facing but not mirroring the 'nuclear concentration camp' on the other side of the wire and linked not to a larger politico-military-judicial state bureaucracy but to an extensive informal network of civil resistants.

The mobilization of a web or network, the image of which is ubiquitous in Greenham literature, visual culture and practice at the wire, predated the use of technological networks vital to the resistance movements of the twenty-first century.[24] The web strung across the diverse camps situated at the gates surrounding USAF Greenham Common – each renamed according to the colours of the rainbow – radiated out from the camp into a national and global Greenham network that encompassed the institutions and traditions of the labour movement, the CND and, most importantly, women's and pacifist groups in the UK and abroad. The camp served as a focus of a broader, virtual network, again prefiguring the linkage between occupations and digital networks characteristic of the emergent contemporary capacity to resist. This network, fragile but also resilient, provided a virtual 'capacity to resist' that could be energized at any moment. The anniversary of the NATO decision to deploy nuclear weapons was marked throughout the life of the Greenham occupation visibly to demonstrate the power of this capacity to the military adversary and to a world public. An important part of the formation of this capacity to resist was the practice of constant historical reflection. The experience of the early years of the occupation is chronicled in *Greenham Common: Women at the Wire,* continued (with a focus on Yellow Gate) in *Greenham Common Women's Peace Camp: A History of Non-Violent Resistance 1984–1995* (ed. Beth Junor) and completed in Sarah Hipperson's narration of the closing years of the occupation in *Greenham: Non-violent Women – v – the Crown Prerogative.*[25]

'*Resist the Military*' was one of series of calls to resist that served to actualize the virtual network that supported the Greenham capacity to resist. Consistent with the genre of 'calls to resist' analysed below in Chapter 5, '*Resist the Military*' articulated the resistant subjectivity of the women at Yellow Gate within a broader virtual network. The call from Yellow Gate was issued to the broader network that it sought at the same time to constitute and enhance: 'Yellow Gate GREENHAM COMMON WOMEN'S PEACE CAMP calls on women to non-violently **RESIST THE MILITARY**'. The call makes visible the ongoing occupation as well as calling for the broader community to manifest itself on this occasion. The text, however, is not just an announcement of an action but also a strategic contribution to a broader struggle; it describes itself as 'A Handbook for Non-violent Resistance, by the Women of Yellow Gate', published as part of an action at Greenham Common on December 9th and 10th 1989 to mark 'The 10th Anniversary of the decision to Site Ground Launched Cruise Missiles in Europe'. The call combines reflection on the history of the occupation with a philosophy of non-violence and practical advice to resistants (on travel, how to dress for the action, and how to deal with legal issues concerning arrest, bail, plea and prison). The combination of philosophical reflection and tactical legal advice also characterizes the first of a series of Zuccotti Park pamphlets, *Occupy*, which combines reflections by Noam Chomsky with pragmatic legal advice to resistants for during and after arrest.

'*Resist the Military*' explores a number of different ways in which the capacity to resist can be constituted and enhanced. The first of the eleven sections of the call provides a history by Katrina Howse of the emergent capacity to resist at Greenham Common. It begins with the occupation of the base at the end of a peace march from Wales and then the emergence of the 'resistance camp' at the base.[26] Central to this history is the emergence of feminine resistant subjectivity for which the 'resistance camp' was the focus. The history situates '*Resist the Military*' within a sequence of calls that mark the NATO decision that ranges from the occupation itself on 5 September 1981 to the magnificent December 1982 'Embrace the Base', action followed by the 1984 'Ten Million Women for Ten Days', 1985 'Widen the Web', 1986 'Reclaim Our Lives', in which 'The theme was reclaiming our lives and land from Rape and War', the 1987 'Take Action on Racism', and finally the 1988 'Re-defining War', in which 'The theme was naming women and children and men of all races to have resisted Genocide and Imperialism…'. This description of the constitution of a resistant subjectivity emphasized the role of the occupation as the catalyst for a wider network as well as acknowledging the tensions between the various 'gates' that emerged during the 1980s.[27]

This chronicle of an emerging capacity to resist is followed by an important statement by Sarah Hipperson on the non-violent character of the resistance. Hipperson traces a continuous history of 'denial of rights, oppression, loss of liberty etc.' that for her testify to the existence of a political and theological evil which it is a civil but also a religious duty to resist. The modern history of evil begins with 'the horrendous occurrences of the concentration camps' and moves to 'the dropping of nuclear bombs on Hiroshima and Nagasaki – the inhuman apartheid laws of South Africa – the segregation of Black people in the United States – the Vietnam War – the present day war in Ireland (the list is endless)…' (*Resist the Military* 4). The recognition of a link between the Nazi concentration camps and the use of nuclear weapons against Japan is a hallmark of Greenham literature, as is the conviction that resisting the nuclear armed military in the 1980s is continuous with the resistance against Nazism during the Second World War.[28] The connection is made directly and without any compromise in statements such as: 'The women who live at Yellow Gate choose the power of non-violence to counteract the power of evil, generated from inside the Base by genocidal nuclear weapons' (*Resist the Military*, 4–5) and: 'The base can best be described as a nuclear concentration camp, where preparations for mass murder are carried out daily' (*Resist the Military*, 5). The neo-Clausewitzian posture of escalating deterrence supported by Aron in France and Kahn in the USA is countered by non-violent but determined resistance: 'Non-violence is neither an easy nor soft option, it is a clearly chosen path of confrontation with the state and the military' (*Resist the*

Military, 5) whose significance was overlooked by them and indeed later by Girard. In her later reflection on 'Non-Violence in Practice' Hipperson acknowledged the precedents of Gandhi's *Satyagraha* or, more precisely, the 'people in Gandhi's resistance, the non-violent women who struggled for suffrage, the civil rights movement in the United States and the women's struggle in Northern Ireland', seeing these struggles as resources or part of a broader capacity of resist that 're-emerged at this time on Greenham Common' (Hipperson, 5).

The Greenham resistance directed itself explicitly against the bipolar posture of neo-Clausewitzian nuclear doctrine, mobilizing a capacity to resist that became capable of opposing the military without entering into an escalating and self-defeating war with it. The capacity to resist is actualized, as in Clausewitz, through energy, but not the destructive energy released by nuclear weapons. It is an energy capable of arresting the evil course of the world, with resistance conceived as an empowering non-violent interruptions of these routines of evil:

> Non-violence is an energy that gives you the power to overcome power-lessness. Whatever the occurrence, you know that there is some action you can take to interrupt, disrupt or stop deliberately, so that the 'occurrence' does not work as it was intended so to do. Evil depends on being thorough and efficient; non-violent action makes it unworkable at the time. (*Resist the Military*, 6)

The interruption also serves to place in relief the banality of evil, showing it for what it is to both its agents and a complicit public and offering 'a chance to change the thinking, behind the ideas, that promote crimes against humanity' (*Resist the Military*, 6). Part of the force of the Greenham resistance issued from this political theology of life opposed to evil and death that mounted an anti-apocalyptic resistance that still challenges many of the assumptions of Girard and other apocalyptic theorists.

The conception of resistant subjectivity described in this and other texts from Greenham characteristically affirms life directly against death. This complements and echoes but also contrasts with the more thanatopolitical versions of resistant subjectivity that affirm life through what Huey P. Newton of the Black Panthers called 'revolutionary suicide'. Faced also with the presentiment of genocide, Newton saw that 'only resistance can destroy the pressures that cause reactionary suicide' (Newton 2009, 6) or the death in life, but insisted that this was not a 'death wish' but the desire fully to live before death and, if necessary, before a violent death at the hands of the enemy. At Greenham, resistance did not take the form of a thanatopolitics, but was understood as realizing a vital capacity to which women for historical reasons were closer than men. In Hipperson's words:

> I believe that non-violence is a spiritual energy – a primitive response of resistance to events and circumstances we find intolerable. It is a precious resource and has an infinite life, if treated with respect. I believe that women especially are suited to act as conduits through which this energy can flow. Most women live without the expectations that the state imposes on its male citizens – we are not directly compelled to do our 'duty' in defence of monarch and country...Therefore without an expected role of 'duty' within the power of the state, we can develop and organise our lives to resist this power and its excesses by allowing the energy of non-violence to direct our actions against the state and the military. (*Resist the Military*, 7)

The necessity of resistance was other than the necessity of the state, the realization of a capacity of life rather than death. Yet the Greenham women and the Black Panthers nevertheless share an opposition to the death in life of 'reactionary suicide', described by Hipperson in terms of the evil and the corruption of the state and of the fearful everyday life under all-pervasive military violence:

> Deep at the root of non-violence is an uncompromising resistance to corruption in all its forms, from it grows a strength to endure the consequences that will follow from challenging the state by non-violent direct action means. Throughout history the spirit of resistance has been kept alive by quite ordinary people refusing to succumb to the imposed corruption of the state. We must keep this resistance alive if we are not to become the walking dead, slaves called upon to endorse any evil the state may impose upon us. (*Resist the Military*, 7–8)

The virtue of courage or fortitude that Fanon, Levine, Newton and Subcomandante Marcos found by placing themselves already beyond death – beyond the death in life of 'reactionary suicide' – is here located in the power of life against violence and deathly corruption.[29]

The demands placed on the non-violent resistant are every bit as great as those assumed by the violent resistance or the Gandhian *Satyagrahi*; it required the sustained work and presence at the camp of 'a small group of women being prepared to keep up a commitment to the continuance of this work no matter what the circumstances or the consequences' *(Resist the Military*, 8). In *Resist the Military* the quality of resistant subjectivity is measured in terms of commitment: 'We work flat out – stretched to our limits', and in terms of time:

> Women who live at Yellow Gate have a record of resistance as individuals that goes back seven years, six years or three years of full-time resistance at Yellow Gate. Some women have a resistance of several years, some several months. (Katrina Howse, *Resist the Military*, 16)

As with Gandhi, a life of truth opposed to the life of corruption is lived under the difficult conditions of the camp, an unalleviated life which requires a constant and uncompromising posture with respect to the authority of the state and its agents. In the words of Abigail Adams, referring to the local police and once again emphasizing the role of energy in realizing a broader capacity to resist and so strengthening resistant subjectivity:

> We hold the work that these police do in protecting nuclear weapons in abhorrence…All our energy must go into *our* work – it would be a massive contradiction to support the police through superfluous or emotional contact which would condone what they do. NO energy must be given to the police. (*Resist the Military*, 16)

Act as if the maxim of your action maximizes the capacity to resist, is the categorical imperative of this subjectivity: 'PUTTING YOUR ENERGY INTO THE ACTION – what is happening at Camp and what is happening on the action shouldn't be kept separate' – or in other words, remembering that 'energy from every woman at the Camp put into an action helps to make that action a success' (*Resist the Military*, 17). The energizing of the capacity to resist, as in *Satyagraha*, requires concentration and single-minded attention to the objective of resisting the military.

The final sections on the pragmatics of non-violent action guided by the categorical imperative of acting according to the maxim that maximizes your capacity to resist give instructions concerning the conduct of resistance. The first involve self-discipline: 'Non-violent direct action always starts with preparing yourself' (*Resist the Military*, 19), and even while conducting actions of criminal damage or trespass it is vital to avoid engaging with the escalating logic of violence: 'Never enter into any paramilitary acts with the police military because then you are instantly a loser' (Janet Tavner, *Resist the Military*, 20). The resistance also requires preparation such as clothing, food, candles and also preparation for the repression that it will provoke. As with Gandhi, the Greenham resistance did not seek to negotiate with the state when arrested or imprisoned. Jean Hutchinson is very clear that accepting repression is part of the resistance:

> Non-violent actions and court cases, as have been described above, are part of the process by which we resist the militarized state. They are an important part of and the basis for working out our non-violent resistance, the work of Yellow Gate. (*Resist the Military*, 28)

Attempting to avoid the consequences that follow the actions or to act with the fear of those consequences 'lowers the resistance to the military' and tacitly concedes legitimacy to the state. The resistant must not make any concession that will 'lower the level of your resistance' but must maintain a disciplined but defiant posture using legal and penal institutions as forums and occasions for public discussion, so ensuring 'resistance is carried through to its climax and then goes on and into the prison experience' (Jean Hutchinson, *Resist the Military*, 34).

The testimonies of Greenham Common chronicle an unremitting campaign of state violence and injustice by military, police and civil authorities against the resistants. The sustained repression was met by fortitude and imagination, the former meeting repeated evictions, provocations and injustice with an extraordinary capacity to resist. This powerful resistance, self-consciously set in a history of non-violent resistance, remains the unacknowledged source of the strategies and tactics of the contemporary capacity to resist, such as the articulation of a visible occupation with a virtual network. The authors and the texts issuing from the Greenham Common resistance testify to a vital but still not fully appreciated moment in both the philosophy of resistance and in the constitution of the contemporary capacity to resist itself.

The Resistant Dead

Perhaps the most internationally visible movement of resistance following the end of the Cold War and the successful completion of the Greenham Occupation was the Zapatista movement of the mid–1990s. The movement clearly learnt from Greenham and benefitted from the developments in communications technology unavailable to the resistants of the 1980s. The communiqués issued from the Chiapas region of South-eastern Mexico after the 1994 New Year's Day insurrection by the Zapatista National Liberation Army (ZNLA) against the promulgation of the North American Free Trade

Area provided a major source of inspiration for a world resistance against global neo-liberalism. For almost six years, until the Zapatista march on Mexico City in 2001, the proclamations to the global media and the communiqués issued on the internet served as the crucible for a fusion of indigenous and global resistance. The declarations and reflections of the Clandestine Revolutionary Committee, General Command (CIRC-GC) of the ZNLA and their spokesman Subcomandante Marcos invented a new figure of resistant subjectivity and a new understanding of the capacity to resist. It did so by aligning the potential offered by the global technologies of internet and media with local traditions of indigenous resistance.[30]

The specific contours of the struggle in the Chiapas region that issued in the 1994 insurrection are complex and difficult to trace. The main lines of conflict that issued in the resistance of the mid–1990s are described in an internal discussion document prepared in 1992 and published after the insurrection. 'A Storm and a Prophesy: Chiapas the Southeast in Two Winds' describes the export of the region's natural wealth: petroleum, hydro-electricity, cattle and agricultural products. The indigenous population did not benefit from this wealth and responded with a locally rooted capacity to resist. The intensification of oppression, and the threat that the neo-liberal NAFTA would intensify it even further, led to a metastasis of resistance, adopting the forms first of the Church and subsequently an alliance with a group of revolutionaries from the North East of Mexico – the Forces of National Liberation (FNL) – motivated by Maoist and Guevarian theories of agrarian revolution. The agrarian revolutionary theses informing the practice of the FNL – armed struggle and the establishment of base areas or focii for the extension of revolutionary action – were transformed by the encounter with the indigenous resistance into a theory of global resistance owing much to indigenous traditions but also to an appreciation of the technological possibilities of meeting global oppression with the constitution of a global capacity to resist. The Zapatista National Liberation Army used the resources of media and internet, staged a local insurrection, forced the national government to sign the San Andrés Accords in 1996 and hosted an international meeting in summer 1996 to debate the role of global civil society in the resistance to neo-liberalism.

The Zapatistas accompanied this strategic campaign with political 'consulta' on issues such as the compliance with the San Andrés Accords carried out complete with polling booths and their own electoral organization and claiming over three million votes. In 2001 after the historic defeat of the PRI, the Zapatistas marched to Mexico City and claimed to have achieved the strategic aims pursued since 1993. What all this shows is a very sophisticated strategic intelligence, one associated with the strategists of the Chiapas movement, of which the masked Subcomandante Marcos became an iconic representative. Marcos works across a number of genres – stories, proclamations, appeals, jokes – that deflate the hierarchy of military command and the vicious solemnity of the enemy.

The communiqués issued between 1994 and 2001 gave a local narration of the constitution of a resistant subjectivity which increasingly oriented itself according to the formation of a global capacity to resist. We will focus here on the former, moving on to consider the latter in more detail in Chapter 5. The resistant subjectivity of the Zapatistas responds to the voices of the dead: as with Levine in the German Revolution but far more elaborately, the Zapatista resistants consider themselves as already among the ranks of the resistant dead. This distinguishes their resistance from that of Greenham Common, which was rooted in an affirmation of life and a virtual community of women. The notion of a continuous resistance stretching from the past through the present to the future was already apparent in the first action of what would become the ZNLA: on October 12th 1992, four thousand indigenous men and women in military formation marked 'The year of the Indian, 500 Years of Resistance' by destroying a monument to the Spanish colonial founder of San Cristobel de las Casas.[31] The construction of a resistant subjectivity on the basis of a retro-active war of resistance became characteristic of the Zapatista movement and its communiqués.

The appeal to resistant subjectivity does not appear in the first of the Declarations of the Lacandon Jungle of 2 January 1994 following the successful New Year's Day insurrection. There the appeal performs the classically revolutionary-constitutional gesture of claiming to be the legitimate representative of the Mexican Revolution and Constitution and formally declares war on the usurping and illegitimate Mexican state through an army that recognizes the Geneva Conventions for the conduct of war. There is no mention of resistance in this declaration addressed to the People of Mexico from a force claiming to be their legitimate, revolutionary army. This has changed radically by the Second Declaration of 12 June 1994, which now addresses not only the People of Mexico but also 'the peoples and governments of the world'. The Second Declaration, following the brutal suppression of the insurrection and the demand from 'civil society' to end military hostilities, is actually made up of two heterogeneous declarations, one which remains close to the constitutionalist language of the First Declaration with the other modulating it into an explicit call for a perpetual resistance.

The second part of the document moves from the language of revolutionary tactics to a reflection upon and a call for resistance. Breaking with the revolutionary project, it claims that the ZNLA does not want to 'impose its proposal on the future' but proposes to struggle for democracy, dignity and justice. With this, it moves from a theory of revolutionary war to one of protracted resistance to the illegitimate power of the Mexican state. In the first use of the word 'resistance' in the declaration, the ZNLA claims: 'We know how to resist to the end' (Ponce de León, 48). The absolute resistance of the ZNLA is affirmed by an evocation of the call of the resistant dead:

'Everything for everyone,' say our dead. 'Until this is true, there will be nothing for us.

'Find in your hearts the voices of those for whom we fight. Invite them to walk the dignified path of those who have no faces. Call them to resist. Let no one receive anything from those who rule. Ask them to reject the handouts from the powerful. Let all the good people in this land organise with dignity. Let them resist and not sell out.

'Don't surrender! Resist! Resist with dignity in the lands of the true men and women! Let the mountains shelter the pain of the peoples of this land. Don't surrender! Resist! Don't sell out! Resist!' (Ponce de León, 50)

This litany of resistance is the injunction from the dead to the living to resist with dignity, and is issued in the name of everyone living, dead and yet-to-live. It begins with the first part of the Zapatista formula for resistance that emerged in 1994: 'Everything for everyone'; the second part of this formula: 'And nothing for us', represented the next step not explicitly declared in the Second Declaration, namely the understanding that a resistant subject is already dead and cannot presume to enjoy the fruits of their resistance. The modality of resistance is ineluctable, with the resistant dead calling on the already dead to resist in the name of all: universal and necessary resistance. The Zapatistas recognize that 'the words of our dead are good, that there is truth in what they say and dignity in their council' (Ponce de León, 50) and call to all fellow Mexicans to 'resist with us'. The capacity to resist includes the dead and living Mexicans; it has not yet extended to the entire world, but the recognition of the universality of the call to resistance will not be delayed for long.

The call from the resistant dead is a recurrent theme in the Zapatista communiqués. This is joined with the further thought that while the resistant dead live and speak – 'In the mountains, the dead live: our dead' (Ponce de León, 102) – the living resistants should live as if already dead. The resistant subject is not free to choose a life of resistance, but is already dead and so *must* resist. This thought began to emerge soon after the

January 1st insurrection, and subsequently became central to the Zapatista vision of absolute, global resistance. It first appears in a communiqué issued under the name of Marcos immediately after the insurrection (6 January):

> 'Dying to Live' says 'enough' to the life of death – death from curable diseases, from poverty – accepting in its place the death in life of a resistant: 'If we die now, it will not be with shame but with dignity, like our ancestors. We are ready to die, 150.000 more if necessary, so that our people may awaken from this dream of deceit that holds us hostage.' (Ponce de León, 17)

The sense of no longer being hostage to life releases the resistant from the passive death in life or 'reactionary suicide' of the vanquished Hegelian slave, but without re-entering the life-and-death struggle of the master and slave, without conceding the master any recognition or legitimacy. The resistant is already dead, and as such has already won their own dignity and courage.

The implications of this view were rapidly unfolded in the communiqués of Spring 1994. On 1 March 1994 Marcos remembers the women commanders and fighters of the insurrection 'Twelve Women in the Twelfth Year: The Moment of War'; he remembers specifically how, during a press conference in the Cathedral of San Cristobal, the Zapatista Comandante Ramona declared: 'For all intents and purposes we were already dead. We meant absolutely nothing' (Ponce de León, 7). This declaration came to mean two things: the predicament of the useless death in life, of suffering the absence of subjectivity, but also the active affirmation of the death in life of the resistant. By affirming death, by saying 'enough', the resistant is no longer hostage to the useless death in life and assumes the dignity of a resistant life without fear of death.

The communiqué issued in the name of the CIRC-CG of April 10th 1994 marking the anniversary of the assassination of Zapata, 'Votan-Zapata Marking Five Hundred Years of History', proposes a remarkable vision of the congregation of the resistant dead. It begins by evoking an assembly of those who endure and endured the 'useless death' of 500 years of misery and oblivion under the Spanish and Mexican flags. They are the ones who endured being 'faceless', having their names ripped from them, hostages who lived and died for 'someone else's future' (Ponce de León, 19). They are united in an assembly before the flag on which the eagle devours the serpent, an assembly that includes the dead, the living and the yet-to-be-born, living in the common hope 'to change the ground and sky that today oppress it' (Ponce de León, 19). The flag hovering between earth and sky on which the creature of the sky devours that of the earth offers the ambivalent hope for a new earth and a new sky and a new relationship between them – the imperial eagle befriending the autochthonous snake, one of the many allusions to Nietzsche's *Also Sprach Zarathustra* that pervades this communiqué.

The assembly of the faceless and the nameless includes those who have now embraced this fate – the everyone and no one or the masked and the nameless Zapatistas. They describe themselves as

> [...] we, the ones without a face and name who call ourselves 'professionals of hope', the most mortal of all, the 'transgressors of injustice', we who are the mountain, we of the nocturnal walk who have no voice inside the palaces, we the foreigners in our own land, the ones completely dead, history's dispossessed, the ones without a homeland and a tomorrow, the ones with a tender fury, the ones of unmuffled truth, the ones of the long night of scorn, the true men and women... the smallest of people...the most dignified...the last...the best. (Ponce de León, 19)

The commitment to speaking truth and the attainment of a place from which to do so – beyond life – comes to define the resistant subjectivity of the Zapatistas. The self-dispossession or becoming completely dead is the renunciation of the hope of freedom in the name of dignity. The resistant is no one and everyone, living but already dead, dead but still living. The communiqué then reveals 'who is behind us, who guides us, who walks in our shoes, who rules our heart, who rides our words, who lives in our death' (Ponce de León, 19). The name, communicated 'in this long night of our death' by our 'most distant grandfathers', is the eternal resistant – the Mayan Votan who died and was reborn in Zapata and all the resistants of Mexican history who died and are reborn in the Zapatistas. The word of resistance came from him through 'the mouths of our dead, from the mouths of the most knowing of our ancient ancestors' (Ponce de León, 20). Votan or the name of resistance is adopted by the assembly of the resistants, among them the ZNLA:

> Arming a tender fury. A nameless name. An unjust peace made war. A death that is born. An anguish made hope. A pain that smiles. A silent shout. A personal present for a foreign future. Everything for everyone, nothing for us. We the nameless, the always dead. We, the Zapatista National Liberation Army. (Ponce de León, 20)

The communiqué ends with the truth that the resistant, in 'Dying death', lives. The walk of the resistant which 'was and was not of these lands' guided by the Nietzschean dancing star becomes the dance of the assembly – the affirmative life of resistance, of the truth received in the 'dancing heart'.

Genet's Resistant Subjectivity

Jean Genet declined the invitation to sign the 'Manifesto of the 121' and remained consistent with this position until the end: 'My situation is that of a vagabond, not a revolutionary' (Genet 2004, 43).[32] He also declined to sign a petition in support of the Black Panthers, preferring to travel illegally to the USA to participate in their life of resistance, later living for similar reasons with the doomed Palestinian fedayeen and carefully chronicling their eclipse. He saw himself first and foremost as a resistant and not a revolutionary, one who led a life of resistance opposed to the self-deceiving rhetoric of both the state and its revolutionary opponents.

What was the object of Genet's resistance? First and above all he saw himself resisting brutality, but then almost immediately – and as part of the same gesture – as resisting the brutalizing of resistance itself. And if we wished to ask in whose name he resisted, the answer would probably be in the name of the delicacy of beginnings. The mark of Genet's resistance to brutality and to the brutalizing of resistance is evident throughout the controversial postures he adopted alongside the Black Panthers, the Palestinians and the Red Army Faction in West Germany. Genet always insisted that he stood beside these movements, never within them. His resistance required that 'wherever I am, I will always feel connected to any movement that will provoke the liberation of men. Here and now, it is the Black Panther Party, and I am here by their side because I am on their side' (Genet 2004, 29). He is connected to movements that *provoke* liberation, that are defiant, but do not promise to deliver it; he stands alongside, but does not join the ranks, and he does so only for the here and now, never for ever. In each of these cases he stands alongside the prisoners, the incarcerated Black Panthers in the USA, the Palestinians surrounded on the West Bank after Black September and the members of the Red Army Faction incarcerated in the maximum security prison of Stammheim.

Genet's fascinated resistance to brutality in all its forms is implicit in his prison novels, but is explicitly stated in his later political positions. It is put most clearly and controversially in his *Le Monde* article 'Violence and

Brutality', where 'the brutal gesture is one that halts and suppresses a free act' (Genet 2004, 171). Brutality suppresses beginnings, ruins futures and confines its victims in an incarcerated present from which there is no hope of escape but only defiance. In his introduction to George Jackson's *Soledad Brother* he describes racism in the prisons of the USA in terms of brutality; there brutality becomes visible for what it is:

> It is there, secret and not so secret, stupid and more complex than a tiger's eye, an absence of life and a source of pain, an inert mass and a radioactive charge, exposed to all and yet hidden away. We could say racism is here in its pure state, tautly alert, radiant and ready to spring. (Genet 2004, 52)

In prison, brutality is tolerated as a well-known secret, predatory; it is stupid and indelicate but also capable of complex, annihilatory calculations 'like a tiger's eye'. It is absence of life and the source of pain, radiant but not with light it thrives under the conditions of incarceration. Racism within or without prison is for Genet one of the ugliest guises assumed by brutality; implacable and all-pervasive within the institutions of the state, it was to be resisted at all costs.

Genet also saw brutality in the oppression of the Palestinians, most painfully in his witness to the massacre of Palestinian civilians in the refugee camps of Beirut between 16 and 18 September 1982, 'Four Hours in Shatila'. He describes the entry of the Israeli Defence Force into West Beirut after the internationally brokered withdrawal of the PLO with the words: 'Their ferocity preceded them', comparing individual resting soldiers to predatory 'boas with two legs stretched out in front of them' (Genet 2004, 212); for him, they appear as hunters who have arrived in West Beirut in search of prey. Genet sets the events in Shatila within a history of brutal violence against the Palestinians:

> Lit by Israeli flares, Israeli ears listened closely to Shatila from the beginning, on Thursday evening. What festivity, what revelling happened there where death seemed to take part in the pranks of soldiers drunk on wine, drunk on hate, and drunk no doubt on the joy of pleasing the Israeli army as it listened and watched, as it encouraged and incited them. I didn't see the Israeli army listening and watching. I saw what it left behind. (Genet 2004, 221)[33]

Genet regarded the brutal attack on the Palestinian refugees after the departure of the armed Palestinians as continuous with a refusal to accept the humanity of the Palestinian enemy. At one moment, and as if trying to escape from the memory of the dead and violated elderly women he saw at Shatila, he digresses with a memory of the cheerfulness of the women he met earlier in Jebel Hussein, a meeting also recalled in *Prisoner of Love*: 'These old women belonged neither to the revolution nor to the Palestinian resistance, theirs was a cheerfulness that has ceased to hope' (Genet 2004, 217). Genet breaks off this beautiful memory with an abrupt return to his brutal present:

> If a Jordanian soldier happened to pass by, he'd be delighted: in the rhythm of their words he would hear the rhythm of Bedouin dances. Without any words at all, an Israeli soldier, if he saw these goddesses, would unload his automatic rifle into their skulls. (Genet 2004, 218)

The point of this comparison is that while both the Jordanian and Israeli soldiers are implacable enemies of the Palestinians, the response of the Jordanian soldier showed delicacy and even a moment of complicity while that of the Israeli soldier was one of detached and mute violence.

In an interview conducted in Vienna on 6–7 December 1983, a year after Shatila, Genet confirmed his view of Israeli brutality towards the Palestinians by illustrating the controversial distinction between brutality and violence that he developed earlier in a 2 September 1977 *Le Monde* article on the Red Army Faction.[34] Refusing to accept the interviewer's assumptions about violence, Genet insisted on the distinction between violence and brutality:

> I'm afraid you are confusing violence and brutality. I'm going to push you – don't be offended. I'm being brutal…now if I hold you back like this to prevent you from falling, I'm no doubt violent, but I'm preventing you from falling. It's not the same thing. You don't think so?' (Genet 2004, 245)

Genet then continues:

> I'm afraid that in your choice of words you're confusing the brutality of the Israelis, for example, and the violence of the Palestinians, which is good, at least in my eyes. They inflict violence not only on the Israelis, but also on the Arab world, the Islamic world in general and even the Western world that refuses them. (Genet 2004, 246)

Yet this distinction is not absolute nor is it a naïve romantic gesture, for Genet is well aware of the potential for resistant violence to become brutality. His *Prisoner of Love* is dedicated to showing precisely this in the specific case of Palestinian violence, showing how it and the Palestinians had become brutalized in the course of their struggle.

In the *Le Monde* article Genet moves between the terms violence/ non-violence, brutality and trial. He sees life as composed of a movement of violence and non-violence:

> If we reflect on any vital phenomenon, even in its narrowest, biological sense, we can understand that violence and life are virtually synonymous. The kernel of wheat that germinates and breaks through the frozen earth, the chick's beak that cracks open the eggshell, the impregnation of a woman, the birth of a child can all be considered violent. (Genet 2004, 171)

When this vital phenomenon of the emergence of new life, the germinal break with what has been and the beginning of something new, is subjected to law and placed on trial, such violence takes on a new, brutal form: 'More or less obscurely, everyone knows that these two words, trial and violence, hide a third: brutality' (Genet 2004, 171). Brutality is a violence opposed to itself, one that steps in to oppose or judge violence – 'by which I mean again, an uninterrupted dynamic that is life itself' (Genet 2004, 172).[35] When violence is brought under judgement, when it is used for some purpose, it risks losing its innocence of becoming in brutalizing itself and its enemy.

Genet begins a list of the 'unexpected forms' assumed by brutality: architecture, racism, colonialism... only to conclude that the forms of brutality are legion and – what is more, self-destructive – 'brutality by its very excess, would destroy itself, would come to wipe itself out, to annihilate itself in the long run, when faced with violence' (Genet 2004, 172). Brutality provokes the violent resistance of life: 'The violence of a bud breaking forth – against all expectation and against every impediment – always moves us' (Genet 2004, 172). The RAF, Genet maintains, never 'allowed their violence to become pure brutality for they know they would immediately be transformed into the enemy they are fighting' (Genet 2004, 173). However, Genet is well aware that violence can very easily mutate into brutality, is always on the point of doing so – a mutation he saw confirmed in the history of the Palestine Liberation Organisation.

Genet stands alongside those who resist, but will in turn resist them when they succumb to brutality, when they lose their delicacy with respect to their enemy and themselves. It is a movement that he sees played out in the mutation of revolt or resistance into organized revolution. Genet, in short, is an anti-revolutionary, a resistant who will continue to resist the revolution that he has himself provoked. In his 1975 interview with Herbert Fichte he is absolutely candid:

> I'm not all that eager for there to be a revolution…if there were a real revolution, I might not be able to be against it. There would be adherence, and I am not that kind of man: I am not a man of adherence but a man of revolt. (Genet 2004, 132)

This confession follows a discussion of the distinction between poetic or artistic and political revolution which elaborated the theme of the 'dual revolution' central to Genet's encounter with the Black Panther Party. In that context, in the 'Letter to American Intellectuals,' Genet called for a 'new vocabulary and syntax capable of making everyone aware of the double struggle, both poetic and revolutionary, of the white movements that are comparable to the Black Panthers' (Genet 2004, 32). The double struggle Genet refers to is an internal struggle between poetic emotion and revolutionary thought; it is present for him both in Mao and the Panthers but perpetually endangered by the revolutionary discipline that it engenders, the threat of the delicacy of beginnings mutating into the brutality of trial and judgement or, in Mao's case, the 'early revolutionary consciousness' of the 1920s mutating into the brutality of the Cultural Revolution.

Genet's last work, *Prisoner of Love* is then a subtle and even elegiac evocation of the transformation of the Palestine resistance into the brutality of the Palestinian revolution. At the very end of the book he reveals his motive for writing it in the search for the reasons for 'the collapse of the Palestinian resistance' (Genet 2008, 425). This collapse was not its military failure – Genet arrived in Jordan when this was an accomplished fact – but the brutalization of the resistance that succeeded it. Paradoxically, this did not consist in an escalation of violence, but in a change in its quality: killing was done under instructions, 'by remote control', merely 'fulfilling an obligation' (Genet 2008, 426). While the Bedouins considered the Palestinians their enemy, the Palestinians did not return the compliment; they seemed to Genet to hunt their adversaries as if they were prey – the Palestinians, in short, 'never considered the Bedouin as enemies' (Genet 2008, 426). The parallel narration of the tinned rations of corned beef consumed by the fedayeen, the product of the distant industrial slaughter of 'the bullock that had been murdered at La Plata' (Genet 2008, 426), with the account of the increasingly brutal quality assumed by the Palestinian struggle emphasizes that the Palestinians considered their enemy to be 'a hunted animal' to be tracked and slaughtered, which is to say that their resistance had become brutalized.

In his narration of the time spent with the fedayeen – time spent with prisoners 'imprisoned inside an area sixty kilometres long and forty wide' (Genet 2008, 256) after the debacle of Black September – Genet returns repeatedly to the mutation of resistance and revolt into revolution. He reflects at one moment that 'I may never know whether I ought to call it the Palestinian Resistance or the Palestinian Revolution' (Genet 2008, 124). This was a shared predicament, and one of which Genet became increasingly suspicious. Later in *Prisoner of Love* Genet is both impressed by the presence of Abu Kassem while suspecting 'he was a present to me from the leaders' – a gift 'supposed to convince me of the seriousness of the resistance. (At the time we couldn't make up our minds which word to use: Palestine liberation, resistance or revolution.)' (Genet 2008, 258). Not even the fedayeen were sure whether they were resistants or revolutionaries, but the distinction was vital for Genet.

Genet looked to see how far the resistance had been betrayed or had betrayed itself, how far it had been brutalized into a revolution orchestrated from above. He was aware of the precedents, mentioning cryptically at one point: 'There's an archaeology of the Resistance which became a revolution in the thirties' (Genet 2008, 230) – one which he had outlined earlier in another reflection on the Palestinian struggle during the 1930s:

The rivalry between the leading families was transformed into patriotism; their senior members became war-lords, regarded as bandit chiefs by England and France, and after 1933, as Hitler's lackeys in the Middle East. The Palestine resistance was beginning. (Genet 2008, 109)

Prisoner of Love performs Genet's perplexity: is he nurturing the beginnings of the Palestinian resistance or mourning its end as it mutates into the Palestinian Revolution? '"What's the point of talking about this revolution?" It too is like a long drawn-out funeral, with me occasionally joining in the procession' (Genet 2008, 219). Genet throughout is reminding himself of the distance between the resistant *voyou* and 'the guardian of law and order' that he might become if he adhered to a revolution. He has to remain alert and remind himself constantly 'of the struggle that has to be put up…against the allurements of rebellions whose apparent poetry conceals invisible appeals to conformity' (Genet 2008, 336).

There is little doubt that Genet considers the Palestinian mutation of resistance into revolution as one that he must resist. But it is a nuanced resistance, directed against the leaders of the Palestinians, the wealthy families and their political representatives; he tried to maintain solidarity with the fedayeen, even if he increasingly came to regard them as accomplices, prisoners of themselves. A macabre if hilarious instance of this insight is a scene worthy of inclusion in *The Balcony*. Following an anatomy of the brutality of a Palestinian intellectual's feigned amusement at the fedayeen's description of a decapitation and other 'acts he himself regarded as brutish or criminal', Genet reflects that this man 'was already drowned in the revolution' (Genet 2008, 267). As an example of the brutalizing of the resistance, Genet describes what he saw as an indelicate custom:

> Like all the other leaders, neither more nor less ostentatiously, he stood up the instant a fedayee came into Arafat's office. Such an obvious and funereal tribute was like a frill around the legs of a piano, or a hastily buttoned fly. The fighter bringing in a telegram, a cup of coffee or a packet of cigarettes was bound to know what it meant: that is you're a hero, therefore you're as good as dead, and so we render you the honours due to a martyr and weep for you in advance. We've got springs under our seats and as soon as a hero comes in we're ejected into mourning. (Genet 2008, 267)

The insincere and mechanical gesture is emblematic for Genet of the transformation of resistant violence and subjectivity into organized, hierarchical and self-serving brutality. It is not only treating another as if they were already dead that is brutal, but also the sense that this is a death sentence accompanied by the self-congratulation of those who issue it and who had no intention of pursuing martyrdom themselves. The victim or 'dead man bringing in the newspaper would see his own open grave with the officials standing all around it, proud both of the hero and themselves and pointing him into the beyond' (Genet 2008, 267). For Genet this was the 'glory of the grave', explaining in a parenthesis that 'I wrote "gravestone" at first but crossed it out because a granite or marble gravestone has words carved on it, and the grave I'm talking about is deep but non-existent and bears no date or name' (Genet 2008, 267). This resistant parenthesis allows the possibility of a named death at the same time as erasing it, making this a brutal death in the name of something else: the revolution was celebrating the dispensability of its own revolutionaries, mimicking in a gesture the accusation made against Israel in 'Four Hours in Shatila': 'It kills men, It kills the dead.'

Genet's resistant posture is sustained by tact and delicacy. It is described using the same botanical metaphors that inspired Luxemburg and to which

Derrida devoted a sustained reading in *Glas*. For it is in the cracks in the facade of escalating brutality that Genet also saw the shoots and buds of new beginnings. A remarkable narrative sequence confronting military and botanical logic appears in an autobiographical meditation towards the end of *Prisoner of Love*. Genet recalls his first visit to the Middle East as a young French colonial soldier in Damascus, along with his first and only foray into military architecture: a gun tower which collapsed on its first trial. It was the cracks in the concrete of that 'tiny, grotesque but monumental disaster [that] prepared me to become a friend of the Palestinians' (Genet 2008, 386). Genet describes how he saw in his prisons that 'one seed, one ray of sunlight or blade of grass was enough to shift the granite. The thing was done, the prison destroyed' (Genet 2008, 386). His doomed gun tower metamorphoses into the France of the German invasion where 'in that ruined temple, mosses and lichens appeared, and sometimes kindness and even stranger things: a kind of almost happy confusion, elemental and classless' (Genet 2008, 387). His resistance became a fidelity to delicate beginnings, to buds rather than swords. His work, in flight from brutality, resists in the name of delicate beginnings, those inaugural acts which, as he described in the May Day Speech, 'have about them a freshness that is like the beginning of the world' (Genet 2004, 37). To approach these beginnings violently is to brutalize them; instead, speaking now to white radicals in his audience, Genet emphasises: 'It is very important, then, for white radicals to act with candour, certainly, but also with delicacy when it comes to their relations with blacks' (Genet 2004, 36). The resistant subject takes a stand against brutality alongside delicate and vulnerable beginnings, keeping open the time promised to and by that beginning, the sacred time Genet confessed in his interview with Antoine Bourseiller 'that was given to me at birth' (Genet 2004, 189). To cut that time short is brutality, while violently crossing the columns of Derrida's *Glas* that divide Genet's botanic erotics from Hegel's philosophy of spirit and reaffirming the illuminated night of spirit betrayed at Shatila is to take that given time and to 'work it almost in a blaze and almost day and night' in what for Genet is the life of resistance.

4 TOTAL DOMINATION AND THE CAPACITY TO RESIST

The theory of resistance received its harshest test under the total domination of the National Socialist Third Reich. The challenge of resisting National Socialism and its Fascist allies posed a limit case for the theory of resistance, raising the question of how to resist in the face of the willed destruction of any surviving capacity to resist. The question of how to resist total domination, or how to preserve the capacity to resist in the face of a conscious, merciless and sustained attack upon it, was at once practical and philosophical. The gravity of the attack and its implications not only for political action but also for what it meant to be a human being were clearly recognized by the first generation of anti-Fascist resistants and theorists, and left a philosophical legacy that survived the defeat of historical National Socialism.

With National Socialism, the equation of total domination and the destruction of any capacity to resist became brutally apparent. The historical experience of total domination exemplifies the inverse law that governs domination and capacity to resist: the more of one, the less of the other; but the very extremity of this limit case showed that this inverse law had always been, and remains, unobtrusively at work in all contexts of what Max Weber described as 'legitimate' domination – whether traditional, charismatic or legal-rational. Arendt's addition of 'total domination' to Weber's typology consciously modernized the theory of domination in the light of National Socialism. Her inquiry in *The Origins of Totalitarianism* addressed itself to the fate of resistance in the face of its reduction to near-zero intensity under total domination. However, her work lacked the concept of the *capacity* to resist – an eminently 'social' rather than 'political' category – an absence linked to her unilateral view of colonial domination and her overlooking of the resistance of the colonized. The underestimation of the capacity to resist is the Achilles' heel of Arendt's political philosophy, but it is one common to many of the attempts to understand resistance under total domination.

A large part of the problem consists in assessing the state of the capacity to resist, whether in societies dominated by National Socialism or in the extreme case of the attempt to extinguish this capacity through the concentration camp system. The capacity to resist survived even the onslaught of police and military repression, finding itself displaced from manifestations of frontal resistance to oblique, even obtuse Schweikian expressions. It is by focusing on the state of the *capacity* to resist that many of the dilemmas surrounding the definition of resistance in terms of conscious intent may be clarified. For instance, Pierre Laborie's question of whether it is possible to 'resist without engaging in resistance' is not entirely pertinent, since what is at issue here is not the motivation of discrete acts but rather the capacity to which they bear witness. Similarly, Laborie's claim that 'acts of resistance are only those accomplished in the consciousness of serving a common objective in the name of a transcendental cause' (Marcot, 35) explains a very small group of actions and overlooks the workings of a broader capacity to resist operating at less transcendental levels. Discrete acts of resistance perpetrated by a resistant subject assume the existence of a broader capacity to resist. The recognition of a continuity between the everyday, unobtrusive formation of such a capacity and the more spectacular events of organized 'conscious' resistance is essential to understanding the survival of resistance under conditions of total domination. This is evident in the historical evidence of direct and indirect resistance in societies under National Socialist domination and even in the camps themselves.[1]

The historical experience of the camps and the possibility of near-zero conditions of resistance has been repeatedly cited in subsequent repressions and resistances. The citation of National Socialist repression and resistance to it was central to the Greenham Common Women's Peace Camp, where the resistants made a direct connection between their own and the historic anti-Nazi resistance by describing a nuclear attack in terms of genocide and the military enclosure as a concentration camp. Even more striking, but harder to understand, is the consistent self-identification of the British state and its police with the memory of the National Socialist oppressor. Beyond the Nazi rhetoric of 'eradication' used by then Prime Minister Thatcher with respect to the Greenham Common women, the authorities could describe their plans to evict the resistants in 1984 as 'The Final Solution' (Junor, 15).[2] The citation, however ironic, of National Socialism pervaded even the everyday routines of oppression at Greenham, with the blocking of the windows to the Portakabin used to confine resistants provoking the police to joke: 'Now we'll shut the door and put the gas on' (Junor, 151). The desire of the police to identify themselves with SS concentration camp guards – at whatever level of tasteless irony – emphasizes the persistence of the memory of National Socialism in the practice not only of resistance but also of its repression in counter-resistance.

Anti-Fascist Theories of Resistance

The reflection on the capacity to resist assumes a particular gravity in the case of total domination. When approaching the limit of zero resistance it is important to remember the diverse discourses of consciousness, violence, invention, virtue and bio-medicine that inform the expression of the capacity to resist. In understanding resistance under total domination it is important not to privilege one of these discourses, such as consciousness. As seen, the expression of the capacity to resist involves various actions: violence, defiant interruptions of the course of the world through strikes, sabotage, diversion, as well as suffering, solidarity and unobtrusive gestures of support. It also has varying relations with respect to 'transcendental aims' such as revolution, reform, liberation and repression with which it can ally itself but on which it does not depend. It is very important to remember this span of the capacity to resist when reflecting on the experience of Nazism and anti-Nazism.

Understanding the limits and possibilities of resistance to Nazism and Fascism was one of the major preoccupations of Marxist theory in the 1930s. But this was a version of Marxism that had already distanced itself from the problem of consciousness that dominated the Leninist experience. The exclusive focus of some early twentieth-century Marxists on consciousness led to the underestimation of the concept of resistance that was met by a critique of consciousness both in the work of Lukács and outside of Marxism by Freud. One outcome of the relegation of consciousness to the margins of political action was the re-emergence of resistance as the expression of the new, the unprecedented, or the messianic – an affirmative understanding of resistance framed in terms of interruption and invention rather than consciousness. Lenin's explosions of resistance doomed to disappear into the night of history if not raised into the light of revolutionary consciousness became the inspiration for Lukács's rethinking of history beyond consciousness. The sparks or explosions of resistance also return in Benjamin's understanding of the 'chips of messianic time' evoked in the *Theses on the Philosophy of History*. Yet we also saw Freud speculating on whether the move from consciousness towards force and the apparently new and unprecedented permitted the emergence of a darker thought of resistance as a necessary ruse for strengthening repression: repression, in short, needed resistance.

What I hope is becoming clearer are not only the difficulties generated by the concept of resistance but also the gravity and complexity of the question of how to resist. This became the specific focus of Gramsci and Benjamin's questioning of how to resist first Fascism and then the total domination of Nazism. What possibilities are available for resisting repressive political regimes that invest enormous organizational and incarceral energies in resisting resistance? One of the significant approaches to this question by Gramsci and Benjamin involved identifying enmity: who or what is the enemy to be resisted? Lukács and Freud realized that resistance did not operate in an environment of undisguised enmity: what or who is to be resisted, by whom, in what way and when was not immediately transparent, nor was it clear whether the enemy was the bourgeois class somehow hidden behind its military and political apparatuses, or the society of reified commodity exchange? For Freud, it was necessary to approach the question in a different way: do we resist a repressed event or fantasy, or is this but resistance working in complicity with repression? In short, any attempt to answer the question of how to resist assumes an opinion on what or who is to be resisted – whether another subject such as the bourgeois class or the Fascist party or the institutional expressions of political and economic domination? Who, what, where and when is the enemy to be resisted?

This question became especially urgent in the resistances to Fascism and Nazism, where the extreme degree of repression *seemed* to clarify what and who had to be resisted. Writing from prison, both Gramsci and Benjamin expressed their doubts concerning this apparent clarity. Both produced their main reflections on resistance to Fascism and Nazism while under confinement: Gramsci's *Quaderni* or notebooks began in jail in 1929, while a version of Benjamin's 'Theses on the Philosophy of History' was completed in a French internment camp and read out to fellow prisoners. Both used the fragmentary, aphoristic form as appropriate to reflection under prison conditions.

Among the most striking features of Gramsci's reflection on the conditions of possibility of resistance are its emphasis on invention, an appreciation of the military logic of obedience and resistance, and a subtle undermining of any focus on consciousness. It is not entirely clear how far his emphasis on invention was due to Croce's Idealism or to Bergson, probably both, but it led him to emphasize the importance of creative action in resistance. It is possible to see already in this early passage from 1915 his movement out the discourses of consciousness and force towards that of invention:

> The International is an act of the spirit, it is the consciousness which the proletarians of the whole world have that they make up a unity… a bundle (*fascio*) of forces united in revolt although with a variety of national attitudes, which has as a common goal the substitution in the dynamism of history of the factor of production for the factor of capital, the violent irruption of the proletarian class, up to now without history or with a history that was only potential, into the vast movement which produces the life of the world. (Gramsci cited in Joll 1977, 33)

This is close to Bergson's *Creative Evolution*, but what Gramsci achieves in this passage is the movement through an 'act of spirit' from a consciousness of force expressed in revolt (resistance) towards the substitution of the proletariat for capital as the possessor of historical initiative. Up to now without history, reacting to the historical initiatives of capital from the position of *ressentiment*, this act of imaginative substitution through a 'violent irruption' initiates the historical affirmation of the working class as the 'life of the world'. Crucial in this passage is the understanding of unity – are the 'bundle of forces' to be united under the tribunal two-headed axe of consciousness as in the image of the *fasces* adopted by Italian Fascism, or are they to be gathered in a way that respects their heterogeneity?

Gramsci took from Bergson the idea that our perception of spatial objects confronting us in the world depended on the prior experience of time, or *durée*. Even the most solid of objects viewed within an expanded time frame will reveal itself as a process, inviting the hypotheses that (a) the world is made up of processes and not things, and (b) such processes only appear thing-like because of the different speeds at which they move relative to each other and to observers. Thus the state appears in one time frame as a thing and in another as a process. An important consequence of this view is that resistance can be understood as an intervention in a process rather than the confrontation with a thing. This understanding of the 'life of the world' in terms of intersecting and conflicting processes moving at different historical speeds allowed Gramsci to develop a very subtle account of political action as a war of movement with different strategic options corresponding to different speeds of deployment. This emerges most clearly in his distinction between 'organic' slow-moving and fast-moving 'conjunctural' change.

The recasting of social into military relations is evident throughout the *Prison Notebooks*, with Gramsci claiming at one point: 'The state was only an outer ditch, behind which there stands a powerful system of fortresses and earthworks' (Gramsci 1971, 238) (what Althusser would later call the SRAs and SIAs). This recasting is essential to Gramsci's understanding of social relations and institutions as dynamic, as defensive positions adopted within a broader configuration of forces. This view puts resistance at the centre of his understanding of political action in both its expansive and repressive forms. The use of a military analogy to understand social relations allows Gramsci to develop a strategic subtlety with respect to class war comparable to Clausewitz's understanding of war between imperial and resistant nation states. This is evident in his descriptions of the different forms of warfare/political action such as the war of movement or manoeuvre that is appropriate to the speed of conjunctural change and the war of position appropriate to the speed of organic change. Gramsci recasts the Leninist distinction of trade union and political consciousness into a far more subtle and differentiated understanding of opposition and resistance played across differing historical speeds. The enemy to be resisted is both a class and its systems of defences, with the consequence that anti-Fascist resistance is understood to take place at many levels and speeds with differing degrees of intensity: what is common to them all is the deployment of strategic invention within an understanding of resistance as already a counter-resistance.

The experience of colonial occupation and resistance plays a central role in Gramsci's understanding of political action. If the proletariat can be said to have been colonized by capital, then the resistance of the European working class has much to learn from the anti-colonial resistance. In this spirit Gramsci offers some shrewd reflections on Gandhi's anti-colonial strategy, thus returning the compliment of Gandhi's own critical interest in Italian national liberation:

> India's political struggle against the English [adopted] three forms of war: war of movement, war of position and underground warfare. Gandhi's passive resistance is a war of position, which at certain moments becomes a war of movement, and at others underground warfare. (Gramsci 1971, 229)

Gramsci understands Gandhi's resistance as a transverse tactical manoeuvre that intersects at various levels and at diverse speeds, ranging from small and symbolic events at the level of everyday life, to sabotage, blockages and overloading of the enemy's movements, to grand strategic movements of the masses in concerted action. The Gramscian scenario is thus Clausewitzian in requiring the formation of a capacity to resist capable of compromising that of the enemy.[3]

Gramsci sees a continuity between resistance and revolution, seeing the difference between them in terms of time, speed and the level of action. His focus on time allows him to develop an understanding of a capacity to resist which emerges at a slower speed than the spectacular events of revolutionary confrontation. This approach permits a sensitivity to the importance of small wars of movement and position at the level of everyday resistance at home, in the street and at work. This is a resistance of the *longue durée*, not settled in the 'decisive blow' of a single battle but engaged over the course of a protracted war conducted at many levels with strategic subtlety and forethought. The rapid movements of revolutionary action are played out on a backdrop of slow and reciprocal movements of resistance and counter-resistance. Consequently the 'modern prince' or political party must always remind its members that they are both besieged and besieging, at once conducting reactive and affirmative resistance:

> In politics, the siege is a reciprocal one, despite all appearances, and the mere fact that the ruler has to muster his resources demonstrates how seriously he takes his adversary. (Gramsci 1971, 239)

Yet Gramsci also cites Marx to the effect that too extended a resistance can be demoralizing and that the timing of an action is critical; in 'On the Eastern Question' of 1855 Marx wrote:

> A resistance too long prolonged in a besieged camp is demoralising in itself. It implies suffering, fatigue, loss of rest, illness and the continual presence not of the acute danger which tempers but of the chronic danger which destroys. (Marx cited in Gramsci 1971, 239)

Here the bio-medical terminology of acute and chronic disease expresses not only the different temporalities of resistance, but also the insight that reactive resistance can undermine or even destroy the resistant subject, while affirmative resistance can strengthen or temper its capacity to resist.

Benjamin's reflections on resistance to Nazism in the 'Theses on the Philosophy of History' take a different approach to the temporality of resistance. Instead of focusing upon the different historical times and speeds in terms of the strategies appropriate to them and to their intersections, Benjamin emphasizes interruption and the potential vested in the future which can serve to energize the capacity to resist in the present. While Gramsci sees Fascism as a conjunctural episode in a much larger and slower colonizing movement of capital and resistance, Benjamin argues for the exteriority *and* immanence of the future experienced as interruption. The final version of the *Theses on the Philosophy of History* has twenty-three theses and two supplements, A and B, which emerged alongside his work on the revolution of the nineteenth century and its capital Paris in the Arcades project. His increasingly urgent question during the 1930s was how this revolutionary history could have had as its historic outcome the Fascism and Nazism of the 1920s and 1930s.

Three groups of theses are of particular interest for understanding Benjamin's views on the possibility of resistance: the first group addresses the future and the 'weak messianic power', the second the Schmittian themes of the enemy and the state of emergency, and the third the question of the messianic. The first group, made up of the sequence of theses II to VI, elaborates the thought that *we* are the future for past generations, that we are those for whose arrival the past longed. This change of temporal orientation with respect to the future and the messianic loosens up the unidirectional sequence of past, present and future that Benjamin insists is more complex and negotiable than it appears. The present generation positions itself by looking backwards and fowards to past and future, but tends to forget that it is as much the future for the past as it is the past for the future. This resistance to what Nietzsche called 'time and its it was' is important for understanding Benjamin's view of the potential and the responsibility for resistance. This thought is expressed in thesis II as: 'Then our coming was expected on the earth. Then, like every generation that preceded us, we have been endowed with a weak messianic power, a power on which the past has a claim' (Benjamin 2003, 390). This is the beginning of the further, difficult thought of the VIth thesis that 'The Messiah comes not only as the redeemer, he comes as the victor over the antichrist' (Benjamin 2003, 391), or again later, as the 'avenger' of the injustice of the past. As the Messiah of past generations, it is we who are expected to redeem that past and to avenge their suffering. These concerns situate this sequence of theses within the Hamlet problem analysed at length in the earlier *Origins of German Tragic Drama*. We should not await the Messiah who will avenge us but realize that we are the Messiah called to avenge the injustice inflicted on those who awaited *us* in the past.

Benjamin shared with Gramsci the Clausewitzian conviction that we are living in a state of war, in his case a war against injustice whose theatre of battle spans past, present and future. From the VIth to the VIII thesis we have various identifications of the enemy – ranging from the ruling class to social democracy. But what is important in these Schmittian theses is the recognition of danger, pointed to already in the VIth thesis. The sense of danger – already recognized as important by Marx in his reflection on anti-colonial resistance cited by Gramsci – becomes a presupposition of the resistance described as the recognition of a state of exception. Benjamin observes in the VIIIth thesis:

> The tradition of the oppressed teaches us that the 'state of exception' in which we live is the rule. We must attain to a conception of history that accords with this insight. Then we shall clearly see that it is our task to bring about the actual state of exception, and this will improve our position in the struggle against Fascism. (Benjamin 2003, 392 translation modified)

Benjamin embraces the implacable thought that Fascism has already declared civil war – that is, it is the counter-resistance to the promise of Communism – and that, accordingly, resistance to Fascism must be pursued on a war footing. Recognizing the real state of exception, i.e. that we are already at war, is the object of this thesis, and it is one that shapes the militant quality Benjamin lends to resistance. It is moreover a war whose gravity emerges from its character as a civil war of vengeance for the oppressed of the past and for the liberation of future generations.

In the third group of theses Benjamin returns to the theme of the messianic and the problem of provoking a resistant event. The arrest of time or the 'messianic cessation of happening or to put it differently, a revolutionary chance in the fight for an oppressed past' described in thesis XVII makes time itself the theatre of action. The sequence of past, present and future is once again disrupted, now opening the possibility for sparks of resistance to emerge; the present in thesis XVIIIA becomes a 'time of the now' or *Jetztzeit* 'shot through with splinters of messianic time' (Benjamin 2003, 397). Here the focus of Benjamin's resistance is the attempt to keep open a future in the face of the National Socialist claim to possess a monopoly on visions of what is to come, 'For every second of time was the small gateway through which the Messiah might enter' (Benjamin 2003, 397). Such insistence was itself an act of resistance against a drive toward total domination that explicitly extended its oppression into a millennial future.

Time is a crucial element in both Gramsci and Benjamin's reflections upon the capacity to resist and specifically on how to resist Fascism and Nazism. By arguing that societies move at different speeds and times,

Gramsci was able to locate resistance in a politics of speed and time. Speed and movement were less significant for Benjamin's resistance to Nazism, which pursued a reorientation of past, present and future in the thought that we are the messianic generation of the past called to avenge the injustices that they suffered with the solidarity of future generations. In both cases a difficulty emerges in thinking through the issue of the enemy – the who, what, where and when of enmity. The Clausewitzian axiom of the continuity between war and politics is important for both thinkers: in Gramsci's analysis of social relations in terms of military structures and with different strategies and tactics appropriate to different speeds of social change, and in Benjamin's view of the actuality of civil war. Common to both Gramsci and Benjamin's thought was the growing sense of the fragility of resistance as well as the realization that enhancing the capacity to resist was distinct from the revolutionary project of realizing freedom, with the consequence that preserving it under conditions of total domination was of critical importance. The fate of resistance under National Socialist domination in many ways confirmed this insight.

The French Resistances

The French Resistance attained the mythical status of an exemplary and successful resistance movement against the National Socialist occupation of northern France and the initially more inconsistent repression under-taken by collaborationist Vichy. By the end of the Second World War the Resistance had assumed a moral gravity which ensured its citation at subsequent moments of crisis in the French state and society: we saw it cited in the Manifesto of the 121 against the Algerian War 'On the Right to Insubordination...' and more recently by Stéphane Hessel in his *Indignez Vous!* (see below Chapter 5). Yet it is important to remember that the mythical, unified French Resistance was in reality the outcome of a complex history of many diverse resistances co-ordinated and unified into a redoubtable and singular capacity to resist. De Gaulle's BBC 'Call for Resistance' of 18 June 1940 understood it not only in terms of military opposition to the German invasion but also as the political and cultural reconstitution of the defeated French nation and state. The desire for the resistance to be constitutive, to outlive the moment of resistance to the invader and to re-found the French nation-state in the capacity to resist, remains in many ways a unique case in the history of resistance.[4]

In De Gaulle's Clausewitzian vision of the resistant nation the physical capacity to resist of what remained of the French army inside and outside France was joined by the moral resistance of French civil society. The early networks of resistance were thus dedicated to disseminating information and creating solidarity to the end of enhancing both the physical and the moral capacity to resist. In the early stages, resistance involved not only the daily practice of resisting – recruiting, gathering and disseminating information – but also a sustained effort of co-ordinating the efforts and structures of the emergent movements and networks. The resistances were from the outset not only different reactions to defeat but also acts of constitutional invention which took several forms and directions, one of which was unification of the resistances under the *Conseil nationale de la Résistance* (CNR).[5]

A key figure in the unification of the military, political and civil resistances into the Resistance was Jean Moulin, who convinced De Gaulle that the emergent movements and networks could serve as the internal complement of the military resistance of the Free French. In the introduction to his superb study of Jean Moulin and the Resistance, *Jean Moulin: La République des catacombes*, Moulin's secretary Daniel Cordier asked the question 'What is the Resistance?'. He shows that while the term was used episodically before 1940 to describe the anti-Fascist struggles of the 1930s, especially in Spain, it was mainly used in the context of military conflict between states. When General De Gaulle in the legendary BBC broadcast proclaimed that 'the flame of the French resistance must not be extinguished', he meant first and foremost the military resistance to the invasion, even if he was already becoming aware of the significance of civil resistance. For Cordier, De Gaulle's proclamation should be understood as a gesture of resistance to Pétain's earlier acknowledgement of the vanquished 'magnificent resistance' of the French armed forces in the face of German military superiority – a gesture which 'fulfilled our obligations to our allies' which now in defeat are no longer binding.[6] The logic of sustained military resistance dominated De Gaulle's vision of the Resistance, even as he became increasingly open to the tactical virtues of clandestine and passive civil resistance as elements within a broader strategic framework of armed national resistance.

Cordier also shows that the use of 'resistance' to designate clandestine and civil resistance emerged surprisingly late: 'The term Resistance evolved slowly to designate the multiform war of the clandestine patriots' (Cordier 1999, 18), adding that it was '[o]nly in the autumn of 1942 that the word Resistance with a capital letter began to be associated with the "movements" and to designate actions of struggle in the current sense' (Cordier 1999,

19). The same timing holds for the use of the term 'resistant'. This points to a process of cohesion and self-identification among the movements and networks opposing the Occupation and collaboration with the constitution of a resistant subjectivity that was very quickly subordinated to political and military logics. In its early years the Resistance moved through the Clausewitzian phases of liquid and vaporous states before assuming solid military and political form. The military and the CNR unified the resistances into a Resistance. It could do so on the basis of a spontaneous cohesion which was then translated through the efforts of Jean Moulin and others into military and political unity.

The movement from resistances to Resistance merits closer examination, especially as it seemed to subordinate a spontaneous capacity to resist to military and political control. Was this a necessary and inevitable process given broader strategic considerations of the War, and how far can it or should it serve as a model for contemporary resistances? The initial period of resistance without a name displayed an enormous and diverse range of sophisticated resistant movements and practices that testify to the formation of a diffuse vaporous but emphatic capacity to resist.

The contribution of Jean Moulin to the French Resistance had many facets and still holds many valid lessons. As Préfet of Chartres in 1940, Moulin found himself between the German occupying forces and the collaborationist government in Vichy. After conducting possible resistance within the changing parameters of his political role – from directly refusing to endorse the slanderous condemnation of French colonial troops to posting French proclamations of the occupying power under the rubric 'Space reserved for the notices of the German military' (Cordier 1999, 80) – Moulin quickly arrived at a point where the office of Préfet was no longer consistent with the exercise of resistance. Soon after Moulin attempted suicide, and in a sense returned from the dead as a resistant subject. Resigning from his post in November 1940, Moulin dedicated six months to investigating the emergent movements and networks of resistance in Occupied and Vichy France.

Held up in Lisbon during a protracted journey to London to meet De Gaulle, Moulin prepared an influential report on the French capacity to resist: 'Report on the Activity, the Projects and the Needs of the Groups constituted in France in View of the Liberation of the National Territory'. The report is a remarkable document which at once describes and constitutes a capacity to resist. Significantly it hardly ever uses 'resistance' as a term to unify the activities of politically diverse movements and organizations that emerged out of civil and military ambiences. He uses instead the term 'movements' and 'groupings' and very rarely qualifies them as 'movements of French resistance' or 'organisations of resistance to the enemy' (Cordier 1999, 207). The report nevertheless gave a full account of the state of the capacity to resist in France, and was prized as such by De Gaulle. In a sense it invented a method of classifying and assessing the capacity to resist that was both descriptive and constitutive: the identification and description of the nascent forms of resistance was a necessary step towards the constitution of the Resistance.

Moulin identifies (and exaggerates) a virtual capacity to resist in the French population (on the whole complicit with Pétain and Vichy) but devotes most of his attention to the work of the militant opposition to the occupation (at this time still consistent with professions of loyalty to Pétain). His description focuses on three major movements of resistance: Libération nationale, Liberté and Libération, assessing their capacity to resist in terms of propaganda – the resistant press and the dissemination of information – intelligence gathering, sabotage and paramilitary action. These criteria had already been articulated within the movements themselves, but Moulin's achievement was to systematize them as a coherent description of an existing resistance as well as the intimations of a resistance to come. After assessing the internal strengths of the movements, he moves on to consider the lateral links between the resistance groups and then with the Free French military resistance in exile (Cordier 1999, 219–21). By describing the movements and their links in this way Moulin not only provided a description of the 'current situation' invaluable to De Gaulle but also recommended specific ways in which the nascent capacity could be actualized and enhanced.

The constitution of a resistance to come was entrusted to Moulin in his missions on behalf of De Gaulle in France. This complicated history is essentially a movement towards the unification of the resistance movements and organizations under the forms of military and political command. The capacity to resist, in other words, was to be actualized under the forms of military hierarchy and the representative system of the state. This emergence of a unified and hierarchically structured Resistance was in its turn systematically resisted by the movements themselves, but they found themselves increasingly subsumed under a forceful and unescapable military-political logic.[7]

The political logic imposed on the resistances emerged from the French socialist party and its response to French Communism's belated conversion to resistance. The invasion of the USSR by Nazi Germany and the de facto termination of the Hitler-Stalin pact released the French Communist party from its posture of strategic inactivity and near-collaboration. The political dimension of the Resistance – present in the concerns about De

Gaulle's democratic credentials – became critical, as did the perception that liberation was inseparable from the reconstitution of French culture and politics. The Resistance was increasingly viewed not only as a military operation against an enemy but also an act of purification or cathartic reconstitution of French society. It was hoped already in 1942 that France would emerge 'cleansed' and transformed by the experience of resistance. The political dimension of this purification could neither be separated from military action nor left to chance. The extension of the main military intelligence-gathering and sabotage institution (*Bureau central de renseignements et d'action*) of the Free French extended its operations under the pressure of the socialist Pierre Brossolette to include a 'non-military' or political section.

While Moulin's mission had been to co-ordinate the resistance movements, Brossolette sought to constitute a virtual polity founded in the Resistance. The immediate military objective of resisting the occupying enemy was joined with the longer-term political objective of reconstituting French state and society in the light of the experience of resistance. The Resistance was increasingly viewed as constituting a democratic and resistant national subjectivity characterized by a solidarity that – as constituent – transcended political differences. The Resistance came to stand for the future French state and society exiled in time. The polity of future French society was constituted in virtual form in the *Conseil nationale de la Résistance* (CNR) whose very existence as the precursor of future, happier days was an act of resistant faith. Yet instituting the Resistance in this way, making it the vehicle for political and cultural reconstitution, was not without its risks.

The CNR united the resistance movements under a political logic dominated by the political parties and trade unions. The founding meeting, called and chaired by Moulin, was held in occupied Paris on May 27th 1943 and assembled eight representatives of the resistance movements, six of the political parties and two representatives of the trade unions. Moulin opened the meeting by reading a letter from De Gaulle which called for the CNR to provide coherence to the Resistance:

Everything that is dispersed, isolated action, particular alliance, in whatever domain that the total struggle unfolds, compromises both the power of the blows brought to the enemy by France and its national cohesion. This is why it is essential that the Resistance on the national territory forms a coherent, organised and concentrated whole. This will be done by means of the creation of a council of resistance that will form an integral part of fighting France and will incarnate all the forces of all kinds engaged in the interior against the enemy and his collaborators. (De Gaulle, cited in Cordier 1999, 708)

In addition to providing cohesion and making a Resistance out of the resistances, the CNR was also required to plan for the liberation and the reconstitution of post-war France. However, it was evident to all, and the cause of some resistance, that while the Resistance would liberate France it could not expect a direct role in its reconstitution. This would be the task of the reformed political parties in a resumed parliamentary democracy whose success entailed the withering away of the movements of resistance. In his *Memoirs* De Gaulle described the role of the CNR not only in terms of giving the Resistance operational cohesion but also in ensuring its rapid and relatively peaceful disappearance after the liberation. It was one of the CNR's signal achievements that the war of resistance did not mutate into a civil war after the victory over the common enemy:

> Without the CNR, there would not have been a resistance, there would have been resistances. At the liberation there would not have been a people in assembly but a divided country. It would have not been possible to prevent the communists from holding parts of the territory. Look at what happened in Yugoslavia and Greece. That would have also happened with us. (De Gaulle, cited in Cordier, 722)

Yet there is a sense in which the Resistance left a more positive legacy, bequeathing an ethos of solidarity or sense of the capacity to resist that survived the dissolution of the resistance movements. At the centre of this legacy was the 1944 programme of the CNR, *Les jours heureux*, which codified the experience of resistance and made it available for the work of reconstituting French society after the Liberation. The document proposes a continuity between the resistance and what is to come after the war. It opens with the premise that resistance was born of the 'ardent will of the French to refuse defeat' and had 'no other reason for existence than the daily struggle constantly intensified' (Heidsieck et al., 13) Yet immediately after this opening, the document claims that 'this mission of combat must not come to an end after the Liberation' and proposes a plan for the reconstitution of France that includes the restoration of democratic rights alongside a number of economic and social reforms to be embodied in the French post-war constitution. It is perhaps not too surprising that this document should have been revived in defence of the French welfare state threatened by neo-liberal reforms and republished in 2011 under the title 'Resistant citizens of yesterday and today – les jours heureux – the programme of the National Council of the Resistance of March 1944: how it was written and applied, and how Sarkozy is accelerating its demolition'. The experience itself has become part of a citable contemporary capacity to resist.

The French Resistance presents the case of a resistance that achieved its goals and largely abolished itself as a resistance. Yet it remained an exemplary experience assuming an aura of myth and adventure to which we saw not even Derrida was immune. But its very success in contributing to the reconstitution of French society meant that it ceased to exist as a resistance. It was only when confronting an adversary that the resistances could thrive – their organization into a hierarchically structured Resistance may have enhanced their operational capacity, but not the capacity to survive the Liberation. Yet paradoxically, the operational disbanding of the Resistance was a condition for its elevation to a moral myth, thus becoming an emblem of a capacity to resist which remains in a virtual state in the French polity.

Resistance and Total Domination

In *Homo Sacer: Sovereign Power and Bare Life* Giorgio Agamben claimed that Arendt's analysis of totalitarian power lacked a 'biopolitical perspective' (Agamben 1998, 4). While certainly problematic, the biopolitical dimension of Arendt's account of total domination is in fact central to her analysis, serving to link the history of colonial domination with the European experience of extreme, genocidal biopolitics.[8] In many ways the problems with Arendt's conception of biopolitics persist in later biopolitical theory and are manifest in an undeveloped understanding of resistance. Her account of total domination excluded resistance by definition – for where there is resistance, domination cannot be total. The underestimation of resistance also shapes the version of colonial history presented in *The Origins of Totalitarianism* – one that silently excluded anti-colonial resistance movements such as those led by Mao and Gandhi. These movements were contemporary with the processes described by Arendt which in Europe culminated in the Shoah and Porajmos or the state-organized mass murder of the Jews and Roma on the basis of the biopolitical theory of race.

As the inauguration of the critique of the biopolitical, *The Origins of Totalitarianism* remains unsurpassed for the way it brings together the emergence of a discourse on race in the nineteenth century with the experience of colonial domination (Foucault was to repeat this gesture less persuasively in his lectures 'Society must be Defended'). Arendt exposes the links between the ideology and repressive technologies of colonial domination, the racial persecution of the Jews and the formulation of the project and administrative technology of what National Socialist administrators called the Final Solution of the Jewish Question in Europe. Yet the absence of any recognition of the innovative role played by the anti-colonial resistances in inventing new forms of defiance and enhancing the global capacity to resist truncates her analysis and fatally orients it towards the problem of domination and obedience rather than resistance and defiance. In *The Origins of Totalitarianism* Arendt remains fatalist in her view of the near-futility of resistance; while mentioning the experience of China and Mao she is clearly ill-informed about his contribution to the tactics of resistance and is almost silent with respect to Gandhi.[9] Colonialism thus appears in her account as a unilateral and unresisted, perhaps even unresistable process tending toward total domination.

Arendt links the experience of violent colonization with the return of the repressive technologies, ideologies and even personnel employed in the colonial periphery to the metropolis. Her sensitivity to the significance of the violence perpetrated at the colonial limit is part of Arendt's debt to the work of Rosa Luxemburg, for whom she maintained an immense and consistent admiration. Arendt describes in *The Origins of Totalitarianism* how the ideology of racism and the techniques of colonial domination involving the separation, concentration and elimination of populations were employed by Nazi Germany in what she describes as a 'vast experiment' to remould human nature, or in our terms, to extinguish any trace of a resistant subjectivity and its capacity to resist. This project is announced in her first preface dated summer 1950:

> The totalitarian attempt at global conquest and total domination has been the destructive way out of all impasses. Its victory may coincide with the destruction of humanity; wherever it has ruled, it has begun to destroy the essence of man. (Arendt 2004, xxvii)

Arendt understands this 'essence' in terms of a capacity for spontaneous action, but does not connect this capacity with the capacity to resist; in a sense she detaches it from its roots in the historical processes she describes and displaces it into a realm of aesthetic and political idealism.

The object of Arendt's analysis in *The Origins of Totalitarianism* is the process of total domination, her addition to the Weberian typology of traditional, legal rational, and charismatic legitimate dominations. Total domination, however, is but another name not just for the extinction of human spontaneity but also the capacity to resist, and for Arendt (as later for Foucault and his heirs) it cannot be understood apart from biopolitical considerations. In the section on 'Totalitarianism in Power' Arendt describes the accession to power of the totalitarian movements as 'the acquisition of a kind of laboratory' focusing on the 'concentration camps as special laboratories to carry through its experiment in total domination' (Arendt 2004, 511). What this entailed is spelt out later in the formal definition of total domination:

> Total domination, which strives to organise the infinite plurality and differentiation of human beings as if all of humanity were just one individual, is possible only if each and every person can be reduced to a never-changing identity of reactions, so that each of these bundles of reactions can be exchanged at random for any other. The problem is to fabricate something that does not exist, namely, a kind of human species resembling other animal species whose only 'freedom' would consist in 'preserving the species'. (Arendt 2004, 565)

Total domination seeks to reduce human diversity to a biopolitical essence, an animal species, except that Arendt went even further in saying that this 'animal life' is itself further reduced to 'a thing' that can be shaped and controlled. Central to this reduction of diversity and the redefinition of human action as reaction and randomness is the institution of the camp, which Arendt clearly understood as a laboratory for the biopolitical experiment of abolishing human spontaneity:

> The camps are meant not only to exterminate people and degrade human beings, but also serve the ghastly experiment of eliminating, under scientifically controlled conditions, spontaneity itself as an expression of human behaviour and of transforming the human personality into a mere thing, into something that even animals are not... (Arendt 2004, 565)

The political technology of the concentration camp is applied to the destruction of spontaneity – its replacement of stimulus by reaction and, with this, the extinction of the capacity to resist. It pursues these objectives not only with respect to the inhabitants of the camps, who suffer it directly and whose experience was subsequently analysed mercilessly by Pasolini in his film *Salò or the 120 Days of Sodom,* but also for the citizens of the societies within which the camps emerged. For the camp is the end product of a segregation, on biopolitical grounds, that involved the destruction of the rights of a minority along with their moral destruction, a step dedicated to rendering the lives of the victims totally insignificant. She describes this operation in terms of a legal-rational administrative process directed toward the goal of total domination and which met with hardly any resistance – indeed, the goal of this process ultimately consists in the destruction of any capacity to resist its implementation:

> After murder of the moral person and annihilation of the juridical person, the destruction of individuality is almost always successful. Conceivably some laws of mass psychology may be found to explain why millions of human beings allowed themselves to be marched unresistingly into the gas chambers, although these laws would explain nothing else but the destruction of individuality. It is more significant that those individually condemned to death very seldom attempted to take one of their executioners with them, that there were scarcely any serious revolts, and that even in the moment of liberation there were very few spontaneous massacres of SS men. For to destroy individuality is to destroy spontaneity, man's power to begin something new out of his own resources, something that cannot be explained on the basis of reactions to environment and events. (Arendt 2004, 586)

Arendt literally extends Weber's insight into the role of consent in legitimate domination to the point of total domination and finds that the destruction of spontaneity coincides with the destruction of resistance. She leaves her analysis at this point, leaving little scope for the analysis of resistance in a work primarily devoted to expounding a theory of domination. Just as total domination involves the extinction of the capacity to resist, so its analysis seems to make invisible the very resistance total domination is directed against. The absence of resistance is perceived by Arendt as a historical fact rather than an effect of a theory of domination which, when projected onto colonial history and the history of totalitarianism, presents a unilateral account of colonial domination that excludes the dimension offered by the anti-Nazi resistance movements and the theory and practice of Mao, Gandhi and others. Arendt does not see that domination is in fact a measure of the power of the capacity to resist, and by emphasizing legitimate domination and the problem of 'obedience' she obscures the role of resistance in determining the quantity and quality of domination. The absence of the capacity to resist remains a weak link in her own and in subsequent accounts of biopolitics, an absence that allowed her political reflection to move away from the alleged heteronomy of the 'social' to the autonomy of the 'political', from the capacity to resist rooted in everyday practices of resistance to a utopian spontaneous revolution and a suffocating fascination with legitimate domination or 'obedience'.

Yet resistance remains a disquieting presence in Arendt's work, which is managed by converting the defiant characteristics of a collective capacity into those of individual conscience or a product of abstract spontaneity; the effect of this is to displace resistance from the socio-political into the ethical or metaphysical realms. The displacement of the capacity to resist is linked in Arendt's work to a broader historical argument about modernity intimated in *The Origins of Totalitarianism* and then developed in *The Human Condition* and the fragments of her Marx project from the late 1950s. This argument, later stated most baldly in *On Violence*, links the disintegration of power and with it a politics based on speech in the public realm with the emergence of violence, technology and war. Violence is instrumental, essentially technological: the destructive application of technology to objects, or human beings thought as objects – what Genet described as brutality rather than violence. It is an aspect of the technological *homo faber* scrutinized in *The Human Condition*, a view of the essentially violent character of technological civilization. Her diagnosis is directly linked to the critique of Clausewitz, who for Arendt is the prophet of the mutation of politics into warfare or the 'complete reversal in the relationship between power and violence' (Arendt 1970, 10).[10] This sombre vision of the overcoming of politics by technological war, the reduction of human actors to objects of violent technological manipulation, leaves little room for the identification of any capacity to resist. In the third and final part of *On Violence* that reflects on violence and life, Arendt links the technologies of violence to the struggle for life, implying the existence of a continuity between National Socialist bio-war (biopolitics at this point would be a contradiction in terms for Arendt) and Fanon's alleged 'praise of the practice of violence' (Arendt 1970, 69) in terms of the struggle for life. The role of resistance in the latter's anti-colonial theory is completely overlooked once again, an omission symptomatic of the near-disappearance of the capacity to resist in Arendt's work.[11]

The implications of the occlusion of the capacity to resist become very clear in the controversial reflection on the Shoah prompted by the trial of Adolf Eichmann. In *Eichmann in Jerusalem: A Report on the Banality of Evil* (1963) Arendt maintained that the prosecution of Eichmann was also the prosecution of diaspora Jews by the Zionist state. Early in her report she wrote:

The contrast between Israeli heroism and the submissive weakness with which the Jews went to their death – arriving on time at the transportation points, walking on their own feet to the places of execution, digging their own graves, undressing and making neat piles of their clothing, and lying down side by side to be shot – seemed a fine point, and the prosecutor, asking witness after witness, "why did you not protest?", "why did you board the train?", "fifteen thousand people were standing there and hundreds of guards facing you, why didn't you revolt and charge and attack?", was elaborating it for all it was worth. But the sad truth of the matter is that the point was ill taken, for no non-Jewish group or people had behaved differently. (Arendt 1977, 11)

The alleged total obedience has here become evidence, for Arendt, of total domination and the absence of any capacity to resist on the part of Jewish citizens in the diaspora.

The lament for an absent resistance in *Eichmann in Jerusalem* is more symptomatic of the absence of a theory of resistance in Arendt than a matter of historical record. Her leading example of an exceptional case of resistance – the heroic actions of Sergeant Anton Schmidt – is presented as an example of the individual moral resistant driven by the imperatives of conscience. For Arendt this is indeed an exceptional, individual and exemplary resistance; for her, the testimony to the actions of Schmidt during the trial bought a ray of light to the sombre proceedings:

And in those two minutes, which were like a sudden burst of light in the midst of impenetrable, unfathomable darkness, a single thought stood out clearly, irrefutably, beyond question – how utterly different everything would be today, in this courtroom, in Israel, in Germany, in all of Europe, and perhaps in all countries of the world, if only more such stories could have been told. (Arendt 1977, 231)

This illumination, of course, links with Arendt's broader concerns with narration and politics, and ultimately with her attempt to rethink Kant's reflective judgement in terms of exemplary narratives, but it leads to a theory of resistance which locates resistance in individual conscience and spontaneity. Schmidt, the resistant German who counters the conformist Eichmann, takes Arendt to the numbing conclusion, which closes *Eichmann in Jerusalem*, that '[p]olitically speaking it is true that under conditions of terror most people will comply but some people will not...' (Arendt 1977, 233). But this frankly banal conclusion overlooks the fact, related by Arendt herself, that Schmidt's resistance consisted in working with 'members of the Jewish underground' and helping 'Jewish partisans by supplying them with forged papers and military trucks' (Arendt, 230) That is to say, Schmidt was not an individual working according to individual conscience, but was participating in a movement of resistance; his actions were only possible given the existence of a collective, organized and historically specific capacity to resist.

Arendt's opening question – why obedience? – and her answer, total domination, concedes the theoretical initiative to legitimate domination and initiated a gesture that continues to inform biopolitics, even in its more recent, radical guises. Arendt and the biopolitical current of thought remains above all a theory of domination; it is not, and in many cases does not have, a defined theory of resistance. It begins with obedience and assumes exceptions to be *dis*obedient rather than beginning with defiance and considering obedience to be the normative exception. In such an approach, the answer to the question of why there was no resistance framed in terms of legitimate total domination actually evades the question. If, on the contrary, resistance is given the theoretical initiative, if it is not put on the defensive before domination, and if its purported absence is approached sceptically and from a strategic rather than a moral perspective, then it might become possible to establish a political philosophy – specifically a biopolitical philosophy – on a theory of resistance.[12]

Near-Zero Capacities of Resistance: the Manhunt Doctrine

Now you'll see something. The hunt. You would never believe it if you did not see it for yourself. (Karski, *Story of a Secret State*)

The attempt to reduce the capacity to resist to degree zero or a point approaching it is not simply a thought experiment but a political and military option that has historically been pursued with monotonous tenacity. It is precisely what Arendt described as the 'total domination' pursued in the Nazi camp system and what Agamben returned to in his descriptions of the Muselmann in *Memories of Auschwitz*. The reduction of the capacity to resist to near-zero not only entails the end of resistance, but also establishes the frontier to the Clausewitzian theory of war. At this point the enemy – precisely defined by their capacity to resist – is brutalized or transformed into prey. Prey does not engage in war, it is not an enemy to be fought according to the laws of war, but is a form of animal life that may be hunted and either captured and put to work in slavery or exterminated. When an enemy is reduced to prey, its capacity to resist approaches zero, a reduction manifest in the last resort of survival through flight.

Grégoire Chamayou's *Les chasses à l'homme* (2010) is an important historical and conceptual analysis of the phenomenon of the manhunt. In this book and in other writings, especially his reflections on the hunt and assassination of Osama Bin Laden, Chamayou insists that the Clausewitzian epoch of declared enemies contesting each other's capacities to resist in warfare is being succeeded by an epoch of the manhunt and the annihilation of erstwhile 'enemies' now reduced to the condition of prey:

> Contrary to Clausewitz's classic definition, such *cynergetic war* is not, in its fundamental structure, a duel. The structure does not involve two fighters facing off, but something else: a hunter who advances and a prey who flees and hides. (Chamayou 2011, 2)

The only option for hunted prey, one adopted by Osama Bin Laden, is survival through flight and concealment; the hunt itself is a police operation conducted outside formal legal structures and devoted to capture or annihilation. The minimal point of the capacity to resistance is thus reached in the transformation of life into survival under conditions of the manhunt.

With this reflection on the transformation of war into the hunt, Chamayou makes a theoretical step of great importance in understanding the reduction of the capacity to resist, giving a mobile dimension to the static account of the total domination of the camp proposed by Arendt and later developed by Agamben in the *Homo Sacer* tetralogy. Cynergetic war conforms to the Arendtian scheme of identification, concentration and elimination of target populations. Locating the prey by means of surveillance is the first step, followed by hunt, capture and either internment or annihilation. It is a strategy that explains the conduct of historic and recent chases, the reduction of the enemy to prey characterizing as much the fate of Jews and other populations during the Second World War, the deadly hunt of Algerian demonstrators by Papon and the Parisian police on the night of 17 October 1961, as the Indian Government's explicitly named 'Operation Green Hunt' dedicated to the physical elimination of the Indian tribal people's capacity to resist and its recent expression in Maoist insurgency.[13] Yet Chamayou, like Arendt, errs in his underestimation of resistance and his unilateral focus on domination or the perspective of the hunter.

At the outset of *Les chasses à l'homme* Chamayou cites as an epigraph an edited version of Aristotle's claim that by 'the art of acquiring slaves, I mean of justly acquiring them, [it] differs both from the art of the master and the art of the slaves, being a species of hunting or war' (Aristotle, *Politics* 1255b, 38–40). This immediately follows a disarming passage in which those who have slaves delegate them to stewards who practice the art of the master so leaving the owners with the leisure to 'occupy themselves with philosophy or with politics'. Later in *Politics (Book VII, Ch.14)* Aristotle returns to the acquisition of slaves in his discussion of the 'whole of life' and the distinction between the rational principle of the soul which commands and the inferior or non-rational principle which obeys. This justification of slavery is supported by a series of further divisions which align war and the institution of slavery and conclude that war is waged 'not with a view to the enslavement of those who do not deserve to be enslaved; but first of all they should provide against their own enslavement' (*Politics* 1333b, 38–40). The study of war is motivated by the need to provide against enslavement, anticipating what Clausewitz would later describe as the preservation of the capacity to resist, but also for the end of gaining 'empire for the good of the governed'. Aristotle returns to the barely concealed assumption in all of this, claiming the study of war for those who 'seek to be masters only over those who deserve to be slaves' (*Politics* 1334a, 1–2). Chamayou is forcefully critical of this ontological definition of worthiness to be enslaved, using it to explain why the rebel slave is hunted to annihilation; however he does not stay with the interpretation of the hybrid character of war/manhunt intimated by Aristotle, effectively separating the two. For Aristotle, slaves may be acquired by hunting them or by means of warfare, which reduces the enemy's capacity to resist by enslaving them.

Chamayou elaborates a historical narrative in which the pursuit of slaves by means of the manhunt is central. He focuses on the Atlantic slave trade and its introduction of the manhunt as a crucial element in the culture of emergent capitalism and colonialism. Central to his account is a powerful and striking critique of Hegel's master and slave dialectic in which Chamayou shows that the master does not risk his life nor the slave choose life over death, that there is no struggle for recognition between them and mediation is secured by the figure of the dog trained to hunt human prey. In Chamayou's reading:

Contrary to the epic legend of the master, their power does not derive from a victory achieved at the end of a free confrontation of consciences. The genealogy of modern slavery is not the duel but the hunt. (Chamayou 2010, 99)

The master does not confront the slave in a struggle for recognition, but simply sets his dogs on him. With this Chamyou deflates not only the pretensions of Hegelian dialectic, but also Clausewitz's art of war, it too being based on the polar opposition of the duel. In the place of war – whether the struggle for recognition or for the preservation of one's own capacity to resist by compromising that of the other – Chamayou finds the hunt, with masters sending their dogs or police/hunters in pursuit of de-subjectified, brutalized humans who are captured, set to work or summarily executed.

The discussion of the Hegelian master/slave hunt in *Les chasses à l'homme* is revealing for its neglect of the experience of the hunted. Chamayou's analysis is conducted largely from the standpoint of the hunter; while criticizing the science of the master/hunter it nevertheless accords it precedence. Yet Aristotle proposed not only an art or science of the master but also one of the slave. The former is the art and science that has historically received the most attention – in doctrines of sovereignty, law and legitimacy – and by criticizing it in the name of the manhunt Chamayou undoes it while tacitly endorsing its priority. But it is important not to forget the art and science of the slave. Aristotle seems to have restricted this to the instruction of slaves 'in their ordinary duties...cookery and similar menial arts' (*Politics* 1255b, 25–6), but it would be possible to extend this art to include the arts of resisting and a new art and science of resisting at near-degree zero levels of resistance.

Chamayou comes closest to developing a genealogy of the art and science of the slave in his critique of Hegel's master/slave dialectic. Yet his account of the consciousness of the hunted subject still gives precedence to the initiative of the hunter. The hunted subject or in this case the fugitive slave

[...] while escaping has certainly reconquered its liberty of movement, but it knows itself to be still pursued. Its new life is that of a hunted existence. This constitutes again, at a distance, a specific form of subjectivisation. The prey is the object of a hunt. (Chamayou 2010, 102)

With the help of Sartre, Chamayou revives dialectic in the art and science of the slave, conforming to Aristotle's assumption that it was but the reflection of the art and science of the master. The hunted subject quickly becomes a haunted subject, surviving only by dint of reflecting and anticipating the initiatives of its hunter:

> To be able to anticipate the reactions of his pursuers, the hunted man must learn to read his own actions with the eyes of his predator. This interiorisation of the look of the other makes him develop an extreme prudence which develops the form of a paralysing inquietude of a paranoic order... (Chamayou 2010, 102)

We have arrived at the point reached by Fanon in his psycho-anatomy of the colonized consciousness, only that Chamayou at this point in his narrative resorts to a dialectical or literally speculative reversal in which the hunted becomes the hunter and the hunter the hunted:

> By integrating in his plan of action the logic of his predator, it is enveloped and interiorised. The prey thus acquires as a result of this first dialectic of the chase the mental capacities of a hunter while it is still but prey. If this new strategic aptitude still permits the prey at this early stage to guess the intentions of its pursuers, it will soon render it capable of something completely different. The art of efficacious flight, insofar as it presupposes intellectual mastery of cynergetic logic, prepares for a reversal of the relation of the hunt. From chased object, the prey makes itself a subject, that is to say, at first, a hunter in its own right. (Chamayou 2010, 104)

Yet there is something too formal and neat in the specular inversion of the hunter and the hunted, a restriction of the art and science of the slave to the status of a dialectical reversal of the hunter/hunted relation (or non-relation).

Chamayou's rediscovery of a dialectical reversal at the moment of near-zero capacity to resist restricts the art and science of the slave to dialectics and what is more a specular dialectics of hunter and hunted. Ernst Jünger's anti-Nazi novel *On the Marble Cliffs* is a subtle and prescient meditation on the limits of this dialectic of hunter and hunted and its disastrous outcome. The dialectic evokes the Nietzschean slave revolt of morals with *ressentiment* lodged in the misfortune that the hunted can only escape by becoming a hunter, by negating and internalizing their oppression by eternal and implacable mastery. With resistance as flight and evasion there is little room for defiance or developing much more than a reactive posture designed to survive the immediately pressing predations of the hunter. Nevertheless, Chamayou does point on occasions to other possibilities, notably in his discussion of the hunt of the poor when he mentions the sheltering of the hunted poor by the people (Chamayou 2010, 119). This points to a different logic, one of solidarity which thwarts the logic of the hunt but not by adopting and inverting it; however, this marks a rare moment in the analyses that make up *Les chasses à l'homme*.

What would an art or science of the slave look like if it were not confined to responding in a specular manner to the art and science of the master? It is noteworthy that the earliest uses of the term 'resistance' in a civil context emerged from the African-American experience of slavery. In one of the first articles of *The Atlantic* magazine following the US Supreme Court's Dred Scott decision that slaves could not become citizens and amid growing civil and political conflict surrounding the extension of slavery, Edmund Quincy asked: 'Is our spirit effectually broken? Is the brand of meanness and compromise burnt in uneffaceably upon our souls? And are we never to be roused, by any indignities, to fervent resentment and effectual resistance?'[14] Yet this resistance, although very often adopting the form of flight and provoking the shameful United States laws permitting the hunt and recapture of fugitive slaves, became more than an inversion of the roles of hunter and hunted. Effective resistance, in other words, should be much more than fervent resentment.

In a sense, the science and art of resistance refuses Aristotle's *choice* of war or the hunt as means of acquiring (and keeping) slaves in favour of a hybrid war/manhunt. The science and art of the slave must resist first of all the temptation to enter into a specular relation with the manhunt by reserving the concept of enmity for the hunter. The hunter would reduce the options of the prey to those appropriate to prey, while resistance consists in recognizing the hunter as enemy and conducting defiant resistance against him on the basis of enmity rather than on that of hunter and prey. It is this insistence that creates a subject that is not just the specular figure of the hunter, and that also enhances that subject's capacity to resist.

Regarding the hunter as an enemy allows other logics of resistance to be engaged beyond those of surviving the manhunt, effectively engaging the hunter in political, cultural and military struggle as an enemy and not as a hunter or potential prey. The African-American resistance from the outset, through the Civil War and the Civil Rights Movement and other actions of the 1960s provides a powerful example of the refusal to accept cynergetic logic or its inversions and of enhancing a minimal capacity to resist through protracted struggle with an enemy conducted on a large number of fronts.[15] Genet's adoption of the perspective of the resistant subject is an exemplary corrective, one which endorsed the Black Panthers' insistence on enmity or the refusal to become prey even while being literally subjected to the manhunt.[16]

Huey P. Newton's *Revolutionary Suicide* (1973) and his 1982 dissertation *War Against the Panthers: A Study of Repression in the United States* theorize the posture of resisting the scenario of hunter/hunted. Newton described this posture as 'revolutionary suicide', or the disciplined refusal to accept the terms of the hunter by adopting the posture of prey. This act of resistance consisted in maintaining the posture of enmity, even when subject to the chase, even to the point of death at the hunter's hands.

> I had faced death before, but under different circumstances. There had been a spontaneity and a suddenness in each confrontation, and the possibility of outwitting death. But when the state kills you, there are no odds; the inevitability of death is absolute. To face execution by the state demands a special kind of courage – the ability to act with grace and dignity in a totally degrading situation. It is the ultimate form of truth. (Newton 2009, 202)

The theory and practice of the Panthers provides an important corrective to the Manhunt Doctrine and its assumption that resistance must adapt to the initiative of the hunter, that it must needs adopt a *ressentiment* posture. Newton indeed used Nietzsche to develop an understanding of affirmative resistance, claiming that the latter's ideas 'have had a great impact on the development of the Black Panther philosophy' (Newton 2009, 173). Newton learnt from Nietzsche the necessity of confronting the hunter as an enemy; instead of suffering the definitions of the oppressor it was necessary to engage in warfare, in this case a 'form of psychological warfare [that] raised the consciousness of the people and also inflicted a new consciousness on the ruling circle' (Newton 2009, 175). The two examples of successful Nietzschean politics were the revaluation of the police as 'pigs' and the invention of the slogan or categorical imperative 'All Power to the People', the latter understood by Newton as a formula for the affirmation of 'a sense of deep respect and love for the people, and the idea that the people deserve complete truth and honesty' (Newton 2009, 180). While remaining painfully aware that they were being hunted, the Panthers refused to adopt the posture of prey, to seek invisibility or to camouflage themselves, thus earning Genet's admiration. In concentrating, as in Chapter 9 of *Les chasses à l'homme*, on the lynch mob chasing the black victim and by situating the lynch as 'the culminating point of a normality comprised of a constant and multi-formed contempt for the life of the dominated' (Chamayou 2009, 150), the Manhunt Doctrine mimics the very reduction of the capacity to resist to zero that its explicit aim and indeed achievement is to contest and at least make visible.

Salò or the End of Resistance

Pier Paolo Pasolini's last film *Salò o le 120 giornate di Sodoma* (1975) is a deliberate attempt to imagine the capacity to resist reduced to near-zero. It can be interpreted as a self-critical reflection on a life of aesthetic, political and sexual resistance scarred at the outset by the brutal paradoxes of the historic Italian resistance. The posture of resisting the resistance exemplified in *Salò o le 120 giornate di Sodoma* was in many ways consistent with Pasolini's overall political profile of total resistance to the moral, political, aesthetic and sexual conventions of Italian society. Born in 1922 in Northern Italy (Friuli), Pasolini lost a resistant brother to the Resistance and was murdered at Ostia in 1975. The often inconsistent positions adopted in his controversial practice of resistance through poetry, films and journalism have in many ways obscured the political consistency of Pasolini's work and contributed to its partial eclipse since his death.

A powerful challenge to this neglect and a meditation on the reasons for it has recently been made by Georges Didi-Huberman in *Survivance des lucioles* (2009), which is also a thinly encrypted critique of the philosopher arguably most close to Pasolini, Giorgio Agamben.[17] While calling for a return to Pasolini's political thought, Didi-Huberman's view of the significance of Pasolini's renunciation of resistance, especially in his last film, is disputable. In many ways it underestimates Pasolini's commitment to resistance, above all to passive or civil resistance evident in his fascination with India and the thought and practice of Gandhi, an interest whose significance has not been fully understood or appreciated. Pasolini's resistance to the adoption of models of armed resistance adopted by Western resistants is informed by his support for Gandhi's positions on non-violent *Satyagraha*. His reading of the Gandhian figure of the non-violent resister back into St Francis and even Jesus is part of a broader project of rediscovering and revitalizing forgotten aspects of the European tradition in the light of non-European experiences. The fecundity of this project is evident not only in his films of tragedy, but also in his intuition of the importance of 'life' and the intimation of concepts and figures later associated with biopolitics and its critiques – *homo sacer* (Pasolini is first to use this term in a modern context, a reference subsequently extended in the work of Agamben), the limits of sexual resistance, and the insight into the anthropological transformation of the life of a population. The difficult equation of life and resistance was Pasolini's theme and preoccupation from a very early date; for him, life, even bare life or survival, was the defiant affirmation of a capacity to resist: at the core of his life and work are the defiant words *io vivo* – I live.

A striking feature of Pasolini's resistance is what might be described as its Socratic character. Pasolini was always in debate with his *polis*, with contemporary Italy as the local manifestation of global transformation. His differences are articulated not only through his poems, his early dialect poems and the influential collections *Le ceneri di Gramsci* (1957), *La religione del mio tempo* (1961) and *Trasumanar e organizzar* (1971) but also through his novels or narrations *Ragazzi di vita* (1955) which adopted the argot of the Roman lumpenproletariat, *Una vita violenta* (1959) and the posthumous and scandalously neglected *Petrolio* (1992). He was also a prolific critic, columnist and political commentator, using the platform of the weekly magazines *Vie nuove* and *Tempo* during the 1960s to engage in a Socratic debate with readers of the magazine (published in Italian as the invaluable *I dialoghi*). These conversations document his almost weekly response to the enormous changes in Italian culture and society during the 1960s, the transformation of a largely peasant agricultural culture to an urban industrial society characterized by internal migration, the tribulations of the largest Communist party in Western Europe, the disputed legacy of the Resistance and the transformation of Catholic Christianity through Vatican II and beyond. Yet his significance as Italy's and perhaps modernity's gadfly was accomplished through his films, *Accattone* (1961), *Mamma Roma* (1962), *Il vangelo secondo Matteo* (1964), *Edipo Re* (1967), *Teorema* (1968) and the *Trilogia della vita* (*Il Decameron* (1971), *I Racconti di Canterbury* (1972), *Il fiore delle Mille e una Notte* (1974)) and finally in 1975 *Salò o le 120 giornate di Sodoma*. All this points to a broad-ranging and intense practice of aesthetic and political resistance, one that seems, in *Salò*, to be subjected to devastating self-criticism.

Because the field of Pasolini's resistance is so extended and internally complex and ambivalent, a valuable means of entry is provided by the single poem *La resistenza e la sua luce* from *La religione del mio tempo* (1961).

So I came to the days of the Resistance
knowing nothing of it but the style:
A style all light, memorable consciousness
of sun. It could never fade
not for an instant, not even when

Europe trembled in the most deathly vigil.
We fled with our stuff on a cart as
far as Casarsa and a village lost between
canals and vines: and it was pure light.
My brother left on a still march
morning by train, clandestine
the pistol in a book: and it was pure light.
He lived longtimes in the mountains, that shone
as if paradisiacal in the sombre blue
of the Friulian plain: and it was pure light.
In the attic of the farmhouse my mother
watched, always lost, those mountains
already aware of destiny: and it was pure light.
Along with a few nearby peasants
I lived a glorious life of one persecuted
by atrocious edicts: and it was pure light.
When the day of death
and liberty arrived, the martyred world
recognised itself anew in the light...
That light was hope of justice:
I didn't know which: Justice.
The light is always equal to other light.
Then it changed: the light became a diffident dawn
a dawn which grew, which extended
over the Friulian fields, over canals.
It illuminated the workers who struggled.
Thus the newborn dawn was a light
outside of the eternity of style...
In history justice was consciousness
of a humane division of wealth
and hope had a new light.

The poem has two unequal stanzas organized according to a kind of *terza rima* (that for Italian readers immediately evokes Dante): one stanza describes the child's experience of the resistance, the other an adult's reflection upon it. The first stanza laces together a series of memories by means of the experience of light, modulating a consciousness of the historical movement of the Resistance with the experience of that resistance for a child and for a people that did not yet have the name or concept of *resistenza*. Thus he came to the days of resistance without knowing anything about it except its style, except the ways in which those days differed from other days: all light, memorable awareness of sun, even when Europe was trembling on '*la piu morta vigilia*'. It is important to be sensitive to the Christian echoes in this internal dialogue. Europe is trembling on the eve of its crucifixion – *vigilia* – rather as Christ in the night of doubt in the Garden of Gethsemane; Europe is also in the Dantean *selva oscura* or dark wood, but in spite of this there is a light which divides it, the light of resistance which did not allow the darkness to become total. Pasolini in this prologue does not accept total domination; even at the darkest hour there is still a glimmer of the light of resistance.

This is both said and done in the poem, especially in the first stanza and notably at the level of rhyme. In the first six lines, the *terza rima* chimes on the open-mouthed 'a' of *Resistenza/coscienza/vigilia*, but then changes to a repeated citation of the word *luce*, ending the refrain *ed era pura luce* – the third triplet chimes o/o/e, ending with *luce*, a scheme repeated twice along with the refrain. In the sixth triplet the o/o/a is disrupted 'e' and 'i' followed by the 'e' of the refrain *luce* and then after this disruption there is an ominous chiming of *morte/luce* in the last triplet of the first stanza interrupted by the 'o' of *martoriato*. This sequence of *luce* evokes the ecstatic Franciscan poem/prayer 'Brother Sun', but serving here to recount the experience of losing a brother. From the reflective first six lines we enter the time of recollection: of flight to a remote village ending with the refrain 'and it was pure light', *ed era pure luce*, to the morning departure of the brother to join the Resistance, *ed era pure luce*, where he fought in the mountains that shone above the plains of Friuli, *ed era pure luce*, and then, with the modulation of the rhyme from 'o' to 'e' with the mother gazing at the mountains from the attic longing for her son's return, *ed era pure luce*, to the glorious life of childhood amid oppression, *ed era pure luce*, to the day of death and liberty – Pasolini's brother was killed in a 'misunderstanding' between Italian and Yugoslavian partisans – when the world saw itself again in the light of resistance.

With the orthography of ellipsis '...' breaking off the first stanza, the recollection is interrupted and the solemn litany of 'it was pure light' falls away, for the light in which the world recognized itself again was not so pure as it was remembered, the world has been martyred, the resistance killed its own, Pasolini lost his brother, his mother her son. Pasolini insists, poetically in the breakdown of the line in an ellipsis and the abandonment of the refrain, that his *ed era pure luce* was a childish illusion about resistance. It is interesting to compare this ambivalence with another great poem of resistance, Elytis's *Axion Esti*, in which any doubt about the purity of the light is not permitted. Pasolini's breakdown of the experience of the purity of the light of resistance is followed by the second stanza of twelve lines – four triplets – which move between the experience of the purity of the style of resistance and the recognition of its impurity. The rhyme provokes almost a physiognomic expression of doubt: 'a/a/e, a/a/e', the repetition signalling certainty but then modulating into 'o/e/e/' before returning to the signature of certainty, but now not sounding quite so certain, 'a/a/e'. The thinking of resistance is taking place as much in the physical movements of enunciation as in what is said. The first triplet makes the gesture of revealing the truth of what the child knew only as style – that light was the hope of justice: it wagers on a platonic Justice whose hope was expressed in the light, adding that all light, all claims for justice are the same. But this experience – and we are following a phenomenology of resistance here – is refined as the light changes: dawn is uncertain, and with it the hope for justice is differentiated and shown to have degrees, dawn grows and extends itself. The light that illuminated the struggles of (resistant) workers was not the pure, platonic, eternal light of style after all… the rhyme has changed, the line again breaks off with an ellipsis. This Nietzschean moment of 'perhaps' expressed in the ellipsis that we saw in Lenin's *What is to be Done* is less a question mark than the breakdown of even the ability to ask a question. If it is a light or hope of justice that is awaited 'outside of the eternity of style', outside of the light that is the same as other lights, if there are different hopes of justice… what then? Or rather, what then…

The poem ends with a wooden reassertion of the opening rhyme scheme of the stanza and a poetic assertion of the Communist appro-priation of the experience of resistance: the party teaches that 'in history, justice was consciousness of the humane distribution of wealth', but note that it was this justice that permitted hope to find a new light, and perhaps a new justice. Pasolini ends by leaving ambiguous the character of this new light or justice – is it more of the same, which is the lesson of the opening of the stanza, or could it be something new and wholly unprecedented?

It is important to look carefully at how Pasolini thought poetically. The subtlety of his poetic thinking was in defiant revolt against any Hegelian appropriation of thinking for the concept, as is nowhere more evident than in his thinking around resistance. Resistance for him is not just the unambiguous answer to the question posed by injustice, but a predicament, one that has to be thought and sung with care. It is in this aesthetic resistance that it becomes possible to escape the conceptual dialectic that afflicts the thinking of resistance. It is precisely this subtle expression of an ambivalence surrounding resistance that he seems to have abandoned at the end of his life – to be precise in 1975 – in a violent, indeed brutal gesture of renunciation that motivates Didi-Huberman's reading of the significance of his work. Didi-Huberman approaches Pasolini's view of the politics of light by contrasting the late journalism, the notorious *scritti corsari* with the early poetry. His reading, which is also a thorough, if sometimes oblique critique of Agamben, focuses on one of Pasolini's last pieces of journalism published in the *Corriere della sera* of February 1st 1975, originally entitled '*Il vuoto di potere in Italia*' (The Void of Power in Italy) but now known simply as '*L'articolo delle lucciole*' (the 'Firefly article'), probably among the most influential articles of twentieth-century Italian journalism. In it Pasolini claims that Italian and Western consumer society is more Fascist than historic Fascism and proposes that post-war Italian history be divided according to the moment of disappearance of the fireflies, driven away by urbanization, industrialization and the prevalence of artificial light.

The fireflies, or Nietzsche's 'dancing stars' with chaos in their hearts (described at one point in *Zarathustra* as fireflies), are unpredictable and fugitive, illuminating themselves for a mating dance (nocturnal prosti-tutes in Italy are also known as *lucciole*). Their disappearance with the spread of artificial light led in Pasolini's view, in 1975, to the passing of this particular fugitive light of the hope of justice and the emergence of the harsh light of control and total domination under which resistance appears futile and absurd. The affinity of the theses of the *lucciole* article and the remorseless and transparent presentation of total domination in *Salò* is patent. Didi-Huberman's strategy consists in restoring the fireflies against Pasolini himself, but also against the 'pessimism' of Agamben that he suggests emerges from the late Pasolini:

> If we extend vision from the horizon that, immense and immobile, extends beyond us and if, on the contrary we concentrate our gaze on the image that, tiny and unstable, passes us by, we will perceive very different things. The image is a firefly of passing intermittence, the horizon however bathes us in a definitive light, the immutable time of totalitarianism or the completed time of the last judgement. To gaze at the horizon beyond means not to see the images that throng around us. The little fireflies give form and illumination to our fragile immanence, the 'ferocious spotlights' of great lights consume all form and illumination – all difference – in the transcendence of ultimate ends. (Didi-Huberman 2009, 69)

Didi-Huberman claims that the 'political desperation' of Pasolini in 1975 that followed his conviction (echoing Arendt) that human spontaneity has been abolished by surveillance and the bright lights of a transparent consumer society is an 'error'. That is, Pasolini's view of the passing of any possibility of resistance in 1975 overlooks that fireflies still exist, resisting extinction, and that it is still possible to find episodic moments of resistance even at the darkest hour. Indeed, the figure of the firefly seems to possess three of the characteristics Schmitt gave to the ideal type of the partisan: its blinking light is not uniform, it is mobile and unpredictable, and finally it is telluric or bound to a territory. Didi-Huberman asserts their presence in Pasolini in spite of Pasolini. Yet even in its own terms his argument does not fully confront Pasolini's 'desperation': Pasolini was not only despairing at the advent of a society of surveillance and control, but also at a society of consumerism where desires themselves have become measurable and predictable objects of exchange. Even those rare moments of 'firefly' intensity in *Salò*, such as the defiance of the young prisoner caught having unauthorized sex who stands naked making the clenched fist salute of resistance before being shot, seem futile to him. Resistance to commodification, or a resistance that does not succumb to the 'justice' of exchange and that stands apart from the exchange of work time for leisure time, seems unthinkable in the holiday camp village that is the Villa in *Salò*. *Salò* was meant as the brutal self-criticism of the 'Trilogy of Life' and the way in which an archaic representation of free sexuality could, without much resistance, be quickly commodified and sold as pornography.

Yet the light of resistance which seems to have been lost in the uniform glare of the consumer/surveillance society that is presented in *Salò* nevertheless persists throughout it; it has been displaced rather than extinguished. The film itself is an act of resistance, proposing to the consumerist cinema audience something that could not easily be consumed or made an object of exchange. Its very resistability places it within a line of ambiguous lights of resistance that flicker through Pasolini's work. *Salò* seen as an *act* of resistance may be contrasted with the *depiction* of resistance in *The Gospel According to St Matthew* – in which Christ is cast as a resistant. The two expressions of resistance complement each other. The latter is a wonderful returning of Gandhi's debt to and interpretation of Christ's thought and example into the Christian tradition. Pasolini's Christ is Gandhian; in one of the exchanges in the dialogues from 1962 Pasolini expresses his enthusiasm for Gandhi and the principle of non-violent resistance:

> Non-violence seems to me a stupendous notion it is extremely aristocratic (Gandhi, Russell, Dostoyevsky…) pre-evangelical origin (oriental) like the greater part of evangelical notions that were christianized with 19th century romanticism and then dechristianized, becoming proudly laical… Non-violence is the highest point of a rational conception

of reality. If every form of thought has need, in practical action, of a concrete manifestation and one based on sentiment and persuasion, non-violence is the sentimental and persuasive attitude that is totally beyond any conformism and is totally free with respect to the instruments of reason and culture. (Pasolini 1995, 221–2)

In his last interview, conducted with Furio Columbo hours before his death on November 1st 1975, Pasolini was sombre but far from desperate. The discussion is haunted by the thought that somewhere, someone is thinking how to kill us; hence the title proposed by Pasolini, 'We are all in Danger'. The conversation opens with the problem of how to resist and the example of Eichmann. Pasolini maintains that '[r]efusal has always been an essential gesture. Saints, hermits, but also intellectuals. The few who have made history are those who have said no...' (Pasolini 2011, 53). Yet this defiant refusal has to be radical, not confined within good sense. For Pasolini, Eichmann was a 'sensible man', perhaps 'a grumbler' complaining about the job he had to do but lacking any capacity to resist, any ability to 'say no, at the outset, when what he was doing was only ordinary administration, bureaucracy' (Pasolini 2011, 53). The 'no' for Pasolini 'has to be big, not little, total, not on this or that point...' (Pasolini 2011, 53), the no of the resistant subject, of Jean Moulin. Yet as the conversation developed and the light faded and the night of his murder approached, Pasolini admits that this capacity to resist is becoming minimal, forever more compromised. Alluding to Eichmann again, 'the SS Nazi' but also to the 'fascist of *Salò*', Pasolini says that it would have been easier for them to say 'no' with 'a little courage and conscience... But now, no' (Pasolini 2011, 55). The Villa in *Salò* is wherever it is impossible to say no, where the hunters play and their captives regress to the level of prey, forget how to resist, forget defiance and learn the pleasures of obedience. For Pasolini it was contemporary Italy and European modernity played in the dress of the Fascist social republic.

5 THE CONTEMPORARY CAPACITY TO RESIST

Stéphane Hessel's influential *Indignez Vous!* (2011) appeals to a continuity between the experience of the French Resistance and the contemporary resistances. Hessel's experience as a resistant and his subsequent view of the achievements of the French Resistance coincided with the phase of its unification in the CNR. As a voice of the institutional resistance, Hessel shows little sympathy for the French resistances that existed before their unification under the CNR, nor in the appeal to this dispersed model of resistance by contemporary movements and networks. *Indignez Vous!* is certainly a call for resistance, but also a warning against spontaneous resistances and, as such, a veiled critique of other contemporary resistance movements and networks.

The experience of the French resistances has become a point of reference for many contemporary practices of resistance, but these also have a number of different qualities that suggest the advent of a new epoch of resistance. Contemporary resistance may be said to have begun with the call for an art of resistant life from within the situationist movement. It assumed a global profile through the *detournement* of communications technologies invented as part of a neo-Clausewitzian effort to ensure the survival of the capacity to resist following a nuclear first strike in the Cold War and emerged as an insurgent capacity to resist able to operate on a global scale. The question concerning the state of the contemporary capacity to resist neo-liberalism requires first of all that we chart some of the contemporary resistance movements and networks and then look to see what forms of co-ordination are emerging between them with the aid of new communications technologies. From this it will be possible to gauge the quality and consistency of the diverse expressions of the contemporary capacity to resist as well as their internal limitations and susceptibility to counter-resistance.

The Other Side of the Spectacle

Genet and Pasolini tested the limits of aesthetic resistance, both as a mode of resistance and as a style for thinking resistance. As a mode of resistance the aesthetic served as a place – or non-place, utopia – from and in which to resist, a place and a possibility that Pasolini pushed to its limits in *Salò*. The erotic utopia of the 'Trilogy of Life' – the affirmation of a vital aesthetic/erotic resistance – was so quickly recuperated under the category of the pornographic that it pushed Pasolini to attempt the unrecuperable in *Salò*. While Didi-Huberman understood the last film as Pasolini's despair, it is possible to see in it hints of something else: an act of aesthetic resistance, a *via negationis* which said no to everything except the unescapable fact that this negation was being staged in a resistant work of art. The thinking of the possibility of resistance through style is taken to its limit in *Salò*, where Pasolini made an unrecuperable film on the impossibility of resistance and in so doing arguably achieved a moment of aesthetic resistance.

This aesthetic of resistance responds to some of the problems encountered at the outset in Sartre's reflections on Lapoujade in 1961. The logic of resistance has the properties of the Hegelian *Reflexionsbestimmung* described as part of the 'logic of essence', or the second major division of Hegel's *Logic* following the logic of being and preceding the logic of the concept. According to this logic, resistance is dependent upon what it opposes and in some sense also complicit with it. This, as we have seen, holds for reactive resistance or *ressentiment* but not necessarily for an affirmative resistance. Yet the latter should not be understood in terms of an attempt to raise resistance up into 'revolution' or some other equivalent in the 'logic of the concept'. It is perhaps in the very indeterminacy of poetry or art – the *ohne Bestimmung* or *die andere Bestimmung* of mood, style and suggestion that is intimated in Pasolini's poem on the Resistance or in the Sartrian streak of colour – that the dependence on the past and openness to the future of affirmative resistance can be experienced. The hospitality of art to the experience of resistance suggests that the Hegelian thesis of the death of art – the idea that art can no longer express the modern concept of freedom but must cede this responsibility to philosophy – is premature and that art can offer a place and an occasion for thinking resistance if not freedom.

The question of the mode and style of aesthetic resistance is appropriate for understanding one of the most determined and influential attempts to sustain an aesthetic resistance outside the confines of the work of art. The situationist adventure extended aesthetic resistance to everyday life in the name of a transition from survival to life.[1] This effort remains contemporary insofar as the failure of situationism left the theory of resistance at a moment of unfulfilled potential, one recently reactivated by the responses of Raoul Vaneigem to the current crisis. In a text given to a meeting of Greek resistants in Salonica, September 2010 – *L'état ne plus rien, soyons nous* – Vaneigem applies situationist theses to the Greek insurrection. Many of these theses return to his *Traité de savoir-vivre à l'usage des jeunes generations* (translated as *The Revolution of Everyday Life*), one of the few sustained theoretical texts on the art of resistance that appeared in the same year as Guy Debord's theory of domination, *La société du spectacle*. The two texts *together* theoretically define the situationist moment of the revolution of 1968, complementing each other as a theory of domination and a theory of resistance and between them opening a theoretical and political space that for Vaneigem in 2010 still remained to be explored.[2]

The two texts define the field of situationist resistance and are literal complements: their authors were writing them almost side by side during the early to mid 1960s, a little like Braque and Picasso in the early days of cubism. Unfortunately, in the legacy of situationism only Debord's treatise on domination is remembered, severed from its defiant twin *Traité de savoir-vivre à l'usage des jeunes generations*. The eclipse of Vaneigem's text has something to do with his withdrawal from the *L'Internationale situationniste* in 1970 and Debord's ambivalent justification of this separation,[3] but it depends also on the character of the two books: texts on domination are more familiar and digestible than those on resistance. Nevertheless they comprised two factors in an equation that did not and does not add up, not specular twins but different and subsequently antagonistic positions on the primacy of domination and defiance. Read together, the two texts together leave us with a Nietzschean perhaps, an elliptical train of dots… Debord expressed this beautifully in a letter to Vaneigem written immediately after reading a draft of the *Traité* on Monday 8 March 1965:

> I believe that the appearance of this book…will mark the end of the 'prehistory of the IS'… Another good thing: our two works evidently deal with the same problem, flow together in the same perspective, pass on this terrain without mistaking themselves; but in crossing so often they always support each other. In a way like ogival arcs. A rare coincidence all the same for two texts that are so different as to details. (Debord, 681)

This beautiful expression of a balance of forces proceeding in different directions but nevertheless intersecting at a number of points is a clear statement that in order to understand situationism, let alone situationist resistance, both texts have to be read, with and against each other. To remember only Debord's anatomy of total domination with its remorseless specularity without its complement in Vaneigem leaves a bleak and one-sided view of the situationist movement and its possibilities. A nameless contemporary described the two texts as 'The *Capital* and *What is to be Done*' of the situationist movement, a parallel provoked by Debord in his *détournement* of the opening lines of Marx's *Capital*[4] at the beginning of *La société du spectacle*:

> All life in those societies in which modern conditions of production prevail announces itself as a vast accumulation of *spectacles*. All that is directly lived distances itself in a representation. (Debord, 766)

Like *Capital*, Debord's text is an objective analysis of the conditions of possibility of living in a society dominated by the spectacle, one which begins with an account of the structures that oppress life then moving to confront these with other forms of possible organization. *The Revolution of Everyday Life*, on the other hand, moves from defiant lived experience towards an intensification of those potentials to live that it sustains in spite of oppressive structures. It begins with what remains of the capacity to resist and then seeks to energize and enhance it.

The prehistory of the IS movement brought to a close by the appearance of *The Society of the Spectacle* and *The Revolution of Everyday Life* began in the early 1950s in proximity to the Lettrist movement – those sombre comedians of a celebratory grammatology – proceeding through critiques of architecture, urbanism and cinema. Lettrism and the prehistoric IS together took a stand against the forces of death, calling for the transformation of life through art, but art understood expansively as politics and everyday life. The situationists brought the freedom of the avant-garde to the question of changing life, but in abandoning the Lettrist indifference – even hostility – to lived life in favour of inscription and the automatic, they wagered their own resistance and hopes for emancipation in an alliance between the situationist and proletarian revolutions.

The limits to situationist resistance are apparent in its concern with the reduction of life to mere survival: both Debord and Vaneigem set out from a life that has been lost: for the one life is abandoned in a 'vast accumulation of spectacles' where the lived 'distances itself in a representation,' while for the other it is a lived experience that has been squandered and must be somehow recovered by those left with sufficient capacity to resist, to still feel its loss. Vaneigem wrote:

My aim is not to make the real experience contained in this book comprehensible to readers who have no interest in reliving it. I fully expect this experience to be lost – and rediscovered – in a general movement of spirits, just as I am convinced that the present conditions of our lives will one day be no more than a memory. (Vaneigem 1967, 7)

Both depart from the melancholy of a lost life, one separated from itself, and make the condition of separation the object of their resistance. Yet the two texts pursue the problem of resistance and restoration along divergent paths: Debord explores the structural conditions of almost total loss and moves towards a remedy at the level of structure and organization, while Vaneigem works through the melancholy of the experience of a lost life, invoking strategies for revivification through the experience of resistance. The one looks for the capacity to resist in the reorganization of life, the other in its intensification through affirmative resistance beginning in everyday life.

The complementarity of the two texts and their dependence on each other is all the more surprising given the very diverse canons to which their authors subscribe. For Debord, the idiom and the content of his text is indebted to Hegel, Marx and Lukács (with the insistent presence of Clausewitz), while for Vaneigem it is Nietzsche, Freud, Reich, but above all Lautréamont and Surrealism (not to overlook a nuanced reading of Sade). Both depart from the critique of consumer society and the question of how to resist it. Debord investigates the mutation of contemporary capitalism into a society of the spectacle and the problem of organizing resistance to it, while Vaneigem analyses the colonization of desire by consumerism, the better to resist it. Debord's treatise is an attempt to reorganize life: it departs from domination or the alienation of life in the repressive mutation of social relations into images, focusing on the role of the commodity in achieving this – 'commodity as spectacle' – and then, citing both Lukács and Schopenhauer, moves to the question of how the proletariat can become the lived world as 'subject' and 'representation'. This question is addressed remorselessly to the problem of organization, with Debord engaging in an implacable critique of what Luxemburg described as the 'organizational questions of social democracy', and in which, like her, he sought an organizational form that would resist the tendency of the proletariat to become a representation, or object for itself and which would keep the revolution alive.

Debord sees the tendency to self-represent at work in the bureaucratization of the revolutionary parties, a tendency he very firmly identifies not only in Lenin but also in Mao and the so-called 'cultural revolution'. (The article '*Le point d'explosion de l'idéologie en Chine*' [IS 1967] shows that he did not share his epoch's illusions with respect to the Great Helmsman.) He sees the possibility for overcoming this separation in the experience of the workers councils and its theorists (Pannekoek and Gorter, see Bourrinet 2001) active during the early 1920s,[5] yet this appeal feels like a theatrical *deus ex machina*, offering but a formal, even specular solution to the problem of life as representation. The air of abstract formality also pervades the analysis of lived time in the later sections of *La société du spectacle*, where the time of the spectacle that condemns life to repetition and survival is met by a formal, rhetorical appeal to resistance that recalls what Walter Benjamin described as 'left-melancholy' or the 'clenched fist in papier-mache'. The *détournement* as the 'fluid language of anti-ideology' capable of disrupting specular representation finds itself quickly set in formal and stereotyped revolutionary rhetoric:

> Self-emancipation from the material bases of inverted truth, this is the self-emancipation of our epoch. This 'historic mission of instituting truth in the world' can be accomplished neither by an individual nor by a manipulated atomised crowd but once and for all by the class that is capable of being the dissolution of all classes in bringing to itself power in the unalienated form of realised democracy, the Council in which practical theory controls itself and views its action. (Debord, 859)

This despairing conclusion – faith in the councils as the organizational form of direct democracy and lived life was to wreck the IS after 1968 – and with the waning of the faith in direct democracy after 1968, all that remains of *The Society of the Spectacle* is an exercise in apocalypse, the specular end of time and life in total domination under the spectacle … *in girum imus nocte et consumimur igni* …

The organizational thought of Debord and the analysis of the structural characteristics of the society of the spectacle left him with very few resources for resistance. If the enemy was so strong and the tendency to represent so implacable, what could possibly serve as an adequate organizational form for resistance? Debord's suggestions, *dérive, detournement*, as styles of thinking resistance sit awkwardly with the appeal to the workers councils as a direct democratic site of resistance to the spectacle. Vaneigem, emerging from the same historic experience of the 'pre-historic' aesthetic resistance of the IS, took a very different approach to resistance that complemented Debord's structural analysis. In emphasizing the economy of desire and affect that informs the society of the spectacle and pointing to a level of lived experience anterior to the representations that fascinated Debord, Vaneigem discovered a capacity to resist that provided the energetic resources for actualizing resistance to the spectacle.

In a preface written for *The Revolution of Everyday Life* following his departure from the IS, Vaneigem retrospectively awards his text clairvoyancy, observing that:

> The stratified past still clung to by those who grow old with time is evermore easy to distinguish from the alluvia, timeless in their fertility, left by others who awake to themselves (or at least strive to) every day. (Vaneigem 2003, 7)

This forms the basic philosophical intuition of the work: the analysis of the 'two moments of a single fluctuating existence in which the present is continually divesting itself of its old forms' (Vaneigem 2003, 7). Already, the dynamic character of Vaneigem's thought contrasts strikingly with the static geometry of *The Society of the Spectacle*. The opposition of sedimented and fertile time runs throughout the book, and is modulated into an analysis of time and power. Only towards the end, after an analysis of everyday life, does Vaneigem arrive at a definition of time and power:

> In the scope of power there is no future other than a past reiterated... Power's crowning achievement, in its attempt to trap people into identifying with such a past future, lies in its resort to historical ideology. (Vaneigem 1967, 238-9)

If power resolves itself in repetition, pleasure finds itself in invention: Vaneigem captures the tension between the two tendencies in his reading of de Sade, which is a premonitory critique of Pasolini's *Salò*, preferring the philosophy of the Boudoir to the tortures of the Villa/Chateau:

> De Sade describes two possible attitudes. On the one hand, the libertines of the *120 Days of Sodom* who can only really enjoy themselves by torturing to death the objects they have seduced (and what more fitting homage to a thing than to make it suffer). On the other hand, the libertines of *Philosophy in the Boudoir*, warm and playful, who do all they can to increase one another's pleasure. The former are the masters of old, vibrant with hatred and revolt; the latter are masters without slaves, discovering in one another only the reflection of their own pleasure. (Vaneigem 1967, 262).

Vaneigem distances himself from Debord and the fascination with domination in looking to the 'masters without slaves' drawn directly and expressly from Nietzsche's distinction between *ressentiment* and affirmative morality. He distances himself from Hegelian dialectic and, implicitly, Debord's reliance on it in *The Society of the Spectacle*, going so far as to affirm a productive possibility in specularity or the mutual reflection of pleasure for the masters without slaves.

Vaneigem sees love and generosity as the bases for a new resistance, but one which does not engage power on its terrain of enmity and opposed force but instead constructs its own new terrain. This terrain is not that of Hegelian dialectic but rather a Clausewitzian duel between the death of power and the life of love, identifying the conflict in the Freudian opposition between the death drive and the pleasure principle – power/stasis and love/creativity. The first of *The Revolution of Everyday Life's* two parts, 'Power's Perspective', presents an analysis of everyday life from the standpoint of power and death. Power confronts life with three impossibilities: participation and constraint (Chapter One), communication (Chapter Two), and realization or power as seduction (Chapter Three), which together conspire to reduce life to survival. Life is what remains after confronting the three impossibilities of power, but it survives in a form scarred by compromise and its conflict with power and death. Part 2, on the contrary, attempts a 'reversal of perspective' in a break with the impossibilities of power by proposing creativity, dignity or masters without slaves, the affirmative experience of time and the triad of self-realization, communication and participation. With this we arrive at resistance and the conclusive challenge 'You won't fuck with us much longer' – an apt reply to the torturers of *Salò*, but one which assumes a surviving capacity to resist which Pasolini (and subsequently Debord) insisted was completely spent in consumer capitalism.

Informing Vaneigem's reversal of the perspective of power is a critique of Freud's death drive and affirmation of the pleasure principle. The triad of participation, communication and realization is revealed as the death drive at work – 'The three elements of the death drive – Nirvana, the repetition compulsion and masochism – and nothing other than three styles of domination – constraint passively accepted, seduction through conformity to custom and mediation perceived as an ineluctable law' (Vaneigem 1967, 166) – precisely the three areas identified in the analysis of the reduction of life to survival in Part 1. The analytic of consumer *Dasein* in Part 1 with its phenomenological descriptions of humiliation, isolation, suffering, of exchange, separation and sacrifice are all aspects of the critique of the death drive; already a decade before Pasolini's *Salò*, Vaneigem was making the equation between consumerism, death drive and the 120 days of Sodom – except that he understood these, following Freud, as resistances to be resisted in an affirmative project of realisation, communication and participation. It is as if, in Vaneigem, it is *The Trilogy of Life* or *The Philosophy of the Boudoir* that succeeds *Salò*, or *the 120 Days of Sodom*.

Yet it is only towards the end of *The Revolution of Everyday Life* that Vaneigem turns to speak directly with Debord, calling for a non-Clause-witzian strategy and tactics of 'spontaneous revolution' and rhetorically praising the creativity of revolutionary spontaneity. Vaneigem, through a critique of the death drive and the endorsement of the pleasure principle, eventually followed Debord into the problem of organization, comple-menting his strategic objective of destroying power with the call for a 'federation of tacticians of daily life' who can 'meet the requirements of the desire to destroy the old society. To equip such a federation, to supply its technical needs, is one of the immediate goals of the Situationist International: strategy is the collective construction of the launching pad of the revolution on the basis of tactics of the individual's daily life' (Vaneigem 1967, 275). Using terms and distinctions that are closer to Clausewitz than he may wish, Vaneigem even foresees a potential military role for the SI:

> Guerrilla war is total war. This is the path on which the Situationist International is set: calculated harassment on every front – cultural, political, economic and social. Concentrating on the battlefield of everyday life will ensure the unity of the combat. (Vaneigem 1967, 275–6)

These attempts to approach Debord at the end of the book forget the opening refusal to engage in the logic of confrontation, and the call for resistance at the level of everyday life and its desire to live provoked Debord's cold rejoinder that everyday life is already under the domination of the spectacle, a gesture later repeated by Pasolini in *Salò*.

Debord and Vaneigem establish a creative tension between their very different attempts to theorize situationist resistance, the one through dialectic and organization, the other through anti-dialectic and the overcoming of the death drive through the release of the pleasure principle. After the approach to Debord towards the end of *The Revolution of Everyday Life*, Vaneigem retreated and entrenched his refusal to enter into the logic of confrontation and its lure of dialectical resolution. This is evident in the *L'Etat ne plus rien, soyon tout* which Vaneigem refused to read at the meeting of direct democracy in Salonica: true to his Lettrist formation he provided a written text, offered as a gift, and refused to enter into the dialectical arena of debate. He gave his reasons, which were, firstly, his desire to avoid becoming part of a spectacle and secondly, his wish to minimize the proprietorial passions involved in debate and the desire for his position to prevail. His text begins with a gesture of solidarity with the Greek insurrection and the corruption of contemporary democracy, moving directly to the problem addressed in Part 2 of the *The Revolution of Everyday Life*, namely the reversal of the perspective of power. His approach to this dimension of resistance – affirmative resistance – this time is followed through without compromise:

> Until now we have had only two alternatives: either the determination to put an end to repressive violence by entering the terrain of the enemy, opposing to him violence of an equal nature, but in the opposite direction, or the passive resistance to tyranny in the manner that Gandhi practised with undisputable success. (Vaneigem 2010, 3)

Vaneigem regards the opposition between Mao or Gandhi alluded to here as by now historic and in the current crisis arriving at its limits of validity. For him a Gandhian strategy could only work because of the residually ethical character of some parts of the colonial power, a quality no longer shared by many contemporary repressive regimes.[6] Nevertheless, this does not entail for Vaneigem that the Maoist strategy with what he calls its repugnant maxim 'all power comes from the barrel of a gun' is the only remaining path of resistance.[7] Vaneigem looks instead to the movement of the Zapatistas and in an open critique of the violence of the Greek insurrectionists he calls for the resistance to learn the lessons of Chiapas or, which is the same, those the Paris Commune:

> The Zapatista communities of Chiapas are perhaps the only ones today to apply direct democracy. Common lands exclude from the outset the conflicts associated with private expropriation. Everyone has the right to participate in assemblies, to speak and to manifest their choice, even children… The Zapatistas have, to define their will to found a more human society, a formula which reminds of the necessity of constant vigilance – we are not an example but an experience. (Vaneigem 2010, 2)

Vaneigem is effectively calling for a rethinking of *Satyagraha* – boycotts, alternative communities, disobedience and creativity; his last words to the Greeks are absolutely consistent with his position in 1967 and a powerful reply to the later Debord and Pasolini's *Salò*:

> I have the conviction that moving beyond the barricades of resistance and self-defence, the living forces of the entire world are awakening from a long dream. Their offensive, irresistible and peaceful, will sweep away any obstacles raised against an immense desire to live that nourishes those, who are born and reborn every day. The violence of a world to be created will supplant the violence of a world that destroys itself. (Vaneigem 2010, 5)

Indigenous Resistances

We saw how in his late work Carl Schmitt was preoccupied by emergence of a global partisan war – one in which irregular, mobile, ideologically driven and telluric struggles are conducted at a global level. What was most striking in Schmitt's diagnosis was an almost apocalyptic vision of a global civil war, a struggle between Empire and world revolution in which ultimately Mao and Maoism would serve as a geopolitical *catechon* against the universalism of Leninist world revolution. This remains a very abstract view of global resistance, since the global capacity to resist has assumed complex and inconsistent forms that combine resistance in the metropolis with struggles at what was once regarded as the 'periphery'. In the constitution of a contemporary capacity to resist and the counter-resistance that it has provoked, the struggles of 'indigenous peoples' have assumed increasing importance. Two very different but, in their way, exemplary expressions of such resistance are the Zapatistas already encountered in Chapter 3 with their vision of resistant subjectivity and the long-standing tribal people's resistances in central India increasingly aligned with the Communist Party of India (Maoist).

Both movements share characteristics that help us understand the contemporary struggle between global resistance and counter-resistance: they are struggles of indigenous peoples forced to the peripheries of their nation-states whose ambient local traditions of struggle and self-determination are now expressed in terms of resistance to global mining and primary raw material interests. With the enormous demand of newly industrializing economies for raw materials, any resistance to attempts to extract these from indigenous lands and their peoples gives local resistances a global significance, putting into question not only the constitutionality of the nation-state but also the imperatives of the repeated gesture of capitalist 'primary accumulation' or violent expropriation present at the birth and recurring throughout the life of capitalism and which has left its mark on the brow of modernity itself. The resistance of the marginalized, excluded and – in many cases literally – hunted peoples who are being violently subsumed and expropriated by global capital contributes to and is supported by an emergent global capacity to resist.

In Chapter 3 we saw how the Zapatistas expressed a profound vision of resistant subjectivity which included the living, the dead and those yet-to-come. What is perhaps even more extraordinary is the way in which this haunted subjectivity was articulated with an emergent global capacity to resist. This was made possible by the internet and the potential it offered of a globally networked resistance. The necessity of resistance is urged by the voices of the dead and the yet-to-live; it is not a question of simply actualizing the freedom of the present generation. The capacity to resist is spread across the living, the dead and the yet-to-live, but in Spring 1994 it spread even further. This extension of the capacity to resist was captured in the Zapatista formula 'Everything for everyone and nothing for us', which from this point in time would be cited repeatedly in Zapatista communiqués, replacing the 'enough is enough' that motivated the 1994 insurrection and its resistance of the indigenous dead. Using the same technology that brought death from the sky and overcoming the distinction between 'modern death versus ancestral life' (Ponce de León, 90), the Zapatistas in a remarkably short period of time brought their 'wooden weapons, the broken feet, and the ancestral philosophy' (Ponce de León, 90) to a world public and worked to actualize a global capacity to resist that would in turn energize their local resistance. Their resistance would be for everyone but not for them; fostering the capacity to resist was an end in itself – in Vaneigem's terms a gift or act of generosity, regardless of what it might bring to the resistants themselves.

As part of their solidarity with a world capacity to resist, the ICRC-GC introduced the *encuentro* for humanity against neo-liberalism of July and August 1996, evoking the specific struggles of the ZNLA and the adoption of the resistant strategy to arm the voice and to hide the face and the name, adopting the Nietzschean strategy of becoming no one in order to become everyone. Behind the mask, behind the weapon, behind the unnameable name, 'Behind us, we are you', are all the names in history, above all those names that have been forgotten: the resistance of the one is in the name of all who have been and will be oppressed and have and will resist:

Behind us, you are us.
Behind our masks is the face of all excluded women.
Of all the forgotten indigenous.
Of all the persecuted homosexuals.
Of all the despised youth.
Of all the beaten migrants.
Of all those imprisoned for their words and thoughts.
Of all the humiliated workers.
Of all those dead from neglect.
Of all the simple and ordinary men and women.
Who don't count.
Who aren't seen.
Who are nameless.
Who have no tomorrow.

The declarations of the IRCG-GC following the *encuentrada* confronted global economic, political, cultural and military oppression with a call to constitute a global network of resistance. The claim that the indigenous resistance is for all becomes a call to constitute a global capacity to resist. What needs to be done is to create

> [...] a network of voices that resist the war Power wages on them... resist for humanity and against neo-liberalism. A network of voices that are born resisting, reproducing their resistance in other quiet and solitary voices. A network that covers five continents and helps to resist the death that power promises us. ('Tomorrow Begins Today' 3/8/1996, Ponce de León, 114)

The Second Declaration of August 1996 goes much further than the mere call to constitute a network by beginning to describe its character and objectives. Beyond the description of the nascent global capacity to resist, the Second Declaration shows a sophisticated strategic awareness of the need to avoid entering into a posture of direct confrontation with power. The proposed network directly addresses the technical possibilities opened by the internet that were still unavailable to the women of Greenham Common Yellow Gate and their network. Building on the political potential of the new technology demonstrated in the resistance to the Russian coup d'etat, the Second Declaration elaborates a vision of a networked global capacity to resist and presages the emergence of the current global capacity to resist based on the internet. The declaration allowed this possibility to be recognized and to be developed theoretically and in practice.

The declaration recognizes that local struggles against global oppression need to draw on the energy available in a global capacity to resist. It calls for 'a collective network of all our particular struggles and resistances, an intercontinental network of resistance against neo-liberalism, and inter-continental network of resistance for humanity' (Ponce de León, 117). Superimposed on the local depth of the capacity to resist rooted in the resistant dead and the yet-to-live is a global network of nodes of resistance, each with their own local density:

> [The] intercontinental network of resistance, recognising differences and acknowledging similarities, will strive to find itself in other resistances around the world. This intercontinental network of resistance will be the medium in which distinct resistances may support one another. (Ponce de León, 117)

The emergent capacity to resist, however, will avoid the trap of becoming fixed in a single place or structured according to a military or political hierarchy: 'it is not an organising structure; it has no central head or decision maker; it has no central command or hierarchies. We are the network of all who resist' (Ponce de León, 117). Listening to and speaking with other resistances itself constitutes the global capacity to resist. The technology is seen to provide a way in which those following different paths of resistance may nevertheless walk together.

The view of resistance as an end in itself, as the goal and not a revolutionary means for arriving somewhere else, is wittily emphasized by Marcos in his October 1999 video message to an international Round Table on Underground Culture, 'From the underground culture to the Culture of Resistance'. In a playful riff on 'the weapon of resistance' Subcomandante Marcos after a few warm-up jokes informed the Round Table: 'I know that you are all anxious to know what the hell I am going to talk about', answering himself: 'So, it is best that I talk to you about weapons. Specifically, I am going to talk to you about the weapon of resistance' (Ponce de León, 166). There follows a discourse on difference which plays with the audience's Maoist expectations about weapons of resistance, only to perform the idea that resistance itself is the weapon, a play with the double genitive 'weapon of resistance'. The text is without *ressentiment* – it relates the terrible conditions of the Chiapas, but then claims: 'Our poverty is the same as the poverty of others, but it is also different; it is an "other" poverty. We are poor because that is what we have chosen' (Ponce de León, 167). The Zapatistas are fighting, 'but for everyone, not just for ourselves'. 'Good, you are asking yourself, but what is the weapon…?'. Well, it is one with which 'we have resisted more than 60,000 soldiers, war tanks, bomber aircraft, artillery, helicopters, cannons, machine guns, bullets, and grenades' (Ponce de León, 167). He means the 'weapon *of* resistance', not a weapon used in resistance, that is to say the struggle in the name of difference itself:

> There are indigenous, there are workers, there are women, there are gays, there are lesbians, there are students, there are young people […] When we say we are fighting for respect for our 'different' and 'other' selves, that includes fighting for respect of those who are other and different and who are not like ourselves. And it is here where this entire resistance movement – whether called underground or subterranean, because it takes place among those below and underneath institutional movements – meets Zapatismo. (Ponce de León, 167)

Resistance itself is the weapon of resistance, as good a definition of the capacity to resist as any and one which can now adopt an international profile commensurate with its globally organized imperial or neo-liberal adversary. The networked capacity to resist actualizes itself not by mimicking or directly confronting the adversary but by avoiding struggle on terrains where it cannot win.

The inventiveness of the Zapatistas and their controlled exercise of violence paradoxically aligns this movement with both the Gandhian and the Maoist movements in India. The Zapatistas seem to propose a contemporary *Satyagraha* which would catalyse change without necessarily pursuing a programme. Politics, in other words, is not destruction and war but invention or peace by other means, and while the Zapatistas opposed the PRI, the Mexican state and NAFTA, and while they defy the state's claim to a monopoly of violence, they have neither a powerful sense of personal enmity nor the sense that their adversary is a dehumanized prey or target. Their enmity is to power itself, and their friendship is with and of resistance. This takes a very different direction to the indigenous or Adivasis's resistance in central India which fights a similar battle, but increasingly within the framework set by neo-Maoism. The Communist Party of India (Maoist)'s 2004 Urban Perspective Plan proposes a programme for taking the struggle of the tribal areas resisting the incursions of global capital supported by the Indian state and its 'Memorandums of Understanding' into the cities, organizing the working class and other sections of the population in order to build a united political front supported by military actions such as sabotage, infiltration and logistical support for armed resistance. While the armed struggle is focused in the countryside and rooted in the capacity to resist of the indigenous peoples, the document proposes to extend it to urban resistance and a wide range of organizational forms, including secret and 'terroristic', open and fractional, cover organizations, and residential associations. The struggle is hierarchically organized with a tightly defined military command structured according to a forceful and implacable definition of the class enemy. The struggle against the class enemy extends into the institutions of the state across terrains ranging from conventional economic and political struggle to cyber warfare. The powerful democratic impulse characteristic of the Zapatistas is subordinated to the organizational imperatives of a rigidly defined military hierarchy pursuing inflexibly defined objectives. The strategic discussion, again unlike the Zapatistas, is conducted according to the axiom of absolute global class enmity

Yet the tactics of resistance proposed in the Urban Development Plan have many other similarities and differences with the Zapatista indigenous resistance. The resistants are to be 'hidden from enemy surveillance', not by wearing obvious masks but by refraining from exposing themselves 'in small demonstrations where all our activities are easily identified and even videofilmed for easy targeting in the future' (Chakravarti, 385). The classically Maoist strategy of protracted war of resistance here guides the tactic of clandestinity of cadres and organization through infiltration and masking, as opposed to the deliberate performative contradiction of the public masking of the Zapatistas. The party also undertakes responsibility for organising and guiding existing resistances:

Constantly living in precarious conditions, the urban poor naturally come together to help each other and unite within organisations to fight for their rights, to secure better living conditions, to solve problems among themselves and to better organise their social and cultural activities. (Chakravarti, 388)

The emergent spontaneous capacity to resist is to be structured hierarchically and then directed to the end of revolutionary class war. Interestingly, while recognizing that 'we should, to the extent possible, make use of the computers and the internet', the document does not fully understand this as part of a strategy to constitute a global capacity to resist, as with the Zapatistas. The internet will be used 'to further' the military objectives of the revolution, with the emphasis placed on traditional warfare by means of the internet. The model of hacking and sabotage seems most prominent in the document, with the internet regarded as a field of battle rather than a resource for constituting a global capacity to resist: 'we should have the perspective of setting up units with the task of damaging the military and other important networks of the enemy' (Chakravarti, 406). The document thus maintains the adversarial posture of classical Maoism with its telluric ideologically driven struggle for the control of liberated territories intended to serve as bases for a protracted war of resistance.

The resistances in India have, however, provoked an immense counter-resistance which has adopted the form of the manhunt. Notoriously identified as the 'greatest threat to the internal security of the country since independence', Indian Maoism and the Adivasis's resistances to which it gives expression has been subjected to an implacable manhunt. The early phase was relatively informal and local – the Salwa Judum (launched in 2005) – which attempted to destroy the Maoist-controlled bases, using irregular Special Police Officers to pursue not only a manhunt, but also the destruction of terrain in which resistants might find refuge. This systematic but informal reign of terror dedicated to destroying the Adivasis's capacity to resist was succeeded by a formal and centrally controlled military operation. The very title of the Indian government's 'Operation Green Hunt' is a stunning vindication of Chamayou's thesis and almost a textbook case of the manhunt doctrine. It is dedicated to the discovery and assassination of resistants and the destruction of their material, territorial and moral capacity to resist. Secretary of the CPI (Marxist Leninist) Comrade Ajith has identified Operation Green Hunt as a 'war on the people' that

> [...] though directed against the revolutionary war led by the CPI (Maoist), is the spearhead of a broader plan to attack and eliminate a wide range of resistance movements going on all over the country. They include movements against privatisation, displacement, environmental destruction and many others. (Comrade Ajith, *Democracy and Class Struggle*, 33)

The analysis is correct insofar as Operation Green Hunt is directed against the very capacity to resist in all its manifestations and above all its expression in the Maoist party, but errs in classifying it as a *war*. The Indian Government has not so much declared war as an open season on the opposition; Operation Green Hunt is exactly what it claims to be, a *hunt* which does not recognize an enemy to be combated but only prey to be eliminated.

A powerful expression of the ethical outrage but also political disorientation provoked by the explicit and implacable implementation of the manhunt doctrine can be found in Arundhati Roy's *Walking with the Comrades*. She too believes Operation Green Hunt to be a war, but correctly intuits that it might be something even more terrible than that: 'What kind of war is Operation Green Hunt going to be? Will we ever know?' (Roy 2012, 12). She gives a clear analysis of the transformation of a relation of enmity into one of hunter and hunted, showing how the very capacity to resist in India is being redefined as a nuisance to be annihilated, referring to

> [...] the concerted campaign that has been orchestrated to shoehorn the myriad forms of resistance taking place in this country into a simple George Bush binary: if you are not with us you are with the Maoists... the State will use the opportunity to mop up the hundreds of other resistance movements in the sweep of its military operation, calling them all Maoist sympathisers. (Roy 2012, 13)

In the case of this specific reduction of resistances to a Resistance, Roy emphasizes that 'tribal people in central India have a history of resistance that predates Mao by centuries' (Roy 2012, 42) and are now grafting this capacity onto Maoist forms of armed struggle in a wholly understandable and in many ways admirable struggle for survival.

In the face of an implacable state-organized manhunt against its resistant citizens Roy confronts an honest perplexity concerning the question of how to defy and resist such an onslaught:

> But what should I suggest they do? Go to a court? Do a dharna in Jantar Mantar, New Delhi? A rally? A relay hunger strike? It sounds ridiculous. The promoters of the New Economic Policy – who find it so easy to say 'There is No Alternative' – should be asked to suggest an alternative Resistance Policy. A specific one, to these specific people, in this specific forest. Here. Now. (Roy 2012, 88)

The urgency of formulating an alternative resistance policy arises from the hunters being often literally minutes behind their prey, weapons in hand; under such conditions Roy is understandably impatient with any talk of launching a *Satyagraha*:

> 'We're approaching the "Border". Do you know what to do if we come under fire?' Sukhdev asks casually, as though it was the most natural thing in the world. 'Yes,' I said. 'Immediately declare an indefinite hunger-strike.' He sat down on a rock and laughed. (Roy 2012, 145)

Roy indeed comes to regard any appeal to Gandhian strategies as the refuge of scoundrels, mere dishonest procrastination under the conditions of Operation Green Hunt, indulged in by those who have but minimal solidarity to offer the oppressed in India. Those who engage in wider resistance 'may strongly disagree with the Maoists – they may be wary, even exasperated by them – but they *do* see them as a part of the same resistance' (Roy 2012, 194). Yet the dismissal of the classic *Satyagraha* and the tolerance of Maoist armed struggle seems symptomatic of precisely the absence of a repertoire of resistance appropriate to current conditions. However ironically meant, there is indeed a need of an 'alternative resistance policy' that is open to all forms of resistance and yet capable of responding to the deadly conditions of a state counter-resistance organized in terms of the manhunt doctrine.

The Calls to Resistance

Any discussion of the Chiapas and Indian Maoist resistances to global capital in the name of the 'indigenous peoples' cannot help but be struck by the similarity of conditions under which both resistances operate and the difference between the bureaucratic and fixed strategic intelligence of the 'Urban Perspective Plan' and the multiformed, imaginative calls for resistance mounted by the Zapatistas. Manifestos, stories, jokes, masks and tricks point to the careful attention the Chiapas resistance paid to the aesthetics of defiance and the need to perform, however ironically, the role of the insurgent. Yet in this we also saw a profound depersonalization of the resistance – the resistants were speaking and acting for and from the realm of the dead and those yet to be born, as the ghosts of Mayan gods and of Mexican heroes such as Zapata and Villa. The masked resistant became both an international star as well as the anonymous voice of defiance. We saw that this movement between personality and anonymity – a resistance for everyone and no one – also mirrored the strategy of moving between local and global resistance.

One aspect of the performative character of resistance that was raised to perfection by the Zapatistas was the genre of the call to resistance. In the last decade, especially since the defiance of Genoa, the call to resistance has become a living genre, certainly inspired by the Zapatista style but also situating itself within a wider, problematic tradition of such calls. The call has been raised in (Tiqqun's *An Introduction to Civil War* of 2001, in the related *Appel* without declared date or provenance but probably from an Italian matrix in the Black Bloc, in the Invisible Committee's *The Coming Insurrection* (2007) and most recently in Stéphane Hessel's *Indignez Vous!* whose widely disseminated call prompted responses in the Arab Spring, in the resistances of *indignados* in Spain and Mexico, the *aganaktismenoi* in Greece and *Occupy!* in the USA.[8] Given the growing contribution of such calls to an emergent global capacity to resist, it is useful first to reflect on the history of the call to resistance and some of the formal characteristics of the genre, secondly to look briefly at the diverse contents of the calls and their family resemblances, and thirdly to show how the calls respond to and distinguish themselves from each other. As an example of the latter property, Hessel's call for a 'peaceful insurrection' will be read as a conservative response to other calls that preceded it, specifically to the call for insurrection of the Invisible Committee.

The formal properties of the genre of the call to resistance have not received the philosophical analysis that they deserve. In contrast to the

Declaration – analysed by Derrida and Arendt in the case of the American Declaration of Independence and the Manifesto, also analysed by Derrida with the example of the Communist Manifesto in *Spectres of Marx* – the call to resistance does not come from a problematically constituted subject of speech. It is not the bringing into appearance of a caller who was previously invisible or inaudible such as the American people concealed by British colonial domination or the Communist League until now clandestine. The calls to resistance on the whole come from nowhere and, rather in the way Nietzsche described his texts in *Ecce Homo* as 'fishhooks', they are not directed to a defined public. They perform a capacity to resist which, once declared, is actualized. They are, put bluntly, not contemporary and not addressed by or to a specific addressee, but are more testimonies to a capacity to resist in the course of actualizing itself.

A plausible candidate for the inaugural call to resistance is the *Manifeste des Égaux* issued in 1796 by Sylvain Maréchal on behalf of Babeuf and the 'Secret Directory'. Addressed to the people of France (the specific addressee will be less defined in future calls for resistance), the *Manifeste des Égaux* called to resist those who would obstruct or divert the course of the revolution. In calling to resist in the name of equality the conspirators of the Secret Directory vow themselves to a counter-resistance, to resist those who resist the revolutionary promise of equality:

> Very well! We want however to live and die as equal as we are born; we want real equality or death. Here is what must be. And we want this real equality at whatever price. Cursed be whoever tries to resist a vow so pronounced. (Mareschal 1796)

Beyond the recognition of the inextricable relation between resistance and counter-resistance, the call of 1796 foregrounds the role of the vow or 'conjuration' in forming a resistant subjectivity, thus anticipating the centrality of the vow in Gandhi's resistant practice. Also interesting is the place of resistance with respect to this vow: it is a resistance directed against those who would resist the vow. In this call, resistance paradoxically holds the initiative. The conjuration continues with a apocalyptic call for the last, messianic world revolution: 'The French Revolution is but the messenger of another, greater and more solemn revolution that will be the last' (Mareschal 1796). The apocalyptic and messianic tone to the call is echoed in the calls of Tiqqun, *Appel* and the Invisible Committee, which are also directed towards the future. The messianic, post-revolutionary future appears in the 1796 call as a proleptic reference to the future's view of the present; the scandal of inequality that will seem unbelievable to our grandchildren justifies the call to found a new republic:

> The moment has come to found the Republic of equals, that great refuge open to all humans. The days of the last restitution have arrived. Families, come and sit at the common table set by nature for all of its children. (Mareschal 1796)

This apocalyptic sense that the moment of resistance has come, that it is no longer to come, no longer possible but actual, no longer messianic but realized, characterizes the temporality of this and subsequent calls to resistance, perhaps at its most explicit in the 1967 Call to Resist Illegitimate Authority's 'Now is the time to resist'. A further salient feature of such calls is found in their anonymity of address and addressee. The 1796 call compromises this somewhat by its appeal to 'the People' and specifically the people of France, but in the sense that these are the people called to resist inequality and to live the exemplary life of equals: 'People of France, open your eyes and heart to the fullness of happiness; recognise and proclaim with us the Republic of Equals' (Mareschal 1796). The affirmative character of the resistance is striking here, in the sense that it locates any opposition to the Republic of Equals to come firmly in the reactive and resistant position of attempting to obstruct the people's initiative.

Many of these characteristics are also to be found in what is paradoxically (but characteristically for this genre) the best and the least well-known of the calls for resistance, the *Appel du 18 juin 1940* by De Gaulle on the BBC.[9] It is in many ways a classic call for resistance being made by nobody, *Moi* (General De Gaulle was an insignificant minister in the last government of France before the German occupation), and being issued in the name of no-one: it was in short neither a manifesto nor a declaration but a call. It echoes the 1796 call while inverting some key elements of its rhetoric. It establishes an apocalyptic, elemental scenario, only to refuse it: 'We have been, we are submerged by the mechanical force, terrestrial and aerial, of the enemy' (De Gaulle 2007). But the last word has not been said, the same technology that overthrew France will in its turn overthrow the enemy. For this is a world – even a cosmic – war for De Gaulle, for whom 'there are in the universe all the means necessary to one day eliminate our enemies' (De Gaulle 2007: 'il y a, dans l'univers, tous les moyens nécessaire pour écraser un jour nos ennemis'). It is very clear from De Gaulle's broadcast that the call itself actualizes resistance, not just calling for but performing it, igniting the flame and itself serving as the 'weapon of resistance': 'whatever happens the flame of the French resistance must not be extinguished and will not be extinguished' (De

Gaulle 2007). This actualization of resistance by appealing to its necessity is followed by perhaps the most moving and almost liturgical moment of the call: 'Tomorrow, as today, I will speak on the radio from London' (De Gaulle 2007) – in effect a signature of an inaugural moment of resistance that initiates the future series of broadcasts destined to ignite but also fuel the flame of resistance.

De Gaulle literally called to nobody: when broadcast, hardly anyone seems to have heard the call. As the first call to resistance it was not expected and therefore not listened for. A recording does not exist, few claimed to have heard it, yet nevertheless it intangibly created the resistance. The model of a call to resist in hopeless circumstances is evoked in the recent calls, which echo the circumstances of De Gaulle's broadcast – without subject, without legitimacy, from no one to no one and breaking with history. Just as De Gaulle's call would retrospectively speak to the first resistance comprising loose networks pursuing sabotage and the dissemination of information, it also looked forward to its subordination under established military and political procedures by Jean Moulin and the second resistance. It is this second resistance of the CNR and its manifesto *Les jours heureux* that inspired Hessel and continues to guide his idea of the resistance.

Stéphane Hessel chose to end *Indignez Vous!* with a deliberately paradoxical call for a 'peaceful insurrection'. With this appeal he mobilizes a term – insurrection – which in the past decade has become increasingly prominent in political debate and practice. Yet as we shall see, the concept of insurrection remains ill-defined, and not only in Hessel's work: it is still unclear just what kind of political action it refers to and what sort of political mobilization it would pursue. Perhaps the success of Hessel's text may be traced to its appeal to an insurrectionary sentiment at the same time that it ventures a powerful critique of the insurrectionary model. In a way, Hessel repeats his own historical experience of the centralization of the anti-Nazi resistances into the hierarchical form of the Resistance – the focus and organization of the insurrectionary energies of the first resistances into the virtual state of the CNR.

The importance of the experience of the CNR is emphasized from the outset of Hessel's call, which begins with a homage to the achievements of the 1944 programme. Yet implied in this seemingly uncontroversial praise of the CNR is an argument for the containment of insurrection, its control and channelling within the forms of the state. Why though, at this moment, would Hessel return with the historical invocation of the myth of a successful insurrection, one which succeeded precisely because it was brought under the form of the state? Perhaps an answer may be sought in the claim that *Indignez Vous!* is in dialogue with an earlier appeal for insurrection – the call by the Invisible Committee for the coming insurrection that was published in 2007. There are many points where Hessel seems directly to refer to *The Coming Insurrection*, working with and against it in an inconspicuous gesture of solidarity and critique.

The ideas of the Invisible Committee became well known in 2008 with the arrest on November 11th of the Tarnac Nine for 'criminal association for the purposes of terroristic activity' in attacking the French transport network, but what is striking about the presentation of their ideas in *The Coming Insurrection* is its evocation of the 'first resistance'. The Invisible Committee appeals to the historical experience of the Resistance prior to its being brought under the discipline of the CNR: a clandestine community, one dedicated to the dissemination of information, to sabotage, and beset by the problem of 'how do we find each other'. The historic Resistance is evoked and brought into the present with the claim 'We live under an occupation, police occupation' and the problem it poses of how to construct networks of resistance to this occupation. Hessel's *Indignez Vous!* contests this appeal to resistance; for him the Republic born of the Resistance was corrupted and its ethos subverted, but enough survives for it to be defended in the name not of the first, but of the second resistance.

De Gaulle's call to resistance of 18 June 1940 and the manifesto of resistance *Les jours heureux* have a completely different tone and character. Like the former, the calls to resistance by Tiqqun, *Appel* and the Invisible Committee depart from a state of occupation, this time by Empire. In spite of their critiques of Negri, prominent in Tiqqun and the *Appel*, the basic premise that we live under occupation by Empire is a shared point of departure. Yet even while sharing hostility to Empire, the calls for resistance differ widely among themselves. Tiqqun (the term is from the kabbalah, and refers to the small practices and rituals for mending creation and hastening the coming of the Messiah) self-consciously inverts the postulates of Schmitt on the *catechon* holding back civil war by following Benjamin in regarding the *catechon* as part of a civil war that needs to be made visible. Embracing a logic of escalation, Tiqqun calls for a civil war understood in terms of a reading of Agamben's *Homo Sacer* tetralogy as one between conflicting forms of life. It contrasts this position with the latent civil war of Hobbes or the war of each against all which it sees as proposing an 'impoverished ethic' of civil war accepted by Schmitt and other conservative thinkers. In section 74 of *The Introduction to Civil War* this is clarified, with reference to the 'imaginary party' and kabbalistic practice:

> Tiqqun means that each act, conduct and statement endowed with sense – act, conduct and statement as event spontaneously manifests its own metaphysics, its own community, its own party. Civil war simply

means the world is practice, and life is, in its smallest details, heroic. (Tiqqun, 181)

This view of civil war is underwritten by a theory of Bloom, the neutralised hero who improbably assumes the mantle of Lenin and Mao as the understated revolutionary in this work. A similar line is pursued in the *Appel*, where the desert of the present combines features of T. E. Lawrence and Nietzsche's deserts but with the critical proviso: 'some have tried to name the desert. They talked about spectacle, biopower or empire. But this also added to the current confusion' (Anonymous 6). *Appel* sees the British Guerrilla gardening movement that plants in waste urban areas as a model of resistance. Like acts of tiqqun for a kabbalist, small actions add up to a life of resistance that may have consequences of an unpredictable scale. As with the messages, graffiti and clandestine flyers of the first French resistance, these calls are to others to find themselves and to join in friendship and resistance – for the *Appel*, it is a call to leave the desert and walk with Nietzsche's Zarathustra on a high ridge between two seas; what is at stake in this resistance is 'the wager of existence of another term, a thin ridge just enough for us to walk on. Just enough for all who can hear to walk and live' (Anonymous).

Hessel's call contests these contemporary calls to resistance, specifically that of the Invisible Committee. It contests the celebration of insurgent youth that pervades *The Coming Insurrection* with an appeal to the serenity and authority of age. Tiqqun describes the resistant Invisible Committee in its closing pages as 'the name given to the ethic of civil war expressed in these pages. It refers to a specific faction of the imaginary party, its revolutionary, experimental wing' (Tiqqun, 193). To its claim that the coming insurrection is a 'vital possibility of youth', Hessel replies in the opening of his call with: '93 Years. It's a bit like the very last stage. The end is not very far away' (Hessel 2011, 9), claiming not only the detachment of age but also the authority of the historical memory of the resistance: 'the years of the resistance and the programme elaborated sixty six years ago now by the *Conseil nationale de la Résistance*' (Hessel 2011, 9). To the celebration of a politics of friendship and the exclusive use of the '*tu*' by the Invisible Committee, Hessel responds with the republican formality of the '*vous*'. The politics of friendship, whose analysis was pioneered by Derrida in the 1990s, pervades all of the contemporary calls to resistance with the signal exception of Hessel. It is the ethical foundation of the 'Imaginary Party' stated clearly by Tiqqun in section 72 of *Introduction to Civil War*:

The only way to reduce the sphere of hostility is by spreading the ethico-political domain of friendship and enmity. This is why Empire has never been able to reduce this sphere of hostility, despite all its clamourings in the name of peace. The becoming real of the imaginary party is simply the formation – the *contagious* formation – of a plane of consistency where friendships and enmity can freely deploy themselves and make themselves legible to each other. (Tiqqun, 179)

This is a powerful expression of what we might, retrospectively, see as a description of the solidarity and friendship that characterized the first French resistance. Friendship is also central to *Appel*, which declares at the outset, from the desert and the emergent world civil war, that '[f]rom now on all friendship is political' (Anonymous, 9). This informs its tactic, again citing the experience of the first French resistance, of starting 'from small and dense nuclei rather than from a vast and loose network' (*Appel* Anonymous, 9), here evoking Nietzsche's understanding of the micro-politics of friendship. The search for the resistant friend also inspires the strategy of the 'imaginary party' for whom sharing among friends constitutes 'a collection of places, infrastructures, communised means; and the dreams of bodies, murmurs, thoughts, desires that circulate among those places, the *use* of those means, the sharing of those infrastructures' (Anonymous, 46–7) – a communism of friendship that Jean Moulin had earlier called, citing in his turn the last days of the Paris Commune, 'the republic of the catacombs'.

Hessel defends the political importance of the sentiment of indignation against the Invisible Committee's dismissal of it as weak and sentimental. *The Coming Insurrection* begins its exploration of the conditions of the possibility of insurrection by expressly rejecting the power of indignation: 'It's useless to get *indignant* about openly unconstitutional laws… It's useless to get *involved* in this or that citizens group' (The Invisible Committee, 95). Such sceptical indignation is shared by Anonymous and Tiqqun who do not 'count on *sentimentality* for pitiful proselytising' (Anonymous, 16). Instead the Invisible Committee make the claim that we are in a state of barely dissembled war and that this war must be made visible. The sentiment of indignation is insufficient to motivate the constructive work of affirmative resistance: what kind of insurrection, in short, would be motivated by indignation? Affirmative resistance is actualized through friendship and the invention of a form of life or a commune that complements the calls for mobility and the removal of 'obstacles' to movement.

It is at this point in *The Coming Insurrection* that the Gramscian inspiration of the Invisible Committee becomes most salient. Their call tries to come to terms with the conceptual tension inherent in very notion of insurrection. It is *stasis* or the state of perpetual uprising understood as a balance between a war of mobility and a war of position. An insurrection works at levels of both surface and depth – mobility across a surface combined with consolidation in depth – or, in the case of the Invisible Committee, with the removal of obstacles to movement across a surface and the development of the commune or society of friendship: 'The commune is the basic unit of partisan reality. An insurrectional surge may be nothing more than a multiplication of communes, their coming into contact and forming of ties' (The Invisible Committee, 117).

Hessel responds to this call with an appeal to a different insurrection. His call for a 'peaceful insurrection' is prefaced by a reference to the Palestinian struggle, but not to the classic insurrection of the *Intifada*, but to a passive resistance that appeals for the support 'of all those in the world who are the enemies of oppression' (Hessel, 2011, 20). It quickly becomes apparent that Hessel's insurrection is an ethical movement manifest at a global level through diplomacy and the work of international institutions as, for example, decolonization, the end of apartheid, the fall of the Berlin Wall or the work of the United Nations. His closing call to insurrection both echoes and substitutes for that of the Invisible Committee; he calls resistent citizens to:

> a veritable peaceful insurrection against the means of mass communi-
> cation that propose to our youth as their horizon mass consumption,
> contempt for the weakest and a culture of general amnesia and the
> extreme competition of all against all. (Hessel 2011, 22)

This is an insurrection launched against the means of communications, but not the physical system of communications allegedly targeted by the Invisible Committee. Hessel is far from calling for the destruction of mass communications technology, but rather an insurrection against the ethical and cultural values proposed by that technology. It is thus an insurrection of debate and discussion, hence a peaceful insurrection, but one which, echoing Gandhi, for Hessel possesses an ethical force. It would resist by reoccupying the times and spaces of oppression through a politics of memory; in reviving the CNR's welfare programme, occupying public space, challenging the content of the media and the culture of mass consumption.

The concept of insurrection has become the shared ground between the very different calls for insurrection issued by Stéphane Hessel and the Invisible Committee. Yet the question remains of what it is about this concept that makes it so prominent in contemporary political discourse. Ironically for Hessel, it is probably the promise of consistency without excessive organization and the combination of tactics and spontaneity made possible by the concept of insurrection that makes it so important for the calls to resistance, from the Secret Directory through the first French resistance to the politics of friendship that emerged after Genoa. Insurrection points beyond individual acts of resistance to a sustained and coherent actualization of a capacity to resist that nevertheless requires a very low level of organization and consequently very little recourse to hierarchical structures. The insurrectional *community* is precisely that: a league of the just or a commune of friends. As a political model insurrection also evokes the gesture of defiance, but emphasizing a sustained uprising rather than the instrumental, goal-directed activity of revolution. Insurrection is resistant but not constituent, opening spaces rather than constituting them and mobilizing a rhetoric of action, even violent action, to inspire its uprisings. Perhaps it is now a more salient term than revolution, with its promise of completed movement, placing beside this a sense of sustained defiance appealing to a capacity to resist that can disappear, return or re-emerge later and elsewhere, always surging up, resistant in the face of counter-resistance.[10]

The Technology of Resistance

Any reflection on the contemporary capacity to resist must consider the question of the technology of resistance, and in particular the contribution of digital technology. But this question is afflicted to an even greater degree by the difficulties and perplexities that already inform the question of technology. It is striking, for instance, that Schmitt does not mention in *Theory of the Partisan* that a 'partisan' was originally a weapon or an innovation in the field of early modern military technology.[11] The question of the relation of resistance and technology, while omnipresent, has until recently rarely been explicitly thematized. It is implicit in the theory of non-violent resistance, which avoids the use of weapons technology, but as part of wider cultural suspicion of the technological. However, the question of the role played by digital technology in the recent resistances of the Arab Spring, the *Indignado*s, Occupy Wall Street and the 'Taksim Republic' has focused attention on the broader question of the relation between resistance and technology. It is important to try and think through this relationship in order to understand and assess the state of the contemporary, global capacity to resist and its possible futures.[12]

The approach to this question is complicated not only by the realization that the concept of resistance is still relatively ill-understood but also that the question of technology itself remains unanswered since Heidegger and Simondon. If we add to this the rapidly changing recent history both of

digital technology and recent resistance movements then the methodo-
logical obstacles to a philosophical reflection on resistance and technology
appear formidable. One way to begin, at least, is to propose some preliminary theses that might guide an approach to the question of technology
and resistance and, with this, help in understanding the emergence of the
technical features now investing the capacity to resist. The first adopts
a position proposed by Simondon in his analysis of technical objects
and taken further by Bernard Stiegler in *Technics and Time*, namely that
technology is a milieu or an ecology: it is not something extraneous to the
definition of the human and used instrumentally, but is constitutive of it.
The human, in other words, is 'essentially' prosthetic; we are in many senses
our own technological objects. Furthermore, technology may be understood as a milieu or medium in which resistance is now crucial; if we listen
again to Heidegger's proposition that 'the essence of technology is nothing
technical', we can add that it is perhaps resistant. If this is extended to the
milieu of digital technology, it becomes possible to view the network as a
technical milieu defined in terms of internal resistances; a network is by
definition a sum of paths and obstacles that realize and restrict movement
and stasis.

To the thesis that the technical milieu is itself a site of resistance might
be added the views of Weber and Foucault that politics, governance, itself
is a technology and that the ways in which we are dominated and resist
are themselves thoroughly technical. A corollary of this is that technology
is inseparably allied with violence, both of domination and of resistance,
and may indeed become an important theatre for the struggle between
them. If with Stiegler technics is 'apprehended as the horizon of all possibility to come and of all possibility of a future' (Stiegler 1998, ix), then
struggles within it and for it entail important consequences for any future
of resistance.

In his analysis of legitimate domination undertaken in *Economy and
Society*, especially the short chapter 'On Discipline', Weber proposed a
typology of legitimate domination comprising traditional, charismatic
and legal-rational domination defined in terms of probable expectations
of obedience. The considerations of probability and expectation situate
legitimate domination within a technical context of reliable and predictable
action and allow the ideal types to be considered as milieus of obedience.
To the quality of legitimate domination may be added its intensity. The
ideal types may also be understood as inverse indexes of the capacity to
resist: a high level of legitimate domination corresponds to a low capacity
to resist, a high capacity to low domination. Where the capacity to resist is
high, the expectation of obedience is correspondingly low. The reciprocal

relation of obedience and defiance is an expression of the density of the milieu or network within which action takes place. The type of legitimate domination may be understood in terms of coherences and stability of networks, with the level of domination depending on the coherence of the network: when coherence is high, that is, when routes within and entry points into a network are strictly defined, then the expectation of obedience or domination is high and the capacity to resist correspondingly low.[13]

The ideal type of traditional legitimate domination presents a coherent and stable network of kin and relations of fealty that infuse military and property regimes (feudalism). The expectation of probable obedience is high and the capacity to resist correspondingly low. Charismatic domination, by contrast, is characterized by a rudimentary unstable network in which obedience is not predictable and has to be repeatedly solicited and rewarded. In 'On Discipline' Weber effectively described the quality, intensity and hence the capacity to resist of the modern network of legal rational domination that he saw emerging in Europe from a ensemble of discrete but interlocking revolutions of the early-modern period. These comprised the military revolution of the sixteenth and seventeenth centuries with technological developments in firearms, partisans, siege and fortifications (see Drake, 2002 for an outstanding study of these developments), new forms of hierarchical organization, the religious revolution of the Reformation inseparable from the technology of print and the dissemination of the printed word, the administrative revolution of the modern state with the creation of bureaucratic forms of rule and its corresponding archives, and the industrial revolution with capital accumulation, the concentration of ownership of the means of production and the institution of hierarchical forms of productive enterprise. Retrospectively the conditions of possibility of all these revolutions appears as an alliance of violence and technology tending towards the creation of networks with a high degree of coherence and stability expressed in a concentration tending towards unification or monopoly. The state is defined by Weber in terms of the monopoly of violence, capital as the concentration of wealth and ownership. Domination, then, is an outcome of the insertion of subjects within a network that tends towards complete subsumption or the 'iron cage', yet without completely extinguishing the capacity to resist.

Domination and resistance can be understood as coefficients of the structure and density of a technological network or milieu. A network facilitates movement at specified speeds along specified routes in specified directions with decreed points of entry and exit and internal linkages. It is embodied memory structured according to past routes and decreeing the range of future passages. Resistance takes place within and against these networks and can be expressed by varying the speed of passage through protraction, acceleration and stasis or through *détournement* or the change of direction by deviating from specified routes, making unsanctioned entrances and exits, feigning position or even exiting the network altogether. These moves stated in the context of a network immediately evoke the internet and hacking, but such phenomena should be viewed as part of a wider phenomenon of resistance conducted on the terrain of the technical milieu or network of domination.

Technology as the organization of events through the disposition of energy adopts many forms, nearly all of which approximate to a particular network/milieu or field. One important technology is writing which, with the archive, becomes the condition of possibility for the development of another network which is law. In its monarchic form, the king is the focus of these networks, which is grafted on to networks of military force, fealty and property ownership. The intersecting revolutions examined by Weber in 'On Discipline' display a greater extension of network/milieus coupled with their intensification. The effect of the meshing of military, economic, political and religious networks is an increase in the probability of obedience and a corresponding reduction in the capacity to resist and the probability of defiance. In the field of governance, the technology of rule known as bureaucracy archivizes a territory, the subjects that occupy that territory and the events that take place on it. The governance of time and space and the enhancement of the probability of obedience depend ultimately on the securing and constant resecuring of a territory by military force or the technology of violence. Bureaucratic governance presupposes the violent securing of its field of operations, the condition of its smooth running is the modern state's claim to a monopoly of the means of violence. Routine resistance to bureaucratic domination can quickly escalate into all out defiance of this monopoly. The securing of rule by means of the bureaucratic/military technical milieu is a condition of possibility for the extension of market relations based on private property that in turn enhance the infrastructure and provide the resources necessary for rule and production. Here we can speak of a network for the movement of property, whether property in goods (raw materials, finished commodities) or property in labour power (movement of populations). Such movement is facilitated and governed by a transport and communications network made up of roads, rail, air routes, telegraph, telephone, wireless, power lines and satellites. The establishment and extension of such networks of movement and accumulation constitutes a traumatic moment of nineteenth-century modernity, which left a technological milieu for the movement of goods, populations and information that served as a technology of rule, but also as a theatre of resistance.

The network/milieu of bureaucratic rule and the movement of living and dead commodities was intensified by the electromagnetic revolution of the nineteenth century pioneered in the work of James Clark Maxwell. The description of the electromagnetic field unleashed a technological revolution that led rapidly to the invention of means of transmitting and receiving energy and information. Central to this revolution was the translation of information into energy and its movement – or transmission via telephone and telegraph lines, radio, television – and subsequent retranslation back into information. This made possible the powerful network/milieus of communication that still underlie the contemporary internet and provide an increasingly important site for resistance. All these intersecting but not necessarily compatible networks/milieus provide the ecology in which human life increasingly takes place: medical, political, educational, cultural, religious subjectivities are dominated and resist, live and/or die in this milieu.[14]

The invention and imposition of such complex and intersecting networks lead to conflicts and centrifugal and centripetal tendencies, towards concentration and monopoly and towards dispersion and plurality, in other words, of domination and defiance. The network of domination is as much a network of resistance, with the Clausewitzian duel appearing as the surface effect of the properties of a network or collision of networks. The coefficient of domination and resistance is determined by the openness and closure of such networks; it depends too on the degree of facility of access and movement within them, making such networks not only the theatre of resistance and domination but also an object to be resisted or dominated. Domination maintains as far as possible the consistency and concentration of the network, controlling the speeds with which it may be traversed, the points of entry and exit and the directions that can be followed, accreditation of identity and assurance of position. Surveillance, control, security are the names given to this consistency. Resistance involves the discovery of unauthorized speeds, directions, routing and place within these networks, or in Clausewitz's terms the opposition of the vaporous warfare of the guerrilla to the concentrated and carefully routed liquid flows of imperial violence. This is the terrain of the telluric that Schmitt identified as the milieu of the partisan; it is the territory on and in which domination attempts to reduce the capacity to resist and is in turn resisted. Keeping such networks, roads, telephones, radio etc. open and traversable is one of the roles of resistance that places it in an alliance with democratic movements which pursue the same aims and use the same means. Such resistance also serves – and this was the insight of Foucault – to refine and test both the resilience of legitimate domination and the capacity to resist.

Digital Resistance

The technical network for the movement of information or the internet has become a crucial site for contemporary resistance. However, it had from the outset a Janus face, enhancing as much the capacity to dominate as the capacity to resist, a tension that quickly assumed a global dimension. A genealogy of the internet quickly makes this clear by showing its origin in the neo-Clausewitzian doctrine of creating a capacity to resist capable of surviving a nuclear first strike. The strategists of the Cold War understood their conflict in terms of the Clausewitzian duel and the actualization of absolute war. The emergence of a war of deterrence placed in the foreground the question of the survival of the capacity to resist and with it this dimension of Clausewitz's thought. In the context of an actualized absolute war made possible by nuclear weaponry, it became vital to ensure the survival of the capacity to resist in the event of a nuclear first strike. The internet was designed to survive a nuclear first strike and by making the survivability of a capacity to resist known to the adversary, would reduce the possibility of that first strike.

The origins of the internet may be traced directly to neo-Clausewitzian concerns with preserving the capacity to resist. The institutional matrix of the early research and development of the web was provided by the strategic nuclear research conducted within the RAND Corporation, founded in 1946 as a strategic think tank for the conduct of nuclear war and largely funded by the US Air Force, and later the US Defence Department's Advanced Research Projects Agency (ARPA), founded in 1958 in response to the Soviet Union's launch of the Sputnik.[15] The RAND Corporation was an important centre for the application of Clausewitzian strategies to the scenario of nuclear warfare. Although this was a very different Clausewitz from the theorist of resistance discussed in this book, the principle of the capacity to resist was carried over into the nuclear scenario. It was transformed into the problem of being able to survive a first nuclear strike and maintain the operational capacity to mount a nuclear 'counter-attack' or resistance.

Central to the constitution of this capacity was the survival of a system of 'command and control', and with it a survivable system of communications. Paul Baran's work at RAND from 1959 addressed precisely this problem and theorized survivable networks, originally AM radio stations and subsequently computers communicating digitally. Baran's work was public domain in order to ensure – in the Clausewitzian spirit of deterrence – that the enemy would know of and also imitate the technical conditions for the survival of the capacity to resist. While emerging directly from a neo-Clausewitzian context, Baran's ideas subsequently joined forces with ARPA's attempts to maximize computer use by researchers by means of remote time-sharing. The capacity to resist a nuclear attack sought in a survivable network subsequently developed in directions which far exceeded the original context of surviving a nuclear first strike.

The conditions of the possibility for the survival of the capacity to resist under nuclear attack were frankly paradoxical. The preservation of a centralized and hierarchical command structure capable of ordering a nuclear counter-attack ('resistance' in this scenario) required the creation of a decentralized and non-hierarchical network of communications that was not vulnerable to attack. The paradox continued and continues to inform the character of the capacity to resist that defines the net. In many ways it repeats Clausewitz's dilemma of resistance: the most effective form of resistance to a solid/static or liquid/mobile enemy was the vaporous, non-hierarchical form of guerrilla warfare, yet he and his contemporaries were aware that this form of resistance could quickly escape the control of the regular army and undermine the very hierarchy that it was intended to defend. An analogous phenomenon informed the early history of the net, with a tension emerging between the dispersed nodes and free traffic between them necessary to sustain a nuclear capacity to resist and the restriction and secrecy required by the military in actualising the state's claim to a monopoly of violence.

The tension between hierarchical enclosure (whether political or commercial) and commons characterizes the history of the net and subsequently the web. From embodying the capacity to resist a nuclear strike, the net and subsequently the web became itself a site for resistance. An early focus of such struggles involved the dissemination of the net and the number of nodes of permitted access. The prototype network of the ARPANET communicating packets of digital information between nodes through a subsystem of message-switching computers connected by telephone lines was joined in the late 1960s by radio-based and subsequently satellite transmission. These systems, developed under military/academic auspices, were further linked to other national and international networks. As a system of military communications – the core of the capacity to resist nuclear attack – ARPANET had to have guaranteed reliability; its reliability had repeatedly to be put to the test and maximized. The possibility of the system overloading and crashing (obviously inconvenient in the context of responding to a nuclear first strike) required that the network be extended and its traffic disposed in such a way that would minimize the probability of it overloading. The obvious way was to extend the network by joining it with others – an 'internetwork' – and devolving transmission and reception of messages to host computers (Naughton 2000, 157–9). The new system worked out by V. G. Cerf and R. B. Kahn involved transmitting datagrams that could move between the different networks but which were indifferent to content. The new system was tested in a simulation of 'mobile battlefield environment' largely because 'the Defence Department was paying for this' (Cerf, cited in Naughton, 164), linking computers in the US, Norway and the UK via radio, satellite and telephone line. The dissemination and devolution intrinsic to the internet was made possible by a transmission control protocol which specified the datagram and the Internet Protocol which identified individual computers. The former were content-neutral while the latter testified to the decentralization of the internet as part of a deliberate strategy to ensure the survival of the capacity to resist in the context of nuclear escalation or the actualisation of absolute war.

The internet provided a solution to the military problem of the reliability and hence the predictability of the network's capacity to resist, but in a way that required the decentralization of the network. This 'vaporization' of the capacity to resist or the creation of a virtual guerrilla network intrinsic to the architecture of the internet had further implications. The principle of basing the network in individual computers with operating systems conforming to internet protocols allowed for the creation of unofficial networks such as the lo-tech Usenet. The launch of Usenet in 1980 antici- pated the later 'social web' in being oriented towards communication, discussion and newsgroups whose content was not subject to any central control. It raised the possibility of a democratic forum which, accompanied by other developments such as graphic interfaces that made entering the net easier and the World Wide Web that widened access to archived files, was believed to point to the actualization of a new, digital democracy.

A capacity to resist the extreme challenge of absolute war required a network that maximized the number of entry and exit points, nodes, routes and speed of passage, or in other words also maximized the capacity for self- resistance. From its origins as a communications network that would ensure the survival of the capacity to resist a nuclear first strike and thus an essential element in the strategy of nuclear deterrence, the net and subsequently the web became a decentralized means of communication and access to memory that constituted a site of resistance in its own right. Resistance within the net/ web can broadly be understood in terms of opposition to the hierarchical tendencies that emerge from political and commercial logics that infiltrate its decentralized military grammar. The intersection but also interferences of the web with and by the networks of government and market produce tensions manifest in attempts to censor or politically control the web and in the prolif- eration of filters reducing access in the name of rationalized consumption.

The tensions are manifest in the two strategies of resistance pursued on the internet: resistance in depth which operates in the terrain of the archive, and resistance on the surface that exploits the proliferation of nodes in order to multiply transversal links. The former works at the level of access to archives or concentrations of information, hacking and disrupting or revealing hoarded and encrypted secrets, as in the case of the work of Wikileaks. Such efforts divert the resources of encryption used in the interest of domination into decryption and the revealing of secrets. The other possibility of resistance does not directly address political or commercial archives, but, by maximizing the number of links between nodes, enhances communication, making it difficult to assure political control of the dissemination and discussion of information. This plays a significant role in delegitimizing domination by making it available for scrutiny and comment from a variety of perspectives, potentially contesting the tendency towards monopolization of information, wealth, power and ultimately violence essential to legal rational or even total domination.[16]

The concentration of power and wealth has become the object of contemporary resistance, whether in the slogans of Genoa 'You are Eight, we are Six Billion' or in Occupy's 'We are the 99%'. These are radically delegitimizing claims, classic gestures of resistance, but are not necessarily revolutionary. While this delegitimation of domination or defiance is enabled by the internet, it is also threatened by it. In *The Revolution will be Digitised: Despatches from the Information War* (2011) Heather Brooke sees very clearly that 'We have the technology to build a new type of democracy but equally we might create a new type of totalitarianism' (Brooke, xi). Yet her 'equally' betrays an optimism that allows her to imagine that the internet will enable 'the world's first global peoples uprising,' the creation of the 'first global democracy' and even 'the next leap of evolution … from a divided to a united species' (Brooke, 238). Her main interlocutor Julien Assange is less sanguine about the 'equally', seeing instead a steady erosion of freedom on the internet; there is the chance of a digital democratic revolution, but it is certainly not equal to the more probable emergence of a 'new type of totalitarianism' or total domination. While there yet remains the possibility of resistance, the revolution is increasingly improbable. Assange sees this 'erosion' – perhaps too neutral a term for the reassertion of domination and the effort to compromise the digital capacity to resist – as taking place primarily at the level of political control with a reassertion of political monopoly over the movement of information. Conversely, Elie Parker and inventor of the World Wide Web Tim Berners-Lee see the tightening of the net in terms of a combination of political and corporate control.[17] In both cases the reassertion of legitimate domination corresponds to a diminution in the capacity to resist, a tension intrinsic as we have seen to the very architecture of the web and net.

The recent politics of resistance has pursued a strategy of delegitimation which is at the same time a politics of the enhancement of the capacity to resist. This was explicitly declared as a political objective in Sharp and Jenkins's influential *Anti-Coup* (2003). *Anti-Coup* describes a non-violent strategy of resistance aimed at delegimizing tyrannical government by making government unworkable and enhancing the capacity to resist over the long term through strikes, public manifestations, dissemination of information and sabotage. The internet can contribute to this in varying degrees, but it is itself subject to the same reciprocal of domination and defiance with which it must engage. In Noam Chomsky's *Occupy* (2012), defiance or the opposition to domination is central to the movement: 'Concentration of wealth yields concentration of political power. And concentration of political power gives rise to legislation that increases and accelerates the cycle' (Chomsky 2012, 28), but the role of the internet in mobilizing, connecting (and infiltrating) the Occupy movement is completely ignored. For Chomsky, '[t]here's nothing to stop all kinds of action, from educating and organizing to political action, to demonstrations. All kinds of resistance are possible, the kinds of things that have succeeded in the past' (Chomsky, 92). The repertoire of tried and tested resistances including industrial resistance, the civil rights movement, the women's movement, anti-colonial resistance and the sexual resistances is now joined by digital resistance and together constitute a capacity to resist with its own history and fate. The newcomer can catalyse existing resistances and enhance their overall capacity, but it should not be forgotten that it is itself engaged in an internal struggle between domination and defiance that in turn requires the support of the broader constituency of resistance.

Contemporary resistance, even in its most technologically sophisticated manifestations, is not an exception to the rules governing the politics of resistance. It is engaged in defiant delegitimization of existing and potential domination but without any prospect of a final outcome in the guise of a revolutionary or reformist result or solution. As reciprocals, domination and defiance are engaged in a perpetual struggle in which resistance can never rest but must adopt a fresh posture with respect to a strengthened counter-resistance. The politics of resistance is disillusioned and without end, one that can claim a lifetime or a life for its pursuit of justice and that requires constant courage, fortitude and prudence. It accompanies the modern adventure of freedom and possibility, but in its ambivalent and ambiguous margins. Yet the defiant life is not negative, not just the reaction to the ruses of an eternally renewed effort to dominate nested within freedom itself, but one with its own necessities, its own affirmations and its own joy.

AFTERWORD: OUTSIDE THE LAW

Only resistance can destroy the pressures that cause reactionary suicide.

(HUEY P. NEWTON)

Kafka's parable *Before the Law,* written soon after the outbreak of the First World War, is among many other things an exemplary meditation on the success and failure of resistance. First published in the journal *Selbstwehr (Self-Defence)* following the debacle of the collapse of solidarity between the Prague Jewish community and the Galician Jewish refugees 'from the country', it reappeared in the 1917 collection *A Country Doctor,* placed between a story of the military occupation of 'the fatherland' that lamented the absence of any capacity to resist the invaders ('A Page from an Old Document') and the story of the futile conspiracy of the Jackals against the Arabs ('Jackals and Arabs'). It appeared again as the object of a commentary in the sermon that marks the end of Josef K's resistance to the court and the prelude to his execution 'like a dog'. As a parable of resistance and counter-resistance, *Before the Law* gives a lesson in how to resist but also in how to be resisted. The Doorkeeper's resistance to the incursion of the Man from the Country succeeds, that of the Man from the Country against the Doorkeeper fails and his compromised capacity succumbs to death.

The opening scenario of *Before the Law* formally parallels the scene of defiance described by Lapoujade and Sartre. Consistent with the etymology of resistance in *stare* or standing, Kafka begins by telling us that 'Before the law *stands (steht)* a doorkeeper'. The Doorkeeper resists entry to the law, and in this capacity arrests the movement of the Man from the Country. Within the first two lines we are in that same peculiar space and time when police and protesters come to a stand evoked by Sartre and analysed by Clausewitz in terms of a duel. The initiative of the Man from the Country is resisted by the Doorkeeper and both find themselves in the predicament described by Clausewitz as war. The Man from the Country is a poor strategist; his first tactical error consists in conceding initiative to the Doorkeeper by *requesting* admittance, meeting a refusal which cleverly invites precaution against escalating enmity. The enmity between the Doorkeeper and the Man from the Country, who find themselves in a classic Clausewitzian duel formation, is defused by the Doorkeeper's reformist gesture of refusing admittance *now* but leaving open the possibility of an entry to the law *later*.

The modality of possibility is not consistent with resistant subjectivity; resistant subjects are not free, they *must* inhabit actuality, and yet the Man from the Country allows himself to be diverted into the realm of the possible. He reflects on the Doorkeeper's reply and, further conceding the initiative, asks if he will be 'allowed' to enter later and whether the possibility that he has been offered will ever be actualized and, if so, when. The Doorkeeper consolidates his diversion of the Man from the Country into the realm of possibility by repeating 'it is possible', thus further testing the Man from the Country's capacity to resist, this time with the feint of stepping aside as if to concede initiative and challenging the Man from the Country to enter. Failing to move, the Man from the Country confirms the growing domination of the Doorkeeper, which is but the inverse of his own waning defiance. The Doorkeeper then augments his domination with an appeal to terror, describing a hierarchy of Doorkeepers united in their enmity to the Man from the Country and of which he himself is but the lowest and weakest. This gesture of deterrence or glimpse of the possibility of an absolute war against an escalating adversary that awaits him if he tries to proceed confirms the Man from the Country's sense of the lonely futility of his own resistance. The Doorkeeper then engages a protracted war of resistance directed against the Man from the Country's fading capacity to resist. In terror he decides to wait while his capacity to resist slowly withers away. He is offered a stool and so finds himself no longer standing before the law and his enemy, but sitting beside it, no longer at the same height as his adversary but below and subordinate to him. In the protracted 'armed observation' that follows, the Man from the Country slowly declines and all his attempts to regain the initiative – questions, bribery, observation – are revealed as but reactive responses to the secured initiative of the Doorkeeper.

The last strategic insight of the Man from the Country emerges only as his capacity to resist approaches its point of exhaustion, that is to say – too late. It marks a last glimpse of the actuality of resistance, the light in the growing darkness not of the law but of the shared predicament of resisting. He cannot be the only resistant, for everyone 'strives for the law', everyone is moving towards the doorway. And yet no one else has come to this door. It is the realization *in extremis* that his resistance has been diverted by being individualized, that in actuality there are many other resistants, perhaps each more powerful than the last, of which he is perhaps 'the lowliest', and that together they would be a match for all the Doorkeepers. Instead of retreating to *ressentiment* and assuming the hunted posture of one closely observing and responding to the initiatives of his persecutor, he should have pursued the solidarity of the other resistants, aligned his own individual with a shared capacity to resist. He should have asked earlier the whereabouts of the other resistants, asked if only he or if the others too had been diverted to this gateway of possibility. He should have sought *them*, and not the law. Had he somehow sought and communicated with the others, perhaps they too arrested in fascinated decline before their own Doorkeepers and gates of possibility, then together they could have realized that those gates were not worth entering and so resumed their movements and lives outside that law. For in this scenario of resistance, the initiative was always with the Doorkeeper: the Man from the Country's resistance fails, this entrance was intended only for him to fail to enter, and his defeat, which is but the inverse of the Doorkeeper's victory, is sealed by the closing of the door.

Athens, July 2013

NOTES

October 27th 1960

1 Cited in Matthew Cobb, *The Resistance: The French Fight against the Nazis,* Simon and Schuster, London 2009, p.159

2 Judith Butler in *Precarious Life: the Powers of Mourning and Violence* (2004) reflects on the implications for the theory and practice of resistance of the dissolution of the juridical model and the elaboration of 'extra-legal powers' exercised through tribunals and detention camps, an inquiry with very different implications from the strategic model intimated by Foucault.

3 One of the rare attempts to elaborate a 'theory of resistance,' Rolf Schroers' *Der Partisan: Ein Beitrag zur politischen Anthropologie* correctly insists that resistance is a 'different category to that of revolution' (Schroers, 18) but underestimates both its ability to graft itself on to other expressions of political power and to persist over extended periods of time.

4 The main theorist of routine, everyday resistance is James C. Scott, whose ethnography in Malaysia disclosed an invisible resistance: 'The resistance I have discovered is not linked to any larger political movements, ideologies, or revolutionary cadres, although it is clear that similar struggles have been occurring in virtually every village in the region...such forms of resistance are the nearly permanent, continuous, daily strategies of subordinate rural classes under difficult conditions...They are the stubborn bedrock upon which other forms of resistance may grow, and they are likely to persist after such other forms have failed or produced, in turn, a new pattern of inequality.' (Scott 1985, 273). This bedrock of resistance, what Vernant would describe as 'cunning' and Scott as 'Brechtian' or 'Schweykian' strategies consist in 'foot dragging, dissimulation, false compliance, pilfering, feigned ignorance, slander, arson, sabotage and so forth.' (Scott, 1985,

29) See also Scott 1990, 172–182 for a reflection on the 'carnival' of resistance.

5   For an example of the carnivalesque in the unlikely context of the German urban guerrilla movement of the late 1960s, see Bommi Bauman's memoir of the June 2nd Movement, an experience cited in recent calls to resistance, *Wie alles Anfing* (1975).

6   Vernant was a charismatic commander in the southern Resistance subsequently honoured by the French state as a *Compagnon de la Libération*. He produced a short memoir of his life in the Resistance, 'Un temps unsoumis', towards the end of his life, included in his collection *La Traversée des frontières 2004*.

Chapter 1: Conscious Resistance

1   See Hahlweg 1986 for an overview of the development of Clausewitz's theory of guerrilla war.

2   Goya's own title for the portfolio of engravings was more specific: 'The Fatal Consequences of the Bloody War mounted by Spain against Bonaparte and other Striking Caprices'.

3   The discovery that Clausewitz was above all a thinker of the war of resistance was made almost simultaneously by the resistant Raymond Aron (1976 and 2005) and Carl Schmitt (1980), both through reflections on Clausewitz's legacy to the Marxist tradition and specifically to the Maoist version of the People's War.

4   The full definition reads: 'War is nothing but a duel on an extensive scale. If we would conceive as a unit the countless number of duels which make up a war, we shall do so best by supposing to ourselves two wrestlers. Each strives by physical force to compel the other to submit to his will: each endeavours to overthrow his adversary, and thus render him incapable of further resistance.' It extends the model of pure bipolar enmity in the duel to all warfare and foregrounds the Kantian notion of capacity or *Fähigkeit*.

5   The most striking example of the application of Clausewitz's lessons to a war of resistance is the Polish resistance first to Tsarist and subsequently National Socialist invasion, central to which was the preservation and enhancement of the present and future national capacity to resist.

6   Paul Virilio is one of the few to emphasise the distance between Hegel and Clausewitz and to propose a neo-Clausewitzian theory of modernity.

Unfortunately his vision of military apocalypse intimated in *Speed and Politics* does not fully account for the dimension of resistance in Clausewitz and as a consequence the second part of his *Popular Defence and Ecological Struggles* (1990) devoted to 'revolutionary resistance' remains abstract and even sentimentally nostalgic.

7   While Clausewitz thinks consistently in terms of opposition, there is little hint of any resolution. Indeed the opening propositions of the first chapter of *On War* theorize the complete annihilation of one pole of what might seem a dialectical opposition. This distinguishes him from Hegel, as does his hostility to Napoleon, in sharp contrast with Hegel's admiration for the 'world spirit on horseback' (an incarnational figure of world history later central to Kojève's influential reading of Hegel in the 1930s).

8   Paret describes the compositional logic of *On War* with characteristic precision: 'Within the eight books and 128 chapters and sections of *On War* dozens of major and minor themes are introduced, developed, compared and combined. Arguments are repeated and tested in different contexts; two or more theses are brought into interaction; an idea is defined with extreme one-sided clarity, to be varied chapters later and given a new dimension as it blends with other propositions and observations' (Paret 2007, 365). It is jazz in place of the Hegelian symphony, a series of skirmishes rather than a linear planned campaign.

9   Paret and Howard's translation is at this point more a gloss than a translation, albeit a very good gloss: *Politik* becomes 'political conditions' and *Energie* 'a degree of energy'.

10 Clausewitz first approached the problem of theorizing resistance through his lectures at the Berlin Military Academy on the established military doctrine of *petit guerre* or the irregular adjunct to regular warfare and the peculiar characteristics of mountain warfare.

11 The painting of the Colossus or Giant complements the *Disasters of War* – but as Todorov in his reading of Goya insists, it is unclear whether it represents the Spanish people, Napoleon, the God of War, or all of these (Todorov 2011, 169). 'Saturn Devouring his Children' can also be viewed as an allegory of actuality consuming possibility.

12 Some of the photographs emerging from the Cretan resistance during the Second World War bear an uncanny resemblance to some of the disasters, see Kokonas 2004.

13 Jake and Dinos Chapman, *Like a Dog Returns to its Vomit* (cat.) White Cube 2005, 35.

14 Todorov's reading of the spatial and temporal disorientation of the image underlines the breakdown of the distinction between military and civil populations: 'Is it the effect of a cannon ball which has destroyed the house?…It is not only human beings that have been massacred but also the space in which they lived – but also those in which the painter and the spectators of the images lived' (Todorov 2011, 155).

15 See the introduction to *Goya Penseur* for Todorov's view of Goya's attempt to think in painting, his 'pictorial revolution' which allowed him to bring into representation the new imagery provoked by resistance to Napoleon. The question of whether the engravings are based on direct testimony is not resolved by the few preliminary drawings that have survived. These seem to be specific studies of the light and shade contrasts of the engravings, with possible exceptions such as the preparatory drawing for engraving 11 (Lecaldano, 31). The sketches for engraving 7 are particularly interesting in this respect, since they seem to move from a very rapid drawing to a blocked out preparatory sketch for the engraving. However, this is one of the few engravings of a specific historic event – an episode from the siege of Saragossa – which it is very unlikely that Goya could have witnessed at first hand (Lecaldano, 23).

16 This text was particularly important for Schmitt's reading of Clausewitz and his revision of the *Concept of the Political* in the direction of a theory of the global partisan.

17 Aron reports Clausewitz's admiration for the Spanish in 1809 who pinned down half of the Napoleonic army through guerrilla warfare (1976a, 54). Clausewitz himself observed: 'So is it in Spain. The French have the half of their entire force in Spain, namely 300,000 men…and they fight their main battles against Wellington with about 40–50,000 men: all the rest are used in keeping the insurrectionary troops apart and preventing the unification of the insurrectionary forces.' (Clausewitz 1966, 732). Paret mentions his considering joining the British to fight in Spain in 1809 when he also began to study 'the possibility of popular uprisings throughout Germany in support of the Austrian armies' (Paret 2007, 144). These studies included papers on the Spanish war and the war in the Vendée.

18 The differences between the warfares of the *ancien* and revolutionary regimes are elegantly described by Howard (2002, 15–19).

19 The understanding of resistant guerrilla warfare in terms of vaporization informed T. E. Lawrence's theory and practice of armed resistance during the 'Arab Revolt'. His 'Science of Guerrilla Warfare' (1929) mobilises Clausewitz's theory of vaporous and condensed violence confronting its solid and liquid forms: instead of viewing the Arabs as a regular army, 'suppose they were an influence, a thing invulnerable, intangible, without front or back, drifting around like a gas? Armies were like plants, immobile as a whole, firm rooted, nourished through long stems to the head. The Arabs might be a vapour, blowing where they listed' (Lawrence, 20). Lawrence was one of the first to realize that *On War* was not the apology for Napoleonic liquid warfare against the solid massed armies of the *Ancien Régime* but a theory of the vaporous resistance of guerrilla war against the Napoleonic innovations on the plane of movement, battle and expenditure of life. The guerrilla was not subject to hierarchical discipline, but actualized a violence characterized by innovation, unpredictability, the avoidance of battle, with a preference for sabotaging military infrastructure and preserving life: 'The death of a Turkish bridge or rail, machine or gun, or high explosive was more profitable than the death of a Turk. The Arab army just then was equally chary of men and materials: of men because they being irregulars were not units, but individuals, and a individual casualty is like a pebble dropped in water: each may make only a brief hole, but rings of sorrow widen out from them' (Lawrence, 22–4).

20 The metaphor of condensation and lightning returns in Nietzsche's evocation of the 'overman' in the prologue to *Thus Spake Zarathustra*, one of the many points of proximity between the two thinkers.

21 In his essay 'The Shame and the Glory: T. E. Lawrence' Deleuze's opening insight into the relationship between perceptual haze and the vaporous arab revolt is abandoned and the essay ends with an evocation of Lawrence as the Jean Moulin of Arabia: 'Lawrence himself helps them transform their paltry undertakings into a war of resistance and liberation, even if the latter must fall through betrayal...' (Deleuze, 125).

22 The war of exhaustion prompted a debate among readers of Clausewitz associated with the historian Hans Delbruck and his assessment of the achievements of Frederick the Great, cited by Clausewitz in I, 2 as anticipating the conduct of a war of resistance. The options for undermining the material and moral forces of the enemy are basically terroristic, aimed at undermining the will of the enemy. The issues at stake in this debate are clearly described by Aron in Chapter III and note xx of *Penser la guerre* 1, but in isolation from Clausewitz's reflections on the People's War and the protracted war of resistance.

23 As proclaimed at the beginning of the Communist Manifesto: 'The History of all hitherto existing societies is the history of class conflict.'

24 Lars T. Lih discerns an evangelical dimension in the social democratic ideology of Kautsky in his comments on the Erfurt programme which persists in Lenin's view of the party in *What is to be Done*. However, he treats it as a largely harmless metaphor, while for Nietzsche it testified to the continuity of Christianity and socialism. The evangelical dimension of social democracy is emphatically confirmed by Kautsky's last work *Foundations of Christanity: A Study in Christian Origins*; Negri too evokes Christian resistance theology in the citation of St Francis in the first volume of the *Empire* trilogy. A fascinating reworking of this dimension of radical thought is Huey Newton's use of Nietzsche's comments on the spread of Christianity in *The Genealogy of Morals* for formulating the tactics of the Black Panther Party, a reading anticipated by Martin Luther King Jr. See Newton 2009, p.175

25 Engels' writings on the war in France have been obscured by the celebrity of Marx's Addresses on the Commune. However his writings for *The Pall Mall Gazette*, especially 'The Fighting in France' of 11 November 1870 are indebted to Clausewitz's theory of guerrilla war: 'During the last six weeks the character of the war has undergone a remarkable change. The regular armies of France have disappeared; the contest is carried on by levies whose very rawness renders them more or less irregular' (Marx and Engels 1986, 163–4). The article traces this form of warfare to the American War of Independence through the Peninsular war to the wars of independence in Italy and Hungary, and describes it as 'popular resistance' that took the place of a regular army that had become 'incapable of resistance' (Marx and Engels 1986, 165). The article concludes with a call for the Prussian army in France to respect the 'legitimacy' of this type of warfare, especially in the case of the reformed Prussian army which itself 'was an attempt to organise popular resistance to the enemy, at least as far as this was possible in an absolute monarchy' (Marx and Engels 1983, 166).

26 Karl Marx and V. I. Lenin, *Civil War in France: The Paris Commune*, p.123.

27 The burning of Paris is likened to the acts which 'the Christians perpetrated upon the really priceless art treasures of heathen antiquity' (Marx 1974, 229).

28 This is confirmed in the rare citation of Clausewitz to be found in a sequence of notes on terror and ruthlessness associated with the composition of *Also Sprach Zarathustra* from the summer and autumn of 1883: '"die Irrthümer, die aus Gutmüthigkeit entstehen, sind in gefährlichen Dingen die schlimmsten" Clausewitz' (Nietzsche 1977, 512). My thanks to Keith Ansell Pearson for bringing this citation to my attention.

29 In his preface to a later edition dated 18 March 1891, Engels tamed the actuality of Marx's thought of a non-state governmentality by distinguishing the immediate 'new and democratic state' of the Commune with the political form of the future generation 'who will be able to throw the entire lumber of the state on the scrap heap' (2008, 20–1).

30 The parallel between the American and French civil wars is sustained throughout these texts: 'The rebellious slaveholders of Bordeaux' (Marx 1974, 201); 'The first attempt of the slaveholders' conspiracy…' (Marx 2008, 69); 'The civilization and justice of bourgeois order comes out in its lurid light whenever the slaves and drudges of that order rise against their masters' (Marx 1974, 226). For Marx on the American Civil War, see Blackburn 2011. The comparison of the two modern civil wars is modulated in the Third Address through references to Tacitus and the precedents of Roman history.

31 For Nietzsche and German Social Democracy see Hinton Thomas (1983); for the Bolsheviks see Glatzer Rosenthal (2002).

32 According to Hahlweg's classic essay 'Lenin und Clausewitz' (Dill, 629).

33 Negri's reading of Lenin is important testimony to the beginnings of a political thinking that, with the *Empire* trilogy, became an essential point of reference for recent debates around resistance to globalization. Yet it also points to problems informing his theory of resistance already evident in the 1970s. The absence of an explicit theory of resistance is as striking in Negri's work from the 1970s as it is in other theorists of workers' autonomy such as Mario Tronti, even while it implicitly organizes the direction and the tensions informing the theory of autonomy. In Tronti's case the Clausewitzian distinction of tactics and strategy is constitutive, and allied to an affirmative but implicit understanding of working-class resistance. Already in his programmatic article 'Lenin in England', capital and the capitalist state are understood as reactions to the initiative of working-class resistance. For Negri it is only in the 1977 *Domination and Sabotage: On the Marxist Method of Social Transformation* that the 'self-valorisation' of the working class begins to be allusively linked, via Foucault, to the discourse of resistance – an allusion spelt out in his introduction to the republication of the text in 1997: 'Guattari and Deleuze's *A Thousand Plateaus* has shown how the indefinite insurgence of molecular resistances can become revolutionary.' (Negri 2005, xlvi). Whether the avoidance of the term 'resistance' was an allergic response to the mythology of Resistance in Italy and its ideological role in the post-war Italian constitution or to the Red Brigades' description of themselves as partisans of a 'New Resistance' is difficult to determine. What is clear is that the reluctance to move towards a thematized analysis of resistance and its place in the logic of workerism led to a severe underestimation of the opportunities and risks presented by this 'concept', one which left the autonomy ineffectual in the face of the armed resistance of the Red Brigades and the repression it invited and which contributed to the near-dissolution of the Italian capacity to resist in the 'Years of Lead'. The lack of explicit theoretical confrontation with resistance alongside a deployment of its rhetoric continues to characterize the work of Negri and Hardt in the *Empire* trilogy.

34 In Lars T. Lih's translation the Russian terms *soznanie & soznatel' nost* classically translated as 'consciousness' here and throughout *What is to be Done* are rendered 'awareness' and 'purposiveness,' so distinguishing the Hegelian moments of consciousness within the term itself. (Lih, 2005, 35) However, it remains clear that it is consciousness that is aware and purposive, these two moments seen as part of the developmental sequence of a class consciousness. Nevertheless, his version of this passage preserves the movement from sense-certainty through understanding to 'embryonic purposiveness' or self-consciousness, see (Lars T. Lih 2008, 701).

35 Lacan's reflections on resistance in the 'Introduction to Jean Hyppolite's Commentary on Freud's "Verneinung"' refer explicitly to Clausewitz to explain the proposition that 'where speech gives up, the domain of violence begins, and that violence reigns there already without us even provoking it?' (Lacan, 313).

Chapter 2: Violent Resistance

1 Sebastian Haffner, 'Mao und Clausewitz' is one of the few attempts to analyse Mao's relation to Clausewitz but unfortunately pays insufficient attention to the Chinese sources of Mao's theory and practice of guerrilla war, namely Sun Wu Tzu, for Mao 'the great military expert of ancient China' (see Dill, 652–63).

2 'On Protracted War' was a series of lectures given to the Association for the Study of the War of Resistance against Japan in May 1938; they are complemented by the tactical lectures 'Basic Tactics' given in the same year at the Anti-Japanese Military-Political University.

3 The cathartic quality of revolutionary violence became evident in the Cultural Revolution as well as in certain alleged actions of the Naxalites in India and the exterminatory purification of the Khmer Rouge in Cambodia. Mao's stance was ambiguous, regarding violence as an end in itself and as a necessary preparation for social transformation: 'Every just, revolutionary war is endowed with tremendous power and can transform many things or clear the way for their transformation.' (Mao 1966, 18)

4   For an account which emphasizes solely the influence of Clausewitz on the Maoist theory of guerrilla war see Heuser pp. 141–3.

5   This can be found in the volume whose title sums up Jullien's wider project *La philosophie inquiétée par la pensée chinoise.*

6   These three tactical slogans are joined in other versions by a fourth 'When the enemy seeks to avoid battle, we attack!'.

7   I wish to thank my friends Udaya Kumar and N. Venugopalan for the conversation in the Blossom Bookshop Bangalore, which challenged many of my assumptions about Gandhi's thought and its role in the Indian War of Independence.

8   In a fascinating aside in *Satyagraha in South Africa* Gandhi doubts whether Christian Europe was really all that Christian. Reflecting on the South African Boers Gandhi wrote: 'I have stated above that the Boers are religious-minded Christians. But it cannot be said that they believe in the New Testament. As a matter of fact, Europe does not believe in it: in Europe, however, they do claim to respect it, although only a few know and observe Christ's religion of peace' (Gandhi 1928, 17).

9   See Chandra et. al.

10   Gandhi explicitly discouraged any exaggeration of the role of Thoreau's notion of civil disobedience in his elaboration of the strategy of *Satyagraha.*

11   As Kojeve noted, 'Quoi qu'il en soit – l'Histoire est terminée?' (Kojeve, 154), a view resuscitated after 1989 and vigorously criticized by Derrida, among others, in *Spectres of Marx.*

12   Collected in *Sur Clausewitz* pp. 13–41 and 42–52.

13   Translated by Mary Baker as *Battling to the End,* Michigan State University Press, East Lansing 2010.

14   Girard cites Kojève and his unavoidable influence at the same time as establishing his distance from this reading of Hegel, see pp. 71–4. He points tellingly to Kojève's post-war politics – 'the idea of Empire' and for him the role Kojève played as the 'inspiration for Gaullist politics after 1945' (Girard 2011, 74). Aron's complex relationship to the latter are thus situated in the context of Kojève and the conservative political consequences of his reading of Hegel.

15 Girard sees a continuity between Lenin, Mao and Al Qaeda as proponents of the escalation of violence to a global level (see Girard 2011, 361).

16 It is these aspects of his thought and especially his unflinching attention to violence and war that makes Levinas a continual focus of discussion between Girard and Chantre in *Achever Clausewitz*.

17 As Derrida warned a propos of Levinas in 'Violence and Metaphysics': 'Peace is made in a *certain silence*, which is determined and protected by the violence of speech. Since speech says nothing other than the horizon of this silent peace by which it has itself summoned and that it is its mission to protect and prepare speech *indefinitely* remains silent. One never escapes *the economy of war*' (Derrida 2009, 185). Derrida was one of the few readers of Levinas to recognize the role of the 'economy of war' in his ethics.

18 The separation of the struggle with the enemy from the manhunt or the struggle with the elements emerges in the Prison notebooks with extreme urgency. The insistence on the enemy is a mark of Levinas's investment in Clausewitz that may be distinguished from Chamayou's explicitly post- or anti-Clausewitzian theory of the manhunt discussed below in Chapter 4.

19 Levinas's notorious comment in a radio broadcast on the Sabra and Chatila murders is thus fully consistent with the understanding of alterity in *Totality and Infinity*:

'Schlomo Malka: Emmanuel Levinas, you are the philosopher of the "other". Isn't history, isn't politics the very site of the encounter with the "other", and for the Israeli, isn't the "other" above all the Palestinian?

'Emmanuel Levinas: My definition of the other is completely different! The other is the neighbour, who is not necessarily kin, but who can be. And in that sense, if you are for the other, you're for the neighbour. But if your neighbour attacks another neighbour or treats him unjustly, what can you do? Then alterity takes on another character, in alterity we can find an enemy, or at least then we are faced with the problem of knowing who is right and who is wrong, who is just and who is unjust. There are people who are wrong.' (Levinas, 1989)

Chapter 3: Resistant Subjectivities

1   'We communists are all dead men on leave. Of this I am fully aware. I do
     not know if you will extend my leave or whether I shall have to join Karl
     Liebknecht and Rosa Luxemburg. In any case I await your verdict with
     composure and inner serenity, for I know whatever your verdict, events
     cannot be stopped' (Leviné Meyer 83).

2   This predicament was theorized by the Black Panther resistant Huey
     P. Newton as 'revolutionary suicide', endorsing Bakunin and Guevara's
     'first lesson that a revolutionary must learn is that he is a doomed man.
     Unless he understands this, he does not grasp the essential meaning of
     his life' (Newton, 3).

3   The second part of Giorgio Agamben's *Homo Sacer* tetralogy
     meditates upon the importance of the vow as a politico-theological
     figure.

4   Hence the importance of autobiographical writing for articulating the
     emergence of an affirmative resistant life, prominent in the case of
     the African American resistants of the United States during the 1960s
     with the autobiographies of Malcolm X and Huey P. Newton. Carson's
     reconstruction of an autobiography of Martin Luther King Jr performs a
     similar service, placing Dr King's life of resistance alongside those of his
     contemporaries.

5   Here as so often paralleling Clausewitz, Fanon cites the Spanish
     resistance to Napoleon as the inspiration for anti-colonial struggle,
     linking it with the American resistance to British colonialism: 'Face
     to face with the enormous potentials of the Napoleonic troops, the
     Spaniards, inspired by an unshakeable national ardour, rediscovered the
     famous methods of guerrilla warfare which, twenty five years before, the
     American militia had tried out on the English forces'.

6   He illustrates this with the case of the Algerian war: 'Terror, counter-
     terror, violence, counter-violence: that is what observers bitterly record
     when they describe the circle of hate which is so tenacious and evident
     in Algeria'.

7   As explicitly stated in his 1967 essay *Clausewitz als politischer Denker.
     Bemerkungen und Hinweise*, 'In the meantime his name has been
     elevated to global fame. World revolutionaries such as Lenin and Mao
     Tse-tung have placed him in the greatest world-political contexts (Dill,
     419). He adds: He remains alive even in the discussions of the weapons
     and destructive means of nuclear war...'

8 Once again evident in the essay on Clausewitz which notes the publication by Hahlweg in 1966 of Clausewitz's 'Vorlesungen über den kleinen Krieg', remarking that in spite of the didactic intention of the lectures 'many of the remarks on the partisan problem are astoundingly contemporary' (Dill, 421).

9 Levinas also followed woodland paths while working as a captive forced labourer; his essay 'Name of a Dog' records how each walk was accompanied by the dread of execution.

10 Subtitled 'Everyman's Guide to Guerrilla Warfare'. An English translation was made by Hans Lienhard of the 'Special Warfare Language Facility' and contains operational recommendations for conducting a contemporary guerrilla war. Written for Swiss military personnel, the 'field manual' begins with the scenario of the occupation of Switzerland and the prospect of 'annihilation' by the enemy. The authors believe 'it is better to resist to the last' and, while seeing this resistance as the responsibility of the army, 'want to show our people a way to resist in case parts of the army are dispersed, split up or encircled'. Beginning with organizational and strategic advice – attacking individual soldiers and small guard posts – the text moves on to offer instructions on how to make homemade grenades out of yogurt pots, how to sabotage roads, trains, telephone and electrical cables, and how to destroy fuel depots and jet planes. It describes how to recruit partisans, establish safe areas and to 'neutralise informers', how to behave during interrogations and how to pursue effective passive resistance. The text usefully includes diagrams on how to conceal guerrillas, mount an attack and the detailed description of how to dispose of guards without noise that particularly struck Schmitt. He was also impressed by the implacable rigour of the author, as in the Closing Remarks: 'If two enemies fight each other to the last – and this is always the case where ideology is involved (religion is part of it) – guerrilla warfare and civilian resistance will inevitably break out in the final phase' (von Dach, 1965, 173).

11 In the context of this conflict, Schmitt fails to mention Hitler's infamous 'Kommissarbefehl', which during the Nazi invasion of the Soviet Union effectively criminalized the Soviet army and the civilian – above all the Jewish civilian – population, effectively defining them a priori as partisans and prey.

12 Although both irregular, Schmitt is on the whole careful to distinguish partisan from terroristic warfare, seeing the partisan as a resistant and distinguished from a terrorist.

13 Schmitt's esteem does not confine the significance of Lenin's notebooks to the twentieth century. 'Lenin was a great expert on and admirer of

Clausewitz. He had studied *On War* intensively during World War 1 (1915), and in his notebooks he copied quotations in German and made comments in Russian with underscoring and exclamation marks. In this way he created one of the most remarkable documents of world history and intellectual history' (Schmitt 2007, 35).

14   Schmitt concludes: 'Mao was many years ahead of Stalin. Also in his theoretical consciousness, Mao took the formula of war as the continuation of politics even further than Lenin' (Schmitt 2007, 41). The latter in the sense that Mao preserved a continuity between war and politics rather than dissolving politics into global class war.

15   This terror is rooted in absolute enmity – interestingly Schmitt turns to the Algerian war and the renegade general Salan to illustrate this pathology: absolute enmity extends from the concrete enemy, in Salan's case the Algerian partisan, to 'his own government, his own commander in chief, his own comrades. Suddenly, he recognised a new enemy in the comrades of yesterday' (Schmitt 2007, 44).

16   'Tilak found the work to be "useless": Gokhale who had long taken an interest in in Gandhi was disappointed, declaring it to be "the work of an imbecile" predicting that it would take only a year in India for him to renounce it' (Attali, 158).

17   Gandhi describes the first steps towards *Satyagraha* in terms of resistance – the measures to control immigration of indentured labour from India to South Africa and to license shopkeepers and finally the proposal to disenfranchise Indians brought the Indians 'to resist this measure' (Gandhi 1928, 28) and Gandhi to recommend resistance: 'I suggested that the Indians should strenuously resist this attack on their rights' (Gandhi 1928, 39).

18   Gandhi explicitly uses the term resistance at this point, mentioning 'measures of resistance' and the 'hardships which such a resistance will bring in its train' (Gandhi 1928, 84).

19   This is not to diminish the effectiveness of passive resistance as a tactic in certain circumstances, as in this example from the Cretan resistance during the Second World War drawn from the official SOE report on the campaign in Crete. Describing an action at the villages of Kouroutes, Apodoulou and Platanos on the night of 6–7 December 1942, the report relates how '[t]he Germans came prepared for resistance, with MG and mortars, ammunition train and medical service and with considerable reserves standing by. They withdrew no wiser than when they started and inclined to distrust the information of their own agents. This was

a signal victory in passive resistance for the peoples of Amari, who
had opened up like a sluice gate, let the Germans pour through their
villages, and closed behind the flood to continue their unlawful careers'
(Kokonas, 2004, 53).

20 'Yellow Gate women call women to Yellow Gate Greenham Common
    Women's Peace Camp to "RESIST THE MILITARY" ON Saturday and
    Sunday DECEMBER 9th and 10th 1989, the 10th Anniversary of the
    decision to site Cruise missiles in Europe' (*Resist the Military*, 10). All
    references to this and other Greenham literature refer to the Greenham
    archive held at the Women's Library, London.

21 For more details of the nuclear Clausewitz see the debate between Kahn
    and Rapaport in Dill, pp. 719–37, see also Rapaport's introduction to the
    Penguin (1982) edition of *On War*.

22 The 1998 Yellow Gate newsletter proclaimed 'Greenham Common
    Women's Peace Camp September 5th, 1998 **17 YEARS** unbroken,
    non-violent resistance'. The camp eventually ceased its resistance in 2000.

23 The controversy provoked by the decision to restrict full participation in
    the Peace Camps to women seems in retrospect difficult to understand;
    the focus made tactical sense (and was indeed at the time justified
    tactically), as well as being theoretically consistent with the objective of
    resisting armed masculinity, and opening the space for the invention of
    an unprecedented feminine capacity to 'resist the military'. In the words
    of one participant, the decision 'suddenly sank in and it became the
    obvious that it was right thing to do' (Harford and Hopkins, 32).

24 While the Greenham resistance pioneered the invention of a capacity
    to resist organized in terms of a network or web, it predated the
    availability of technological communications networks. Unlike the
    neo-Clausewitzian internet, the Greenham web was a patching together
    of existing civil society networks including the women's movement, CND
    and the broader international peace movement, religious organizations
    and the labour movement. The Greenham Network's capacity to resist
    was actualized through dissident actions in the military, media and
    legal forums. The first resistance to exploit the resources of the new
    communications technology was the resistance to the attempted coup
    d'etat in the USSR on 18 August 1991. Both resistances are important as
    prefigurations of the digital resistance networks of the late twentieth and
    early twenty-first centuries. The fusing of the Greenham virtual network
    with the digital web was announced in the creation of a Greenham
    website in the 1998 Greenham Newsletter. The mass resistance to the

coup in Moscow, orchestrated by traditional resistance techniques of leafleting but also using radio and the new media, directly inspired the uprising of the Arab Spring through the theoretical work of Gene Sharp and Bruce Jenkins. Their *Anti-Coup,* referred to by Arab resistants, draws the theoretical and strategic lessons for resistance from the successful neutralization of the Russian coup by popular non-violent defiance and the denial of legitimacy and co-operation to the putschists.

25 The contemporary reflections on the invention of the Greenham resistance are complemented by Anne Pettit's account of the origins of the occupation, *Walking to Greenham,* a thoughtful and often uproarious memoir which emphasizes the role of chance and improvisation in the early history of Greenham.

26 Pettit describes how the traditional CND tactic of the march spontaneously transformed itself into an occupation which then assumed its own momentum.

27 Katrina Howse's chronicle may be supplemented for the early years of the occupation by Harford and Hopkins and for the decade 1984–95 by the volume written and edited by Beth Junor. The latter focuses properly on the magnificent resistance at Yellow Gate, but it may be supplemented by the work of Sasha Roseneil, which gives the perspectives of the other gates, emphasizing the invention of novel forms of female subjectivity. Sarah Hipperson's elegaic history *Greenham: Non-Violent women – v – the Crown Prerogative* completes the chronicle of the history of the sustained resistance at Yellow Gate. Fairhall (2006) offers an overview that unfortunately does not do justice to the occupation as a self-conscious and sustained act of resistance that saw its historical role as continuing the anti-Nazi resistance.

28 The impact of reports on and images of the Nazi concentration camps recur in the women's autobiographical reflections on their paths to resistant subjectivity: Sarah Hipperson describes how 'during the war years much of my leisure time was spent at the pictures (the cinema). Pathé News was always an important short film before the feature film. When the troops began to liberate the concentration camps, we began to see images from the concentration camps for the first time – we hadn't seen any of this during the war. I was shocked and haunted by those images… It was the loss of my innocence and, I can see now, the beginning of my political awareness – which would be a long, drawn-out process' (Hipperson, 8–9). Ann Pettit in her memoir weaves together the anti-Nazi past and anti-nuclear present in a family history set within the context of anti-nazi resistance.

29 For a powerful fictional evocation of the passage from the life of a 'walking dead' to a feminine resistant subject see Sarah Hall's *The Carhullan Army*.

30 James C. Scott (1986 & 1990) provides invaluable analyses of the subtle character of the kind of peasant resistance that underwrote the constitution of a networked global capacity to resist in Chiapas; he is however critical of the very notion of a resistant subjectivity, preferring to focus on forms and spaces of mutual resistance: 'If we are to understand the process by which resistance is developed and codified, the analysis of the creation of these off stage social spaces becomes a vital task. Only by specifying how such social spaces are made and defended is it possible to move from the individual resisting subject – an abstract fiction – to the socialization of resistant practices and discourses' (Scott, 1990, 118). However, with respect to the concept of the capacity to resist, both approaches are complementary.

31 See Ana Carrigan, 'Chiapas, the First Postmodern Revolution', in Ponce de León, 419.

32 One of Derrida's last works is an examination of the politics of the vagabond or *voyou*, of which Genet is a self-proclaimed exponent.

33 Genet returns to the aftermath of brutal violence against non-combatants two pages later, emphasizing the 'ferocity of the carnage' (Genet 2004, 223).

34 Written as a preface to a collection of RAF texts *Textes de la "Fraction Armée Rouge" et dernières lettres d'Ulrike Meinhof*, Maspero Paris 1978.

35 Walter Benjamin in his earlier 'Critique of Violence' (a text important for the members of the RAF) described violence brutalized by judgement as 'law preserving violence'.

Chapter 4: Total Domination and the Capacity to Resist

1 This is the lesson of James C. Scott, applied in the context of National Socialism by Detlef Peukert's study of the arts of resistance practiced by the German population during the Third Reich. Drawing on Gestapo archives Peukert describes the emergence of a capacity to resist in everyday life and in youth subcultures, one expressed in tastes in

music, dance, 'swing,' dress, the 'Edelweiss Pirates' and other indirect expressions of dissent. The parallels with Scott's study of peasant resistance in Malaysia are striking, with the difference that the National Socialist authorities were very well aware of the defiance, surveyed it constantly and obsessively and subjected it to both routine and spectacular repression.

2   The citation of the 'The Final Solution of the Jewish Question in Europe' agreed at the Wannsee Conference is in a sense parodically appropriate, since the Greenham 'final solution' also seems to have emerged from a conference of official parties interested in the question of suppressing the protest. In Parliament on 5 April 1984 MP Bob Clay referred to a 'conspiracy' of MOD, MOT, Berkshire County Council and the police to disrupt protest through a road-widening scheme.

3   Paul Virilio's neo-Clauswitzian studies of the importance of speed and politics are an important complement to Gramsci's analyses, especially his *Bunker Architecture* and the notion of defence as the arrest of movement and the capacity to resist as an expression of historical deacceleration.

4   There are of course parallels with the Polish and Italian resistances, the former self-consciously dedicated to the re-constitution of Polish democracy and the latter retrospectively called to serve as a source of ethical values for the post-war Italian constitution (see Peli). It is instructive to compare these cases with the divided Greek resistance which destroyed itself in a bitter and often horrific civil war (see Close 1995).

5   Martin Evans in his thought-provoking oral history of the French resistance to the colonial repression of Algeria describes how this process of unification continued into the construction of the mythic historical memory of *The Resistance*: 'The image of the Resistance as a regular army stood in opposition to the image of the Resistance as an irregular, transgressive force, involving illegal, subversive activity. The fact that this illegal, transgressive side of Resistance was downplayed, consciously effaced even, is testament to the "normalisation" process which began at the Liberation when partisan troops were sent into the regular French army. In bringing maverick partisans under the control of career officers, the autonomous action and culture which had marked so much of the Resistance experience was eclipsed. What was constructed was a unified view of the Resistance in which the interior Resistance was more akin to a regular army, closely identified with De Gaulle, and fighting for an uncomplicated patriotic image' (Evans, 186). Evans also underlines how this unification also imposed a specific gendering of the resistance,

equating it with masculine military subjectivity and erasing the role of women in establishing and maintaining networks of resistance.

6 Cordier 1999, vol. 1 p. 17.

7 The military logic of the resistance co-existed with the political logic in spite of tension, distrust and even conflict between civil and military resistance. A specific prism through which to view these tensions and their sometimes deadly expressions is the history of the British Special Operations Executive (SOE) whose purely military missions perforce intersected with the formation of a civil capacity to resist: for the complex and still controversial case of France see the work of M. R. D Foot (1966 & 1993) and for the perhaps more successful and theatrical case of the SOE's interventions in Crete, Kokonas (2004).

8 Arendt represents the turn of phenomenology (she was a student of Heidegger and Jaspers) to political theory, largely motived by her work with Jewish refugee organizations in the 1930s. She escaped to the USA via Port Bou, a week or so before Benjamin unsuccessfully tried the same route, and in the post-war years set herself to the attempt to make sense of National Socialism and the camps that resulted first in *The Origins of Totalitarianism* and then *The Human Condition* and the fragments of the abandoned work on Marx – *On Revolution, Between Past and Present*. These concerns emerged to full public view with her report on the Eichmann trial *Eichmann in Jerusalem: A Report on the Banality of Evil* (1963).

9 The banal comment on Gandhi's strategy of resistance in *On Violence* is indicative of this underestimation: 'If Gandhi's enormously powerful and successful strategy of non-violent resistance had met with a different enemy – Stalin's Russia, Hitler's Germany, even pre-war Japan, instead of England – the outcome would not have been decolonisation, but massacre and submission' (Arendt 1970, 53). Arendt's endorsement of this judgement is meant to support her argument for a distinction between power and violence, with power rooted in a political community while violence relied on the possession of the 'instruments of violence' and the disintegration of power.

10 Needless to say, Arendt's reading of Clausewitz shows no sign of exposure to the rediscovery of the resistant Clausewitz by Aron, Hahlweg and Schmitt. He is for her the theorist of the primacy of war over the political, of violence over power, a precursor of total domination rather than resistance.

11 Arendt implicitly extends the lineage to include the New Left of the 1960s: 'the categories in which the new glorifiers of life understand themselves are not new. To see the productivity of society in the image of life's "creativity" is at least as old as Marx, to believe in violence as a life promoting force is at least as old as Nietzsche, and to think of creativity as man's highest good is at least as old as Bergson' (Arendt, 1970, 74). It is a lineage which Arendt traces back to Clausewitz, and the alleged primacy in *On War* of violent action over speech and politics.

12 An important step in this direction is Dillon and Reid's *The Liberal Way of War* (2009) which deliberately confronts bio-politics with Clausewitzian theses on chance and violence in politics and war. Their account of the growing and inextricable relationship between resistance and counter-resistance, global government and global terror, points to an intensification of the disorientation intrinsic to the notion of resistance. They show the uncanny complicity and exchange between domination and resistance to be a form of Clausewitzian speculative escalation and try to point beyond it to the emergent figure of the resistant *voyou* or rogue, the parrhesic 'good for nothing' who resists by not engaging in the specular game of resistance and counter-resistance. The figure of Tom Paine who haunts *The Liberal Way of War* is just such a rogue, an exemplary figure for the call to save 'the honour of politics' with which their book concludes.

13 For Operation Green Hunt see Roy 2012 and the selection of articles from Democracy and Class Struggle *Operation Green Hunt: India's War on the People* (2009). For further discussion see Chapter 5 below.

14 Edmund Quincy in *The Atlantic Special Commemorative Issue: The Civil War*, Introduction by President Barack Obama, March 2012, 12–13.

15 The African-American resistance is notable for its duration and the quality of its internal debates concerning the art of resistance and the formation of a capacity to resist. The work of Douglas, Martin Luther King Jr, Malcolm X and Huey P. Newton emerged from a matrix of a sustained experience of resistance and counter-resistance. The differences between Dr King and Malcolm X are particularly important for the issue of violent or non-violent resistance and the constitution of a capacity to resist that breaks with the specular relations urged by the art of mastery. For Dr King, inspired by Gandhi and Nietzsche, non-violence was tactically and ethically justified as a break with the structures of *ressentiment*: 'Non-violent resistance had emerged as the technique of the movement, while love stood as the regulating ideal. In other words, Christ furnished the spirit and motivation while Gandhi furnished the method.' (Carson, 67). What Dr King meant by love was precisely the breaking of a specular relationship between hunted and

hunter, between civil rights resistants and the counter-resistance of the men with dogs. Dr King replied forcefully to the criticisms of Malcolm X and others of his position, seeing it as a powerful and formative rather than a weak and reactive option: 'I'm not saying that you sit down and patiently accept injustice. I'm talking about a very strong force where you stand up with all your might against an evil system, and you're not a coward. You are resisting, but you come to see that tactically as well as morally it is better to be nonviolent.' (Carson, 266)

16   The fate of Huey P. Newton is sad testimony to the brutalizing and destructive effects of the manhunt on the even the most resistant of the hunted, see Pearson 1996.

17   Agamben's fidelity to Pasolini becomes increasingly evident as the *Homo Sacer* project approaches completion – the figure of St Francis and the politics of renunciation are prominent in the fourth part of the tetralogy.

Chapter 5: The Contemporary Capacity to Resist

1   Raoul Vaneigem very clearly states the difference between life and survival in terms of creativity and generosity in his recent wide-ranging interview with Hans Ulrich Obrist (Vaneigem 2009).

2   In the interview with Obrist, Vaneigem concedes that he has 'never ceased to rewrite' the *Traité de savoir-vivre à l'usage des jeunes generations* (Vaneigem 2009).

3   For Vaneigem's perception of the break, see 2009.

4   'The wealth of those societies in which the capitalist mode of production prevails presents itself as a vast accumulation of commodities' (Marx).

5   Another figure, Heinrich Blücher, associated with the Left Opposition in German Communism, became the single most important interlocutor of Hannah Arendt and was acknowledged by her to have contributed fundamentally to her thought during the 1950s.

6   A judgement that would be endorsed by Arundhati Roy in the case of her critique of Gandhian strategies of non-violent resistance to the brutality of the contemporary Indian state. Both are close to Arendt in conceding an ethical potential in domination and underestimating the power of non-violent defiance.

7   Arundhati Roy takes a very different position to Vaneigem, moving towards Maoist armed struggle out of the discredited ruins of Gandhi's tactics and strategies in contemporary India.

8   The Mexican *indignados* were resisting less the state than its corruption through the market for drugs and the devastating social and cultural impact of this corruption on Mexican civil society. The call for a civil resistance to organized crime has also been prominent recently in Italy with the widely followed work of Roberto Saviano (2007).

9   Recently commemorated on a 2 euro coin and included in UNESCO's register of global memory.

10 The politics of insurrection is most suggestively if not explicitly theorized in Giorgio Agamben's tetralogy *Homo Sacer,* most openly in Chapter 8 of *The Kingdom and the Glory* but also in the opening citation of the secession of the plebians.

11 The 'partisan' appears at the beginning of Hamlet when Marcellus asks 'Shall I strike it with my partisan?' For an illustration see the Folger Shakespeare Library edition, Simon and Schuster Paperbacks, New York 1972, 16.

12 The beginnings of a reflection on the political promise and threat of digital technology can be found in Assange et.al., 2012 which foregrounds the role of cryptography in sustaining a digital capacity to resist (see also Neal Stephenson's 1999 novel *Cryptonomicon*) as well as the risks intrinsic to the technology. A networked insurrection for example 'needs to happen fast, and it needs to win, because if it doesn't win then that same infrastructure that allows a fast consensus to develop will be used to track down and marginalise all the people who were involved...' (Assange et.al., 2011, 24)

13 The analysis of social action in terms of networks and coherences was pioneered by Simmel in his still-underestimated *Soziologie* (1992).

14 As Assange pertinently observes, while an increasing proportion of humanity 'has thrown the inner core of their lives onto the internet' it becomes ever more urgent to recognise that 'There is a battle between the power of this information collected by insiders, these shadow states of information that are starting to develop, swapping with each other, developing connections with each other and with the private sector, versus the increased size of the commons with the internet as a common tool for humanity to speak to itself.' (Assange 2012, 22)

15 See Naughton (2000), Chapters 5 and 6.

16 Assange notes that the internet is not only underwritten by the material foundation of fibre-optic cables and satellite technology, but also by the

'whole neoliberal, transnational, gloabalised modern market economy' (Assange 2012, 27) and for now more inconspicuously by state violence: 'We are all living under martial law as far as our communications are concerned, we just can't see the tanks – but they are there.' (Assange 2012, 33)

17 'While the Internet can give us new opportunities to grow and experiment with our identities, the economics of personalisation push towards a static conception of personhood. While the Internet has the potential to decentralise knowledge and control, in practice it's concentrating control over what we see and what opportunities we're offered in the hands of fewer and fewer people than before' (Pariser 2011, 218). Or stated even more starkly: 'Technology designed to give us more control over our lives is actually taking control away' (Pariser 2011, 219).

BIBLIOGRAPHY

Agamben, Giorgio (1998) *Homo Sacer: Sovereign Power and Bare Life,*
    trans. Daniel Heller-Roazen, Stanford University Press, Stanford
    California
—(2010) *The Sacranent of Language,* trs. Adam Kotsko, Polity Press, Cambridge
Anonymous *Appel Call*
Arendt, Hannah (1970) *On Violence,* Harcourt Brace and Company, San
    Diego and New York
—(1977) *Eichmann in Jerusalen: A Report on the Banality of Evil,* Penguin
    Books, Harmondsworth
—(2004) *The Origins of Totalitarianism,* Schocken Books, New York
Aron, Raymond (1976a) *Penser la guerre, Clausewitz I L'âge Européen,*
    Éditions Gallimard, Paris
—(1976b) *Penser la guerre, Clausewitz II L'âge planétaire,* Éditions Gallimard,
    Paris
—(2005) *Sur Clausewitz,* Editions complexe, Bruxelles
Assange, Julien et al. (2012) *Freedom and the Future of the Internet,* OR Books,
    New York. London
Attali, Jacques *Gandhi ou l'éveil des humiliés,* livre du poche, Paris
Babeuf, Gracchus (2010) *Le Manifeste des plébéiens.* Éditions Mille et Une
    Nuits, Paris
Baumann, Bommi (1975) *Wie Alles Anfing,* trs. Helene Ellenbogen and Wayne
    Parker, Pulp Press, Vancouver
Benjamin, Walter (2010) *Über den Begriff der Geschichte,* Suhkamp, Franfurt
    am Main
Bensäid, Daniel (2002) *Marx for our Times,* trs. Gregory Elliot, New Left
    Books, London
Blackburn, Robin (2011) *An Unfinished Revolution: Karl Marx and Abraham
    Lincoln,* Verso Books, London
Blanchot, Maurice (2010), *Political Writings 1953–1993,* trs. Zakir Paul,
    Fordham University Press, New York
Bourrinet, Phillipe (2001) *The Dutch and German Political Left,* International
    Communist Current, London
Brooke, Heather (2011) *The Revolution will be Digitised: Despatches from the
    Information War,* William Heinemann, London

Brown, Judith M. and Anthony Parel (2011) *The Cambridge Companion to Gandhi*, Cambridge University Press, Cambridge

Budgen, Sebastian et al., (2007) *Lenin Reloaded: Towards a Politics of Truth*, Duke University Press, Durham and London

Butler, Judith (2004) *Precarious Life: The Powers of Mourning and Violence*, Verso, London and New York

Carson, Claybourne (2009) *The Autobiography of Martin Luther King, Jr.*, Abacus, London

Caygill, Howard (2013) 'Philosophy and the Black Panthers' *Radical Philosophy 179*, May/June 2013, 7–14

Chakravarti, Sudeep (2008) *Red Sun: Travels in Naxalite Country*, Penguin Books, New Delhi

Chamayou, Grégoire (2010) *Les chasses à l'homme,* Le fabrique éditions, Paris

—(2011) 'The Manhunt Doctrine', trs. Shane Lillis *Radical Philosophy* 169, September/October 2011, 2–6

Chandra, Bipan et al., (1989) *India's Struggle for Independence,* Penguin Books, New Delhi

Chapman, Jake and Dinos (2005) *Like a Dog Returns to its Vomit (cat.)* White Cube, London

Chomsky, Noam (2012) *Occupy*, Penguin Books, London

Clausewitz, Carl Von (1966) *Schriften – Aufsätze – Studien – Briefe, Erster Band,* hsg. Werner Hahlweg, Vandenhoeck & Ruprecht in Göttingen

—(1982) *On War*, Anatol Rapaport (ed.), Penguin Books, Harmondsworth

—(2010) *Vom Krieg*, RaBaKa Publishing, Neukirchen

Close, David H. (1995) *The Origins of the Greek Civil War*, Longman, London and New York

Cordier, Daniel (1999) *Jean Moulin: La République des catacombs,* Gallimard, Paris

Dach, H. von (1965) *Total Resistance,* trs. Hans Lienhard, Paladin Press, Boulder Colorado

De Gaulle, Charles (2007) *The Flame of the French Resistance*, foreword by Antony Beevor, Guardian, News and Media, Manchester

Deleuze, Gilles (1998) *Essays Critical and Clinical*, tr. Daniel W. Smith and Michael A. Greco, Verso, London and New York

Democracy and Class Struggle (2009) *Operation Green Hunt: India's War on the People*, London

Derrida, Jacques (1993) *Spectres de Marx*, Galilée, Paris

—(1998) *Resistances of Psychoanalysis*, trs. Peggy Kamuf et al., Stanford University Press, Stanford

—(2007) 'Penser ce qui vient', in René Major (ed.) *Derrida – les temps à venir*, Edition Stock, Paris

—(2009) *Writing and Difference* trans. Alan Bass, Routledge, London

Didi-Hubermann, Georges (2009) *Survivance des lucioles*, Minuit, Paris

Dill, Günter (1980) *Clausewitz in Perspective: Materialen zu Carl von Clausewitz: Vom Krieg,* Ullstein, Frankfurt am Main

Dillon, Michael and Reid, Julien (2009) *The Liberal Way of War: Killing to make life live,* Routledge, London

Douzinas, Costas (2013) *Philosophy and Resistance in Crisis,* Polity Press, Cambridge

Douzou, Laurent (2010) *La Résistance: Une morale en action,* Gallimard, Paris

Drake, Michael (2002) *Problematics of Military Power: Government, Discipline and the Subject of Violence,* Cass, London

Dreyfus, François-Georges (1996) *Histoire de la Résistance,* Éditions de Fallons, Paris

Evans, Martin (1997), *The Memory of Resistance: French Opposition to the Algerian War,* Berg Publishers, Oxford

Fairhall, David (2006) *Common Ground: The Story of Greenham,* I. B. Tauris, London

Fanon, Frantz (2011) *Oeuvres,* Preface D'Achille Mbembe and Introduction Magali Bessone, La Découverte, Paris

Foot, M. R. D. (1966) *S O E in France: An Account of the Work of the British Special Operations Executive in France 1940–1944,* Her Majesty's Stationary Office, London

—(1993) *S.O.E. The Special Operations Executive 1940–1946,* Arrow Books, London

Foucault, Michel (1976) *Histoire de la sexualité: La volonté de savoir,* Gallimard, Paris

—(2001) *Dits et écrits I, 1954–1975; II, 1976–1988,* Éditions Gallimard, Paris

—(2003) '*Society Must Be Defended*', trs. David Macey, Picador, New York

—(2006) *Psychiatric Power,* trs. Graham Burchell, Palgrave Macmillan, Basingstoke

Freud, Sigmund (2001) *The Standard Editition of the Complete Works of Sigmund Freud,* vol. 21, trs. James Strachey, Vintage, London

Gandhi, M. K. (1928) *Satyagraha in South Africa, The Collected Works of Mahatma Gandhi,* vol. 34, New Delhi

—(2009) *An Autobiography or the Story of My Experiments with Truth,* Vasam Publications, Bangalore

—(2010) '*Hind Swaraj*' *and Other Writings,* Anthony J. Parel (ed.), Cambridge University Press, Cambridge

Genet, Jean (2003) *Prisoner of Love,* trs. Barbara Bray, New York Review of Books, New York

—(2004) *The Declared Enemy: Texts and Interviews,* trs. Jeff Fort, Stanford University Press, Stanford

Giap, Vo Nguyen (1972) *La guerra e la politica,* Emilio Sarzi Amadé (ed.), Mazzotta Editore, Milano

Girard, René (2011) *Achever Clausewitz: Entretiens avec Benoît Chantre,* Flammarion, Paris

Glatzer Rosenthal, Bernice (2002) *New Myth, New World, From Nietzsche to Stalinism,* Pensylvania State University Press

Gramsci, Antonio (1971) *Selections from the Prison Notebooks,* trs. Quintin Hoare and Geoffrey Nowell Smith, Lawrence and Wishart, London

Greenham Common Women's Peace Camp (1989) *Resist the Military,* Newbury

Guevara, Ernesto Che (2005) *Guerra per bande,* trs. Adele Faccio, Mondadori, Milano

Hahlweg, Werner (1986) 'Clausewitz and guerrilla warfare' *Journal of Strategic Studies,* 9:2–3, 127–33

Hall, Sarah (2007) *The Carhullan Army,* Faber and Faber, London

Harford, Barbara and Hopkins, Sarah (eds) (1985) *Greenham Common: Women at the Wire,* The Women's Press, London

Hegel, G. W. F. (1956) *The Philosophy of History,* trs. J. Sibree, Dover Publications Inc., New York

—(1977) *Phenomenology of Spirit,* trs. A.V. Miller, Oxford University Press, Oxford

Heidseck et al., (2011) *Les jours heureux: Le Programme du Conseil Nationale de la Résistance de mars 11 1944: Comment il a été ecrit et mis en oeuvre, et comment Sarkozy accelere sa demolition,* La Decouverte, Paris

Hessel, Stéphane (2011) *Indignez Vous!* Indigène éditions, Montpellier

Heuser, Beatrice (2002) *Reading Clausewitz,* Pimlico, London

Hinton Thomas, R. (1983) *Nietzsche in German Politics and Society, 1890–1918,* Manchester University Press, Manchester

Hipperson, Sarah (2005) *Greenham: Non-Violent women – v – the Crown Prerogative,* Greenham Publications, London

House, Jim & Macmaster, Neil (2006) *Paris 1961: Algerians, State Terror, and Memory,* Oxford University Press, Oxford

Howard, Michael (2002), *Clausewitz,* Oxford University Press, Oxford

Jullien, François (2009) *La philosophie inquiétée par la pensée chinoise,* Éditions du Seuil, Paris

Junor, Beth (1995) *Greenham Common Women's Peace Camp: A History of Non-Violent Resistance 1984–1995,* Working Press, London

Kant, Immanuel (2003) *Critique of Pure Reason,* trans. Norman Kemp Smith, Palgrave Macmillan, Basingstoke

Karl, Rebecca E (2010) *Mao Zedong and China in the Twentieth Century,* Duke University Press, Durham and London

Karski, Jan (2012) *Story of a Secret State: My Report to the World,* Penguin Books, London

Kojève, Alexandre (1980) *Introduction á la lecture de Hegel: leçons sur la Phénoménologie de l'Esprit professées de 1933 à 1939 à l'École des Hautes Études,* Paris

Kokonas, N. A (2004) *The Cretan Resistance 1941–1945*, 'Mystis' Manouras G.-Tsintaris A. Co., Iraklion

Kurlansky, Mark (2006) *Non-Violence: The History of a Dangerous Idea*, Vintage Books, London

Lacan, Jacques (2006) *Écrits*, trs. Bruce Fink, W.W. Norton & Company, New York

Lawrence, T. E. (2002) *Guerrilla*, ed. Marco Dotti & Simonetta Franceschetti, stampa alternativia Roma

Lecaldano, Paolo (1976) *Goya: Die Schrecken des Krieges*, List Verlag, München

Leigh David et al. (2011) *Wikileaks: Inside Julian Assange's War on Secrecy*, Guardian Books, London

Lenin, V. I. (1962) *Collected Works Volume 11 June 1906–January 1907*, Lawrence and Wishart, London

—(1975) *What is to be Done: Burning Questions of Our Movement*, Foreign Languages Press, Peking

Levinas, Emmanuel (1989) *The Levinas Reader*, Seán Hand (ed.), Basil Blackwell, Oxford

—(1990) *Difficult Freedom: Essays on Judaism*, Seán Hand (ed.), The Johns Hopkins University Press, Baltimore

—(1999) *Totality and Infinity: An Essay on Exteriority*, Duquesne University Press, Pittsburgh

—(2009) *Carnets de Captivité et autres inédits*, Bernard Grasset/IMEC, Paris

Leviné Meyer, Rosa (1973) *Leviné; the Life of a Revolutionary*, Pluto Press, Farnborough

Lih, Lars T. (2008) *Lenin Rediscovered: What is to be Done? in Context*, Haymarket Books, Chicago, IL

—(2011), *Lenin*, Reaktion Books, London

Lloyd Geoffrey and Sivin, Nathan (2002) *The Way and the Word: Science and Medicine in Early China and Greece*, Yale University Press, New Haven and London

Loraux, Nicole (2006) *The Divided City: On Memory and Forgetting in Ancient Athens*, tr. Corinne Pache and Jeff Fort, Zone Books, New York.

Lukács, Georg (1971) *History and Class Consciousness*, trs. Rodney Livingstone, Merlin Books, London

—(1977) *Lenin: A Study in the Unity of his Thought.* New Left Review Books, London

Luxemburg, Rosa (1970) *Rosa Luxemburg Speaks*, Pathfinder Press, New York

Mao Zedong (1966) *Quotations from Chairman Mao Tse-tung 1924–1964*, http://www.campbellmgold.com/ accessed 28/6/2013

—(1966a) *Basic Tactics*, trs. Stuart R. Schram, Frederick A. Praeger, New York

—(1967) *Selected Works of Mao Tse-tung*, Languages Press, Peking

—(2004) *Mao's Road to Power: Revolutionary Writings 1912*–Vol. 6, ed. Stuart R. Schram, East Gate Book, New York

Malcolm X (1999) *The Autobiography of Malcolm X*, Ballantine Books, New York

Marcot, François (ed.) (2006), *Dictionnaire historique de la Résistance*, Éditions Robert Laffont, Paris

Mareschal, Sylvain (1796) Manifeste des Egaux, www.bataillesocialiste. wordpress.com accessed 6/8/2013

Marx, Karl (1973), *The Revolutions of 1848*, trs. David Fernbach, Penguin Books, Harmondsworth

—(2008) *Civil War in France: The Paris Commune*, International Publishers, New York

Marx, Karl and Engels, Friedrich (1980) *Collected Works* Volume 16, Lawrence and Wishart, London

—(1983) *Collected Works* Volume 40, Lawrence and Wishart, London

—(1986) *Collected Works* Volume 22, Lawrence and Wishart, London

Merlio, Gilbert (2001) *Les résistances allemandes à Hitler*, Éditions Tallandier, Paris

Muller, Jean-Marie (2004) *Il principio nonviolenza: una filosofia della pace*, trans. Enrico Peyretti, Pisa University Press, Pisa

Naughton, John (2000) *A Brief History of the Future: The Origins of the Internet*, London

Negri, Antonio (2004) *Trentatre lezioni su Lenin,* Manifesto Books, Rome

—(2005) *Books for Burning: Between Civil War and Democracy in 1970s Italy,* trs. Timothy S. Murphy, Verso Books, London

Newton, Huey P. (2009) *Revolutionary Suicide,* Penguin Books, New York

Newton, Isaac (1999) *The Principia: Mathematical Principles of Natural Philosophy* trs. I. Bernard Cohen and Anne Whitman, University of California Press, Berkeley

Nietzsche, Friedrich (1969), *On the Genealogy of Morals,* trs. Walter Kaufmann, Vintage Books, New York

—(1968) *The Will to Power*, trs. Walter Kaufmann and R. J. Hollingdale, Vintage Books, New York

—(1977) *Nietzsche Werke Kritische Gesamtausgabe, 7 (1) hsg.,* Giorgio Colli und Mazzino Montinari, Walter de Gruyter, Berlin

Paret, Peter (2007) *Clausewitz and the State: The Man, his Theories and his Times*, Princeton University Press, Princeton and Oxford

Pariser, Eli (2011) *The Filter Bubble: What the Internet is Hiding from You*, Penguin Books, London

Pasolini, Pier Paolo (1980) *Poésies 1953–1964*, trs. José Guidi, Gallimard, Paris

—(1992) *I dialoghi, Edizioni Riuniti, Roma*

—(2011) *L'ultima intervista di Pasolini*, Furio Columbi and G. Carlo, Avagliano editore, Roma

Peli, Santo *Storia della Resistemza in Italia*, Einaudi, Torino

Pettit, Ann (2006) *Walking to Greenham*, Honno, Dynas Powys

Peukert, Detlef (1989) *Inside Nazi Germany: Conformity, Opposition and Racism in Everyday Life*, trs. R. Deveson, Penguin Books, Harmondsworth

Rose, Jacqueline (2007) *The Last Resistance*, Verso, London and New York

Roy, Arundhati (2012) *Walking with the Comrades,* Penguin Books, New York

Sartre, Jean Paul (2009) *Portraits*, trs. Chris Turner, Seagull Books, London New York Calcutta

Saviano, Roberto (2007) *Gomorrah: Italy's Other Mafia*, trs. Virginia Jewiss, Pan Books London

Schmitt, Carl (1980) 'Clausewitz als politischer Denker. Bemerkungen und Hinweise,' in Dill 1980

—(2007) *La guerre civile mondiale: essais (1943–1978)*, Céline Jouin (trs. and ed.), Éditions ère, Maisons-Alfort

—(2007) *Theory of the Partisan: Intermediate Commentary on the Concept of the Political*, trs. G. L. Ulmen, Telos Press Publishing, New York

Schram, Stuart (1974) *Mao Tse-Tung Unrehearsed: Talks and Letters 1956–71*, trs. John Chinnery and Tieyun, Penguin Books, Harmondsworth

Schroers, Rolf (1961) *Der Partisan. Ein Beitrag zur politischen anthropologie*, Kiepenhauer und Witsch, Köln and Berlin

Scott, James C. (1985) *Weapons of the Weak: Everyday Forms of Peasant Resistance*, Yale University Press, New Haven and London

—(1990) *Domination and the Arts of Resistance*, Yale University Press, New Haven & London

Semelin, Jacques (2011) *Face au totalitarisme, la résistance civile,* André Versailles éditeur, Paris

Service, Robert (2010) *Lenin: A Biography*, Pan Books, London

Sharp, Gene and Jenkins, Bruce (2003) *The Anti-Coup,* The Albert Einstein Foundation

Simmel, Georg (1992) *Soziologie: Untersuchingen über die Formen der Vergesellschaftung, Gesamtausgabe*, Suhrkamp, Frankfurt-am-Main

Stiegler, Bernard (1998) *Technics and Time: The Fault of Epimetheus*, trs. Richard Beardsworth and George Collins, Stanford University Press, Stanford

Sun Tzu (1971) *The Art of War*, trs. Samuel B. Griffin, Oxford University Press, Oxford

Tartakowski, Danielle (1997) *Les manifestations de rue en France 1918–1968,* Publications de la Sorbonne, Paris

The Invisible Committee (2009) *The Coming Insurrection,* Semiotext(e), Los Angeles

Thoreau, Henry David (2004) *Walden and Other Writings*, ed. Joseph Wood Krutch, Bantam Dell, New York

Tiqqun (2010) *Introduction to Civil War*, Semiotext(e), Los Angeles

Todorov, Tzvetan (2011) *Goya à l'ombre des lumières,* Flammarion, Paris

Vaneigem, Raoul (1967) *Traité de savoir-vivre à l'usage des jeunes générations*, Gallimard Paris; trs. *The Revolution of Everyday Life*, trs. Donald Nicholson-Smith, Rebel Press 2003

—(2009) *Hans Ulrich Obrist in conversation with Raoul Vaneigem*, e-fluxjournal, 6, May

—(2010) *L'État n'est plus rien, soyons tout,* rue des cascades, Paris

Vernant, Jean-Pierre (2004) *La Traversée des frontières,* La Librairie du Seuil, Paris

Virilio, Paul (1990) *Popular Defence and Ecological Struggles*, trs. Mark Polizzotti, Semiotext, New York

—(2006) *Speed and Politics*. trs. Mark Polizzotti, Semiotext, New York

—(2010) *Bunker Archaeology*, trs. George Collins, Princeton Architectural Press, New York

Weber, Max (2009) *From Max Weber: Essays in Sociology*, ed. H. H Gerth and C. Wright Mills, Routledge, Abingdon

Weil, Eric (1955) 'Guerre et Politique selon Clausewitz', *Revue française de science politique* 5, 2 1955, 291–314

—(1998) *Hegel and the State*, trs. Mark A. Cohen, Johns Hopkins University Press, Baltimore

INDEX